# CHIAROSCURO

## AN ANTHOLOGY OF VIRTUE & VICE

Edited by

## NORTHERN COLORADO WRITERS

Print ISBN: 978-0-578-97661-7

Ebook ISBN: 978-0-578-97662-4

Cover design by Maggie Walker

Edited by Bonnie McKnight, Lorrie Wolfe, Sarah Roberts, Joe Hutchison, Tara
Szkutnik & Veronica Patterson

# CONTENTS

# INTRODUCTION

*Virtue itself turns vice, being misapplied,*
*And vice sometime's by action dignified.*
—*William Shakespeare,* Romeo and Juliet

When we consider vice and virtue, we do so through a moral lens, in part because both terms are defined in relation to morality. The seven deadly sins and seven heavenly virtues come immediately to mind. And yet, morality is simply a system of values and principles of conduct; the extent to which an action is right or wrong.

Who decides?

Given the diversity of thought, culture, and religious practice found around the world, who is to say which system of morality is the right one. Which system should apply to all people. Clearly this is a question for the ages; one that cannot be easily answered. Perhaps, it shouldn't be answered at all. Perhaps questions of vice and virtue are non-universal, appearing differently for individuals, groups, and communities.

Maybe the labels, vice and virtue, merely communicate a comparison between extremes. The distance between what is right and wrong, good and bad, but within the framework of our own lives and cultural beliefs.

For this year's anthology, we asked contributors to think about these concepts in terms of contrast.

Simple?

Not really.

As we opened for submissions, our country began to shut down amid a global pandemic. Racial tensions reached a crescendo, and the fight for equality and human rights in our country spawned protests and debates, violence as well as beautiful acts of compassion.

At home, families struggled to cope with school shutdowns, work closures, sickness, and death. Businesses scrambled to react to changes, with many shutting their doors for good. The last two years have seen incredible innovation and adaptation, but also significant crisis and division.

In other words, the contrasts have been profound. What better time to ponder the concepts of virtue and vice, light and dark, good and evil?

We hope the pieces contained in these pages will make you think and feel and perceive in new ways, opening your heart and mind to the subjectivity of vice and virtue and where these attributes fit into your own life and understanding of morality.

Thank you for reading.

Amy Rivers

Director | Northern Colorado Writers

# MATINS

## MEGAN E. FREEMAN

the woman with her cigarette
on the front porch
outside to protect her family from the smell

her inauguration of morning
perfuming the cul-de-sac as surely
as the priests perfumed the ancient cathedrals
with their incense and their Latin

hers is a meditation in smoke
worshipping the dawning day
with the devotion of mystics

the cigarette is just an excuse
the guise of courtesy her accomplice

# THE HUMAN CONDITION MIGHT BE
## LEW FORESTER

two Jamaican women selling
fruits and juices in a muddy,
vacant lot in south Chicago
as traffic grinds by on Cicero Ave.
Wearing flashy jewelry and bright
floral dresses, they stack
clear plastic containers of fresh-cut
pineapple, mango, melons,
blue and red berries on folding tables—
a rainbow set below a bruised
and swollen sky, as if to defy
the surrounding landscape
of litter, crumbling tenements.
Glass dispensers of juices on ice—
mango-cherry, strawberry-kiwi,
guava-grape—await those who thirst
for the exotic, want to quench
something they can't name.

The women wait, laughing heartily—
themselves in their prime, ripe
with hope that their fruits will entice
before the ice melts, like a spell.

# WHY I THREW MY DAUGHTER

## LAURA MAHAL

She was playing in the center of a planting bed, and for a moment, she seemed to shimmer.

Her hand reached toward the bird bath, the bowl bone-dry on top of its concrete pedestal, when I realized what gave her the full-body halo, like a fairy from a distant and long-forgotten land.

I abandoned my shovel and raced for her, clearing the dozen feet between us in two bounds. Her face, confused, swung from birdbath to my hands, which gripped her small body and then *threw*.

Aiming for a spot of ice plant, away from metal edging, the black protective cap long torn away. Away from roses, from black-berry canes, away from anything that might cut, pierce her . . .

Away from the ground wasps that now electrified me with a thousand sharp currents, wasps that covered my body, piercing me through my gloves and long-sleeved shirt. Stinging me again and again on my thighs, my calves, my face.

She was wailing and I could not go to her, to see if my child was hurt, to see if she had indeed landed on the rusty edging, to see if her shimmer of yellow jackets was gone.

I prayed I would not die as my daughter lay crying, within range of me but outside my scope. I prayed, if I did die, that someone would find her quickly, scoop her into a safe, loving embrace.

Survival instincts drove out thought. I wrenched and twisted birdbath to the earth, trapping wasps under bone-dry concrete ceiling. Ran for garden hose. Spun metal dial mounted on wall. Flicked setting on nozzle to "jet."

I blasted hair, ears, eyes, neck. Water hot from resting in hose. Boiling yellow jackets, drowning them as they tumbled downward but not without a fight, stinging me again and again in their forced retreat. If they made a war cry, I could not hear it. I heard only water, from hot hot to ice ice. And screaming. Two pitches that fused. Hers, and mine.

Soaked, wasps waterfalling from my body, I crawled to her, as my daughter crawled to me.

"Baby, are you all right?" I asked through swollen, distended lips, reaching with unrecognizable appendages, medical gloves inflated as makeshift balloons, rubbery hands the size of eggplants.

"Mommy," she cried, snot streaming over mouth and onto chin, "Mommy, Mommy."

*She can speak*, I thought as I lay back on the grass, afraid to pull her into a hug, lest any wasps cling to my skin or clothing.

My eyes swelled close, but not before I saw that she no longer shimmered.

# HOW TO MEASURE A HEART
## HOLLY COLLINGWOOD

The corporate glass door is heavy and cool under my palms. I push against its thickness and step onto the quiet street. The impulse to waltz teases me, but they might be watching from their upstairs window. When the interview ended, both suits smiled, shook my hand, and looked me in the eyes.

They want me. *But don't dance too early.* Wait for the official offer.

My left boot clicks against the concrete. The right one lands softly, as it's more sock than sole. The hems on my dress pants are frayed but tucked deep in the boots for the interview. Hiding desperation is my specialty.

I'm almost to the Mandatory Exercise Station. This MES diagram shows twenty burpees, twenty squats, and twenty calf raises. I throw all my post-interview energy into the first burpee. My chest nearly touches the platform before I leap to my feet and jump-reach.

*One. Repeat.*

*Two. Repeat.*

With every reach, my sleeve slips past my elbow and the

cardiomometer implanted in my forearm sticks out beyond my sweater, just far enough to see the digital numbers increasing. I peek over my shoulder toward the third-story window. Are they still watching me? Will their hiring decision be based on my MES compliance? Did they notice I took the stairs to their office instead of the elevator? My cardiomometer had blinked an increase of 103 ticks after the stairs, but I know I used those extra beats while my heart crazy-raced through their interview questions.

I finish the burpees and move on to squats. Hands on my hips for balance, I dip low.

*One. Repeat.*

*Two. Repeat.*

My glutes and hamstrings burn. I squat again. I need this job. My squat is low, but my credit balance is lower.

My cardiomometer blinks an increase of 178 ticks. I bust out the twenty calf raises while the elderly man waiting in line behind me stacks his groceries in a pile before taking his turn on the platform. He rolls up his sleeve and checks his cardiomometer before he begins.

The next airtram departs in three minutes; if I sprint, I'll make it. The people in front of me in line are already executing their line-waiting lunges in synchronized form. I join them, and our heads bob an even cadence. Aboard the airtram, an official poster for Vita-Bev promises "200 ticks in every bottle." The corner is peeling, and a tiny note advertising underground sugar peeks from behind it. I push the poster back into place between shoulder shrugs. No one should buy that sugar. Or consume it.

Years ago, the Health Hierarchy assigned arm circles to airtram passengers but switched to shoulder shrugs after complaints of unintentional whacking, and intentional groping, in the cramped space.

At my stop, I depart the airtram and walk past the Health Hierarchy Hospital. A family exits with an antiseptic rush of air. Their young child is bundled in blankets. "Health to you," I greet them. "Did he turn one?"

They nod at each other. "Just received his cardiomometer. Two trillion ticks."

"That's all?" I bite my lip and suck air through my teeth. I shouldn't have said that aloud. I have more heartbeats left than this tiny baby.

The curly-haired father's forehead shows deep creases, and the mother's eyes are rimmed by deep red.

"Sorry," I mumble.

"It's the diabetes. Runs in his family," the mother shoves her thumb at the father.

I wish the diabetes serums worked as well as the cancer ones. "My daughter's appointment is in two weeks," I tell them.

The picture on the electronic billboard above the hospital's entrance rotates to a close-up of an infant's face. The slogan flashes under the baby's pudgy cheeks and long, dark eyelashes: "Live Long. Live Healthy."

"The implantation. Was it painful?" I ask.

"He hasn't woken yet," the father whispers. The handle of the paper bag he carries rips, and its contents roll across the concrete.

I squat and help retrieve the items: white sterile bandages wrapped in plastic, antiseptic wipes, and three large bottles of liquid pain medication. "Will he need this much?"

As if on cue, the baby whimpers, arches his back, and stretches his arms out of the blankets. A fresh red oval spreads across his bandage.

"Health to you." The mother clutches her son tighter and they hurry toward the airtram.

I have two more MES platforms to complete before I reach my building. I take the stairs to the daycare on the second floor. My baby stands at a table banging two blocks together. I call to her. "Jubia."

She recognizes my voice, drops to her knees, and speed crawls across the rug. I scoop her up and squeeze tight. She smears my neck with baby slobber while I breathe deeply and refill my heart with Jubia. A long, raw rug burn streaks her cheek. "What happened here?" I ask the health provider in the pastel scrubs.

"She tipped over doing downward dog today. Landed on her face. Didn't cry much though."

"Yoga already?"

"Youth Exercise Requirements." She points to a poster on the wall, clears her throat, and hands me a pink paper. "Invoices turn overdue tomorrow."

"Hope this doesn't scar." I rub her cheeks with my thumb and ignore the reminder of another late bill. I heft Jubia's bag to my shoulder to carry her up six more flights to our tiny apartment. This is always the biggest gain of my day. Plus 587 ticks because of the nineteen-pound baby and her twelve-pound bag.

A yellow eviction notice sticks to my front door, but I've been ignoring it all month. Inside our apartment, I'm unpacking soiled clothes from Jubia's bag when my COM vibrates with a message. **Congratulations, Senova. Your new position at Health Hierarchy Hospice begins in three days. Kartis will supervise.**

I swing Jubia to my hip, cue dance music, and spin her in circles. We foxtrot. She squeals. We two-step. She giggles. Plus 134 ticks.

---

The schedule for Patient #7328 shows: 2:00 Rotate, 4:00 Nutrition, 6:00 Sanitary. Kartis leads the way to the first bed. "Remember how to roll one over?" he asks.

"Support the neck and head, push from the hips and shoulders."

"Right. Do this one yourself. I'll watch."

I introduce myself to #7328. "Health to you. I'm Senova and

I'm here to rotate you." Between saggy skin and sheets, my arm squeezes through. Bracing, my white shoes squeak against the industrial tile. I put my body weight into the push. He rolls. Too easy. Too far. Too close to the edge of his narrow bed.

Kartis catches #7328 at the last moment. "Slower next time. Drop a patient to the floor and you'll be filling out forms for a month."

"I didn't expect him to be so light."

"It's how they are at the end."

I pick up #7328's arm and check his cardiomometer. 12,381 ticks left. "His last day?"

"Yep. Another will take his place tomorrow."

I straighten the sheets around the patient's shoulders, smooth his thinning hair, add a blanket, and stare at the wrinkles that surround his eyes like a flowing river. "Can he hear us?"

"No. Don't bother introducing yourself to the next one. Now, check his ass for bedsores."

---

Rebetha waits at a table in the far corner of the crowded café.

"Sorry we're late. Long wait at the MES." I wipe sweat off my forehead and adjust the biting strap of my sports bra.

"If I take Broadhealth to Walnut, I don't pass any MES plat-forms. 'Course it's eighteen blocks longer." She laughs.

"Probably equals out." I shrug, but I can't believe she would avoid an MES. I only skipped one once, eleven and a half months ago, on the way to the birthing hospital after Jubia kicked so hard my water broke.

Rebetha holds Jubia while I take off my coat and set up the high chair. "How's the new job?" she asks.

"Good change. I was tired of entering data all day. And I can almost afford this place now."

"Is it sad? The dying and all?"

"I'm day shift. They usually go at night."

The server arrives with our order. Green 10-Veg Juice for Rebetha. Kale Citrus Blend for me. He also brings a bowl of peeled jicama sticks for Jubia to teethe against.

When he leaves, Rebetha pulls a container from her purse. Inside is a frosted pastry, a rainbow of sprinkles decorating the top. Rebetha grins. "It's Jubia's birthday donut."

My mouth waters. I swallow hard to fight the temptation. "Where'd you get it?"

She leans close and whispers, "Woman in my building makes them."

"But the illegal ingredients? Where does she find them?"

"I don't ask. She'd never tell me anyway."

I hate arguing with friends, but this is unacceptable. "Jubia can't eat it."

"Why not? Only one chance in life for a first-birthday donut."

Pink goo drips off the edge in delicate icicles. A waft of sugar infiltrates my nose. I lean forward and inhale deeply. Jubia mimics me. Her baby nostrils open wide and she bangs her fists on the high chair's tray.

Rebetha's grin is mischievous. "See. Your gal's a smart one. Knows a tasty thing when she smells it. Besides, you'll never know how many ticks she loses because she doesn't have her cardiomometer yet." Rebetha holds Jubia's arm and runs her finger across the spot where it will be implanted next week. "So soft." She blows a raspberry on the spot and Jubia kicks with joy. "She can try a tiny bite. Or three."

"No." My fingernails dig into my thighs.

"Watch me." Rebetha dips her finger into the pink frosting and waggles it in front of Jubia's face before licking it. Her eyes close with delicious pleasure. She pulls up her sleeve and waits for the total. "Look. Only down 48 ticks for that sweet lick."

I glare at her and grind my teeth.

She shrugs. "So, I'll croak a minute sooner. Or I can eat an apple and do double MES workouts today to earn them back." She checks over her shoulder and whispers, "Outside the city, they probably eat like this every day."

"Except everyone knows that farmers are the only ones that live outside the city. And they have cardiomometers too. Anyway, I don't want her to enjoy that crap and start craving it." I'm about to boil over but trying not to show it.

"One minuscule lick, her face will be so adorable. Get your camera ready." She dips her finger into the frosting again and holds it close to Jubia's lips.

I smack Rebetha's hand away. "I said NO!" Hauling Jubia out of the high chair, I balance her on my hip, throw eight credits on the table for my drink, and weave around crowded tables.

"Brose would have let her," she yells after me.

Brose. I don't want to think about Brose. Raising Jubia alone is hard enough without letting myself miss him. Stupid seizures. Stupid empty apartment after his grand mal.

The bright sunshine makes me squint. Kneeling, I buckle Jubia into her jogging stroller. I've got plenty to run from.

We run past tempting underground markets.

Past the dance studio. "We can merely exercise to earn heartbeats, or we can apply grace," the instructors repeated every time they adjusted my posture and position.

Past the performance theater that rejected me. Seven times. "We know you love dancing, but your precision is inept." Whatever. Screw them.

Past the data depository I'd then been assigned to. Screw them too. Adrenaline pushes me to outrun Rebetha's invasion and every unbearable memory of Brose.

The trail is narrow along the river, and I slow to lift the stroller over a bumpy mess of tree roots one wheel at a time.

My heart thumps loud in my chest. Plus 2,091. *Whew. Worth it.*

Jubia's thumb plugs her mouth and her drowsy head lolls to the side. Mossy green foliage hangs from the trees, and tiny white wild-flowers grow in bursts along the path. I wipe sleepy baby drool from Jubia's chin.

Laughter, not far off, weaves through the thick forest. The high pitch of a toddler and the rusty tones of a grandmother mix with middle-aged voices. Closer.

The voices transform from mirth to worry and a child says, "I can do it."

"This trail is rough," an adult argues.

"But I'll be careful," the child begs.

"Yes, go ahead. We need a few moments together," the elderly voice says.

A group of adults come into view. One man carries a toddler on his shoulders. They walk a tentative pace, looking over their shoulders every few steps.

"Health to you," I offer.

Their silent nods are curt.

A few moments later a child appears, pushing an elderly woman in a wheelchair who points into the trees. "There. In the pines. Purple wings."

"Oooh, that's the rarest kind, right, Granny?"

"Does she have polka-dots on her tummy? Purple wings too? If you spot her, she's the Queen." The grandmother winks at me.

"Oh Granny, she does. She's the Pixie Queen!"

They're still on their imaginary search when they hit the rooty section of trail. The wheelchair stops and the child leans forward, shoving hard to force it over the ruts. But only the left wheels move. The right side remains wedged and the chair lurches. Flailing her arms, the grandmother lands on the ground with a grunt.

"Granny!" the child cries and falls to the dirt next to her.

I sprint to the pair. "Can I help?"

The grandmother rolls to her back. "Let me catch my breath a minute."

The child's eyes are wide. "Are you okay, Granny?"

The grandmother takes another deep breath and rounds her shoulders, feeling for injuries. "Of course. That's the most thrilling thing that's happened to me in a long time." She touches her granddaughter's cheek with her palm. A black elastic sweatband surrounds her wrist, and purposefully, without looking at the screen, she adjusts the band up her forearm to cover her cardiomometer completely.

The child sags. "Those roots were bigger than I thought."

"I'll help your grandmother. Don't worry, I do this at work."

Together, we straighten the wheelchair and set the brake. I put one arm under the grandmother's shoulders and another under her knees. Once the grandmother is settled, the child adjusts her grandmother's sweater, and we both brush twigs and pine needles from its fibers.

"I probably could've caught myself, but I didn't want to mess up my new polish." The grandmother holds up her fingers, which are painted neon orange. The polish extends from her tips past the cuticles and all the way to her knobby knuckles. They clearly represent the artistry of the child.

The granddaughter grabs the elder's hands. "They're still beautiful."

"Beautiful," I agree.

The grandmother winks at me again.

"Health to you," I call after them as they disappear up the trail.

Jubia wiggles on my lap in the waiting room. The Health Hierarchy monitor blinks, "1 of 21 e-forms complete." Another pops up. I skim it, press my thumb in the signature box, and wait for the next.

"They promise you'll heal quickly," I whisper in her ear. Jubia twists her fingers into my hair. She yanks hard. I tilt my head backward to relieve the pressure. The plaster ceiling is smooth and seamless.

"4 of 21 e-forms complete." I offer my thumb print again.

Another blinks on the screen. "This one's for your cancer serum," I tell Jubia, who's about to cry. She's agitated in this unfamiliar setting. "Kiss, kiss," I say and smooch her cheek twice to calm her. She puckers like a goldfish to mimic me. I'd do anything for that fishy-face.

"Live Long. Live Healthy," every e-form promises above the signature box.

"This one prevents asthma." She doesn't care and sucks her thumb harder. No one remembers what asthma was, but we still medicate against it.

Finally, we finish the forms.

They are coming for her. I turn my back to the door and memorize the petite, paper-thin nails of her fingers. Not a single hangnail breaks their perfection. I won't see them again for forty-eight hours.

A hand squeezes my shoulder. Damn. Not enough time. Jubia's eyebrows and cheeks are perfect too. I trace the soft flesh of her forearm for the last time.

They take her. My arms are empty.

---

"I've got to send the afternoon reports. Connect the 2:00 Nutri-Vita lines," Kartis says and disappears into his glass office.

When he powers his monitor on, the glare from the screen

reflects onto the window behind his desk. I struggle to figure out the columns in reverse as the numbers blink. When I squint, the reflection comes into focus. Clear numbers and their labels shock me. But I can't read for long; a full room of patients need me.

In the first bed, Patient #21670 has twisty silver hair that spreads out on the pillow like rays of moonlight. I connect the NutriVita-bag to the IV line and mark the monitor.

*One. Repeat.*

*Two. Repeat.*

I'm about to connect the line for the third patient when she mumbles, "Blanket?"

I jump back and gasp. "What?"

"Can I have a blanket?"

"You can talk?"

She strokes the thin sheet. "Of course. And I'm cold."

I open the cupboard above her bed and shake out thick blue folds. When the corners of the blanket are tucked in, she reaches down and pulls it up to her chin. Her fingernails. Orange. The polish is chipped and cracked but still brighter than a sunrise. A black sweatband covers her cardiomometer.

"I know you. We met in the woods."

"I'm Jain." She presses her hand into mine. Her skin is calloused, and her palms are warmer than I expected.

"You were with your granddaughter, right?"

Tears fill her lower lids. "That sweet one is going to miss me."

I nod. My lips twitch but form no words.

"She has the imagination of an inventor, for sure."

"Will she visit you?" No one else has visitors, but maybe her family would.

"It's not allowed. We said our goodbyes in the woods. Our last pixie quest."

"Visits aren't allowed?" I'm surprised, but not surprised.

"No," she confirms and curls a finger at me, indicating I should lean close. "Can you bring me a chocolate bar?" she whispers.

My jaw drops, but before I can answer, she asks Patient #48209, in the second bed, "You still awake, Lira? Anything you want Senova to bring tomorrow?"

"Hmm?" The woman answers without opening her eyes.

"Do you want anything tomorrow?" Jain repeats, louder.

"Sorry. Sleepy meds are knocking me out again." She points to the IV line I just connected.

"The IV is only nutrition and pain relievers." I correct her automatically, but even as the words come out of my mouth, I wonder. The bag in my hand, ready for the next patient, is suddenly heavier.

Lira fights sluggish lips and mumbles a challenge. "Try one yourself and see if you can stay awake." She yawns twice. "A pack of smokes. That's what you can bring me."

I gasp. "Cigarettes? But, you'll lose heartbeats."

Both women glare. Lira shrugs one shoulder. Jain waves me away with her hand.

---

I balance Jubia on my hip. Her sleepy head leans against my shoulder and bounces with every step. Aisle three. Almost there. The shelves are lined with medical supplies. My eyes scan the sterile boxes. I should've purchased the Infant Cardiomometer Cleaning Kit before picking Jubia up, but I didn't want her to wake at the hospital without me. Green box. Found it.

On the way to the front of the commissary, I grab whole grain bread, protein flakes, and beet sauce. Next to the automatic credit register, a row of carob bars is on display. Sixty credits each. The sin tax quadruples their cost. Even for fake stuff. Honey Cocoa. Almond Butter. Dark Diva Toffee. I'm curious. I've always been tempted. But never enough. Too many ticks and credits at stake. I finish nineteen line-waiting lunges before it's my turn to pay. Plus 201.

Jubia squirms and whimpers in my arms. Blood seeps through her bandages. We have to get home for her next dose of pain medication.

We're nearly home when the alley vendor behind my apartment building heckles, "Bacon. Weed. Soda. You want it. I got it."

Usually his offerings are easy to ignore. But today I pause in front of his cart. "Chocolate?"

He lifts a row of exercise magazines to show me a red box of chocolate-covered cherries. Mixed with fruit, maybe Jain and Lira won't lose as many beats.

---

Double-check. Kartis' office door is still closed. I gawk at the numbers reflected from his monitor on the window again and run my finger around the edge of my cardiomometer.

Jain's in the third bed, with her blankets pulled so high under her chin that her toes stick out the bottom. Her thick toenails are painted orange too. I tuck her feet in and show her the chocolate-covered cherries. "Jain, are these okay?"

She opens the box and smells. "Mmm." Her moan is low and long.

"I didn't get any cigarettes, so can you share with Lira?"

"She's gone."

I look at the next bed. Jain's right. Someone new with short black hair is there. He looks young. Maybe my age. The monitor says Patient #89893.

"When?"

"Middle of the night. They wheeled Lira out, changed the sheets, and brought him in ten minutes later."

My toes curl inside my shoes. "I'm sorry. Were you close?"

"Close as two old ladies who met in a waiting room of death."

I inhale, unsure of appropriate words. This is why I was told not to engage with the patients.

"Lira knew it was time. Kept checking her cardiomometer all night."

"And yours?" I reach over and pull her sweatband down.

Jain slaps my hand. Hard. I shake out the sting.

"Don't," she hisses. "I've never looked."

My jaw drops. "Never?"

"Not since I lost my baby. She was four. Didn't want to know how much longer I had to live without her."

Cramps wring my heart. Why did I want to work in hospice?

Her voice is full of memories. "It's been sixty years, but she was my first. Dark curls. Easy giggle. Mischievous eyes."

"You had more children after her?"

"You saw them in the woods."

The outline of my cardiomometer shows under my thin sleeve. I can remove Jubia's bandage tonight. How many beats will she have? Soon I'll know. The face of the devastated mother in front of the hospital slams my brain and ricochets from one side to the other.

Jain sighs and drops a chocolate in her mouth. "Pass these around." She points down the row. Each patient takes one and the sound of their savoring fills the room.

The door swings open. "Why does it smell like chocolate in here?" Kartis demands.

I sneak the empty box under the closest pillow and lie. "Don't know about chocolate, but I'm cleaning a Code Brown."

Kartis exits as fast as he entered. Once I hear his office door close, I ask Jain, "How did you know it was time to check in here, if you never look at your cardiomometer?"

"I didn't." Her voice cracks. "They came for me. Told me I had twenty-four hours to appear."

"But how did the Health Hierarchy know?"

She licks the last of the chocolate from her lips and taps her covered cardiomometer. Her voice is condescending when she finally speaks. "It tracks more than heartbeats."

"You believe that?" My words are hollow.

"I know that. How do you think they found me? I was at a friend's house for dinner when they knocked."

I glance at the door over my shoulder. Pretending to rearrange her pillows, I lean in and admit, "I know now, too."

She's right. I've seen the transmissions. Every day, Kartis's monitor displays the hundred nearest cardiomometers. All my patients in this room. The patients on the next floor. His. Mine. The other aides and supervisors. It's all on his screen. Location. Body temperature. Daily tick total. Remaining heartbeats. MES compliance. Six more intrusive columns.

My fingers trace the edge of Jain's black band. "They told us it only collected information. But it transmits too." I rub my forehead with my palm, trying to fathom the magnitude of admitting the truth to her. And myself. "My daughter's was implanted two days ago."

Jain nods. "My children have theirs too. And my grandchildren. If they didn't, we would have snuck away from the city years ago."

"Everyone knows that only the farmers live outside the city." But my gut twists as I say the words. Is it possible to leave the city?

She points out the window. "I know there's something beyond the farms."

I avoid her eyes and keep my hands busy tucking her sheets close. "Your baby? What happened to her?" Jain will fall asleep soon and I must know.

"Remember the 107 Airtram Crash? Slid off the tracks. Cardiomometers can't predict everything." Jain twists the sheet in her fingers. Only flecks of the orange polish are left.

I nod. Brose's cardiomometer didn't foresee his grand mal, either. Until it started. Seizing in my arms, thrashing against my pregnant belly, his body quaked. His numbers crashed. And bottomed out. At zero. On our bathroom floor.

———

On my commute home, the airtram is packed; a small boy standing near me slips his hand into his pocket and pulls out a tiny wrapped package. Without stopping his shoulder shrugs, he unwraps the green paper and slips the candy into his mouth. His lips pucker around the sweetness, and he steals sideways glances at his mother until the sugary scent betrays him.

She scowls at her son. "Spit it out. Where did you get that?"

Eyes down, he holds it out for her. A saliva string still connects it to his mouth.

The mother swats it to the floor where it rolls between the traction grooves. She grabs her son's arm and yanks his sleeve up. "Negative 82. Just for a piece of candy." Her eyes are narrow with disgust.

The boy's chin drops.

"You disappoint me. Keep doing your shoulder shrugs. And march in place. Earn those beats back," the mother hisses.

My gut twists. I could be that mother.

Wait.

I already am.

———

The jogging stroller is packed with everything I can think of. What didn't fit is rolled inside my backpack. It's time to leave this city. I measure Jubia's pain medication and squeeze the pink liquid between her cheek and gums. Then, I pour another and double dose her. Twenty minutes until maximum potency.

But I'm first.

The skin around my cardiomometer is scarred. Thick. Protective of the foreign implant. With tongs, I lift the first spoon from the boiling water. While it cools, I pour clear liquor over my forearm. It cost me 180 credits from the same alley vendor who sold me the chocolate-covered cherries. I try one mouthful. Flames twist in my throat. It threatens to come up, but I swallow against the reflex.

The second and third gulps burn less.

With the edge of the spoon, I pry the corner of the cardiomometer closest to my wrist. I dig with determination. Must block the pain by pretending this is someone else's arm.

Doesn't work.

The first creek of blood runs down my arm and drips from my elbow. Push the spoon deeper. I change the angle and pry again. Harder.

Finally, the edge pops loose. So does the pain. Black clouds spin at me while blood stains the blue kitchen tablecloth.

But the cardiomometer is still attached. Wires extend far into my body. I pull on the first one. Inside my wrist it gives way and slips out. Like the time I held the tip of a long spaghetti noodle, swallowed it, then pulled it up my throat.

The last wires extend up my arm. How long are they? I have to risk it. This is no way to live. I grab the cardiomometer and yank. Under my shoulder I feel the wires stripping themselves from my vessels. Muscles cramp and my arm jerks. With the final tug, my heart twitches and the wires slide out.

I'm free.

If I could, I'd jitterbug across the kitchen. But there's no dancing now. I'd pass out. Or slip on my own blood.

The mess of wires lies on the floor in a tangle. Zeros flash across the screen until a grey puff of smoke erupts from the cardiomometer.

It's dead.

I'm alive.

My hand shakes but I pour liquor into the hole in my arm. An invisible blaze erupts and I suck long breaths. I wrap my arm using bandages from Jubia's Infant Cardiomometer Cleaning Kit, then stare at the floor and pant. Cracks in the tile look like veins.

*One. Repeat.*

Jubia sleeps in the stroller. I try not to wake her as I unwrap the bandages from her arm. I'm tempted to peek at Jubia's count. So tempted.

But if I look, this is all for nothing.

I resist.

We have to live. And dance. Every day.

Her spoon waits in the boiling water. When it cools, I dig deep and fast into her flesh. She whimpers and her back arches.

I jerk on the tiny wires and pull my daughter out of this life, and into our new one.

# RAVEN FAITH
## ERIN ROBERTSON

before swinging
you must trust
you will keep your seat
there's enough lignin
in the branch's tracheids
the ropes will stay strong
the knots will hold
as will your hands
and the roots will keep you
knitted to earth

then you step out
into sky
striding across treetops
butterflies doing loop-de-loops
in your own trunk
the reward for your faith:
seeing the world
with a raven's sight

# ASPEN LEAF ULTIMATUM

## LAURA MAHAL

It wasn't the first time she'd seen naked young men lounging in trees—this was, after all, Boulder, Colorado—a college town with plenty of pledging fraternity brothers and those who got an extra-strong handful of gummies from the medicinal dispensary. But it was the first time the young man in question looked like her son. If it weren't for the spider monkey tattoo on his left buttock, she really wouldn't have been able to tell the difference.

"You, young man! Come down this minute," she said.

He peered past delicately placed aspen leaves. Wide-lobed oak leaves would have done a more thorough job. His auburn beard caught the light, and then caught on a branch. "Ouch," Aspen Man said, tugging fruitlessly, snarling his facial hair, his pale buttocks flailing like a fish seeking a path to the sea. "Could I maybe get some help, lady?"

She climbed atop a concrete turtle, meant for the entertainment of children whose parents foolishly brought them to witness the carnival-like atmosphere of Pearl Street, and reached up. Her keen eye for snow-weakened tree limbs was as honed as her ability to spy a shortstop with overly tight hamstrings or a pitcher not yet adequately recovered from Tommy John surgery. Rather than attempt to free the beard, she broke the branch at its base, wielding it, young man still attached. He dropped to the ground as effortlessly as a circus acrobat, or Troy Tulowitzki fielding a ground ball.

"Have you any clothes handy? We need to talk," she said, as she seesawed the wood from the thicket below Aspen Man's chin, evaluating the candidate before her. About six foot two, two hundred pounds, with a glorious curly mane cascading over his broad shoulders. Oh yes. This young man would work perfectly. Lean, muscular. Endowed with, um, all the right qualities.

He shrugged and wrapped himself in a tattered blue beach towel he pulled from beneath an overflowing recycle bin. The towel featured a large red *C*. Alas, she noted, not the *C* of a Colorado sun pressed against a mountainous skyline, but the logo of the cursed Chicago Cubs.

She snatched the towel from his waist and snapped him with it, for good measure, leading to an adorable wince on his adorable face. He wiggled and weaved a few steps away from her, in what could pass as a victory dance, under the right circumstances. She flung the towel as far away as she could throw, which actually wasn't shabby for a woman her age. "That won't do! I'll buy you something."

Taking him by the hand, then thinking better of it, given his extraordinary nakedness, she pushed his shoulders down so the concrete turtle hid most of his lower body. Like it or not, he was crouched like a catcher behind home plate. "Wait here. I'll be back before you can sing 'Take Me Out to the Ball Game.'"

She hustled to the All Things Colorado store across the way and purchased him a complete set of Rockies gear, from socks to sweatpants to jersey plus a ball cap. Boxer shorts were only available in Denver Broncos colors, but that would have to do. Blue and orange were a darn sight better than Cubs colors, for mercy's sake. No one would ever know if the young man looked like a Detroit Tiger underneath his Rockies uniform. Besides, the last time the Tigers won the World Series was 1984.

As to shoes—or better yet, cleats—they could figure that out later. They had a few hours to play with. Fortunately, the "no shoes, no shirt, no service" rule was loosely applied in a town that considered dogs and service donkeys perfectly welcome patrons at bars.

The pedestrian-only zone was mercifully quiet at this hour. She crossed to Aspen Man, whose eyes appeared to be closed. Probably meditating. She promptly upended the All Things Colorado reusable cloth bag on his head.

He snatched the boxers off the ground with admirable speed. Good eye. "Look, I can explain—"

"No time. Get dressed," she said. "I've a proposition for you."

He looked up, alarmed. She was at least twice his age.

"No, not that. After all, I'm asking you to get dressed, right?" She frowned. Did she look that old? She pinched her cheeks to add a bit of color and assessed her stomach. She hadn't missed a Barre fitness class in months. But whereas his freckles were adorbs, her sunspots were dime-sized and the color of a breaking-ball bruise. *Focus*, she reminded herself. *You're on an important mission that could make or break the postseason. You've got to sell this and sell it hard.* She shook off her thoughts and forgot about her abs, which were not bad for pushing fifty. As to the sunspots, well, she had spent a lifetime outside, cheering on her favorite teams.

Time to sweeten the pot.

"It's about a job. We'll talk over a good meal. My treat. Shake a leg and robe yourself, Your Highness."

She realized, in retrospect, that might have sounded like a slight. He didn't appear to be stoned, simply fond of aspen trees and the superb view these must certainly afford. For all she knew, tree climbing was his own form of Spring Training. As to his nudity, she'd never asked any of the naked young men she'd met in Boulder about motivation.

He dressed and followed her somewhat meekly to a burger joint around the corner, where they both ordered a mushroom Swiss with sweet potato fries and an iced tea. *Great minds think alike,* she thought.

She waited for the server, Candy—who looked like she wanted to ask the young man for an autograph—to quit hovering. "Here's the scoop," she said without preamble. "I've got a problem. I need you to help solve it. There's good money in it for you, and it's one night only."

He looked frightened for a moment, like the twentysomething he was. "Look, lady. I make an honest living. I'm not interested in a life of crime."

She grabbed his hand and squeezed it. He squeezed back—a good firm grip. Yes, he would do just fine.

"I'm not asking you to commit to a life of crime. Just one night of baseball. Your name, well, not your name, but someone else's name called—you run out—wave at the crowd, doff your cap, that sort of thing . . ." Her voice trailed off.

"Lady, I'm a street performer, not a sports guy. I climb ladders balanced on concrete turtles and do handstands on the top. I juggle bowling pins and bottles and occasionally flaming torches."

"Yes," she interrupted. "I've seen you. You're good." *Even if you are a Cubs fan,* she thought. "I've paid you $5 on occasion, because you've got skill. The key thing is you can catch." She emphasized the word. "You've never once dropped a thing when you've juggled."

The food arrived. The young man was distracted as the server stood at his shoulder, twirling a corner of her tavern T-shirt.

"You want his autograph, I take it?" asked the woman. The girl, cute enough but far too young, nodded shyly. This would take some managing. Fortunately, the woman had a wealth of experience when it came to shielding superstars from overly enthusiastic fans.

She cleared her throat. "Well, he has a game at seven tonight,

Candy, so Major League rules say he can't sign autographs. But this is your lucky day. I happen to have a spare poster here in my bag if you'd like." She reached into the silver-clasped Michael Kors portable suitcase that had appeared out of nowhere (no different than good-looking young men manifesting in aspen trees, if you think about it). Her Kors bag was embossed with the Coors logo. She tugged out what looked like a roll of parchment, unfurling it and pressing it flat on the table. "But I suppose we can make an exception, let him write a 'To Candy, my biggest fan'?"

She shoved a Sharpie at her unsuspecting tablemate. "You heard me. 'To Candy, my biggest fan.'" He moved in slow motion, staring down at the face—and beard—that so closely resembled his own. She almost said, "Yes, you're twins. Get over it." Except darn Minnesota clinched first in the AL Central last year. She could not say the word *Twins* to save her life.

To her unabashed joy, he reached for the marker with his left hand. *Mercy me, he's a leftie*, she thought, suppressing her desire to give him a quick peck on his cheek. (The one on his face, not the one sporting a spider monkey. What kind of story do you think this is?)

He wrote, "To Candy. Call me." Then scrawled a 303 phone number. Candy hustled to the kitchen, face flushed with pleasure, poster held close. Aspen Man followed her with his eyes, then shook his curls so they wrapped around his ears for a moment frozen in time. A *Sports Illustrated* photographer could have captured that image for the cover of next month's newsstand issue and no one would be any the wiser. *If his own mother wouldn't know the difference, then what could be the harm?* Her plan was brilliant. She was batting a thousand.

The young man took a deep pull of iced tea and said, "I need to understand what you're asking of me."

She tut-tutted. "Isn't it obvious? You're an exact replica of my son, down to—" She thought of the inadequate aspen leaves but forced away the image. The last time she'd given her son a bath, he'd been six and a lot must have changed since then. It was unfair to compare. She might have sunspots—anyone who called these liver spots was going to get an umbrella upside the head—but she had eyes, and she hadn't forgotten how to use them. She was, um, a scout. Yes, that's it. A baseball scout. Evaluating a potential candidate for his, um, fitness.

She waved Candy away, who was bustling toward the table with a basket of fried pickles.

"We clean you up properly, the fans will never know, and neither will the ball club." She leaned closer and lowered her voice. "He's on probation. If he shows up inebriated one more time, he'll be suspended for the season. I stopped by his house this morning with a fresh apple pie . . . you know, baseball, hot dogs, apple pie? The all-American symbols of wholesomeness, good fortune, all that?"

She saw the young man's confused look and said, "Never mind. The point is, he's going to be in no shape to play tonight, and you are in fine, err, shape." Her eyes drifted sideways. Candy was tittering next to the bar with a gaggle of college girls, cell phones out. Or maybe high schoolers. It was hard to tell, and she couldn't afford to take any risks with an underage server. Why oh why had she let him hang on to the Sharpie instead of grabbing it away, limiting Aspen Man's likely on-base percentage? *Focus*, she reminded herself. *You're on an important mission.*

"All you need to do is come over to my place, have a shower, let me get the twigs out of your beard, then you slip on a uniform and show up at Coors Field by 4:30. I'll walk you in the players' entrance, and, voilà! You get to hit the big-time tonight."

"But I couldn't hit a ball off a tee in Little League," he protested.

Golly he was cute when he was nervous. He would look marvelous on a jumbotron.

"Doesn't matter. My son's in a terrible hitting slump. Just stick the bat out—you might get lucky—then run like the dickens toward the base on your right. All that really matters is you catch any balls that come to center field.

"I believe in you," she continued after a lengthy inhale, honed by Pilates. "Last month, I watched you juggle baby hedgehogs. You managed to outrun the PETA people when they showed up. You've got decent speed, and your route efficiency isn't bad. We could go over running routes and fielding strategies this afternoon, if there's time. I've tried to advise my son [who shan't be named lest the author of this story be sued] on geometry, but he's a bit of a hard-head, it turns out."

He sighed, seeming to give the idea serious attention. He undoubtedly got propositioned every week during tourist season. *Not that that's what I'm doing,* she was quick to assure herself. *Though it isn't unheard of, surely. I'm not dead, for heaven's sake.* Her attention had wandered. She looked out the window of the restaurant to the crown of an aspen tree headed toward golden-yellow glory, reminding herself to concentrate on the tree as a whole and not as the sum of lovely individual parts.

"What's in it for me?" he asked, his eyes now focused on hers.

"Sign a contract that says you'll never ever spill the beans, and I give you $5,000 now." She looked him over carefully. "$5,000 after you've showered, that is," she amended. "Another $5,000 after you flash my son's pass at Coors Field and confidently stroll to the workout room, and $5,000 more when I pick you up at the end of the night."

His eyes bulged.

"Five grand once a month for the next two years, or as long as my son's contract holds out. That's *if* you keep your word about our deal and don't blab to the *Daily Camera* or the *New York Times.* Plus you clear your schedule on home game nights, just in case. If you play, you make a flat $7,500 per game. I'll throw in free medical care, in case you ever fall off your ladder or drop a flaming torch on your toe."

He leaned toward her, his purple, silver, and black jersey rippling in all the right places. "And what if I don't take you up on this deal of a lifetime?" he asked, arms crossed over his chest, looking for all the world like a major league baseball player negotiating a contract.

Her voice became arch and prim as she delivered the ultimatum. "Well, then, young man. That'll be twenty-five dollars for that mushroom Swiss burger you're shoving in your mouth, to start with. If I tell Candy you're a regular old street performer and not a sports star, she and her friends aren't likely to ring you up on your cell, are they? Or offer you free dessert?"

The server seized that exact moment to lean over the young man and smile, whispering, "Shh . . . It's on the house," while placing an extra-large hot fudge sundae before him. Candy had fashioned a baseball diamond out of peanuts, then filled it in with whipped cream and added pink candy hearts for the bases.

It was time to clinch the deal.

"The fine for public nakedness is $500, payable immediately, cash only. I'm on the Boulder City Council! Your nakedness is—" she was going to say shameful, but really, his body was taut and toned and easy on the eye.

"Providential, if I must say so myself. Welcome to the Rockies."

# 7

# IN PRAISE OF SLOTH

### ERIN ROBERTSON

to lying in the purple hammock's curve
gazing at lemon-yellow green ash leaves
outlined by bluebird sky
head lolling on the pillow
not even pretending to read

to frumpy flannel pjs
baked warm as toast
by the idling heat of a body
under more flannel under wool under down
under the full bright beam
of mid-morning sun

to languorous lunches
dirtying only one plate
and a single sharp knife
summer sausage, cheese, grapes, strawberries
the newspaper
silence

to evening sunset ritual
putting the day to bed in the west
feeling the last light on your eyelids and cheeks
watching the sumptuous palette change
awaiting the first star

to squeezing the barbell balloon of time
til past and future disappear
and all that's left is now
the beat in your chest
and the buzz in your wires
breathing in space
and exhaling joy
thankful for being
despite anything else

# 8

# PENIS ENVY

## BARBARA "BO" JENSEN

I didn't really want the penis itself, mind you; I just wanted the penis lifestyle. The specific equipment didn't matter so much to me. However, the physical reality was clear: boys have a penis. And I didn't have one.

And I was a boy.

Except, to the world, I was a girl.

When my little sister was born, my parents had both a girl's name and a boy's name picked out for her, since they didn't know the sex of the baby beforehand. In those days, it was a surprise. Which I think is a more accurate way to view your baby, honestly. Gender reveals could just be rolled in with bar mitzvahs and quinceañeras later, at a more appropriate time. Let your child take their body for a test-drive first, see how it handles. Let *them* tell *you* who they are.

But that wasn't how it worked back in the seventies. We weren't even close to that. Schools had just stopped forcing left-handers to switch and use their right hands, as if left-handedness was inherently wrong. I am, of course, left-handed. My litany of sins is endless.

Peering through the bars of the crib, looking at my baby sister, I asked my mom about those name choices and learned that if Beth had been a boy, she would have been Bret. Or maybe Brett. They hadn't decided on a spelling.

I didn't understand spelling yet and didn't care. Instead, I felt my small self falling into a tailspin of longing: if only I could be named Bret. Suddenly, I had a brilliant insight. "What was my name going to be?" I stood on tiptoes, leaning toward my true name.

Mom looked off, then frowned. "I don't really remember. I don't know if we ever picked out a boy's name for you." She looked at me and half-smiled. "You were just going to be a girl, I guess." I slowly lowered from hopeful tiptoes to flatfooted reality.

Crushed. Both me and Mom. I was clearly not the daughter she had hoped for. She told me throughout my childhood, "Here I was, dreaming of a little Shirley Temple with all the curls and  the dresses—and instead, I got a red hot sweaty kid who wants to go outside and play in the rocks." She thought it was a funny line. She didn't really pick up on subtle clues well, my mom. Or blatant clues, like me wearing my brother's hand-me-down clothes instead of the girl clothes from my cousin. No, against my protests, Mom dressed me in a navy blue sailor dress for kindergarten. A girl in my class pointed to the gathered bell shape and laughed. "You look like you're gonna have a baby!" I was mortified, and refused to ever wear that dress again. By first grade, it was any dress. Everyone called me a tomboy. I tried to be satisfied with that.

I remember watching the animated movie *Pinocchio* at this age. The Blue Fairy appears in the night, granting toymaker Geppetto's wish for a real boy by making his wooden puppet Pinocchio come to life. Pinocchio can move, can speak. "Am I a real boy?" Pinocchio asks the Blue Fairy.

"No, Pinocchio," she replies. "To make Geppetto's wish come true will be entirely up to you."

The Divine Feminine had spoken. That did not seem fair to me.

I resented this Blue Fairy; she clearly had the power. While manipulating Jiminy Cricket with her irresistible charms, she tells Pinocchio the essential traits needed. "Prove yourself brave, truthful, and unselfish, and someday you will be a real boy." He's so excited, he's all in, thinking he can prove himself. He can learn to choose between right and wrong. He'll always let his conscience be his guide.

Maybe it could be that simple. In second grade, I decided to take the Blue Fairy's challenge. My best friend had known me since we were three years old. Pulling her aside on the playground one day, I said, "I have something to tell you. It's really important." I looked around, then took a deep breath. "My parents made a mistake. I was supposed to be a boy. I'm supposed to be in a boy body." I looked at her expectantly, waiting for her reaction.

Her eyes widened . . . and then rolled. "You're so crazy." She laughed. "Come on," and she ran back to the playground toys. I ran after her, bewildered, wondering how I'd ever get to be a real boy if even she couldn't see it.

But no one could see it. Except the older girls at school, who twice kicked me out of the restroom. "You can't be in here!" No boys allowed. I was so furious, not because they thought I was a boy, but because I had to go to the bathroom, and I knew I wouldn't be allowed to use the boys' toilets. My anger flared as I retorted through clenched teeth: "I'm not a boy; I'm a girl." I hung my head, cheeks burning, ashamed of myself.

I felt like I was lying. I wasn't yet sophisticated enough to know what a half-truth was. I didn't know how to explain, to myself or anyone, that I was a boy on the inside, and a girl on the outside. It was all so confusing, I just continued telling the half-truth for decades.

Meanwhile, the messaging I received, at home and in society, was that a girl needed to find herself a man. The Women's Liberation Movement of the seventies was interpreted by Middle America to mean, "Oh yeah, boys? I'll show you." The rub: in order to show a boy your equality, you first had to have a boy's attention. The idea wasn't so much to be liberated as to be impressive. I switched from ignoring being a girl to aggressively being a girl. I chased all the boys I secretly wanted to be: rough, rowdy, smart, funny. We were equals, I thought. But even if I momentarily piqued their curiosity, I was never feminine enough to keep their interest. I wasn't really their kind of girl. Or mine.

By high school, I threw myself into sports. I'd always played basketball and softball and run track, setting records in hurdles and sprints. Always the fastest kid on the playground, now all the boys started surpassing me with greater muscle mass, strength, and speed. Their shoulders broadened. Their jaws squared. My female body began to betray me. I grew breasts. I grew hips. I grew soft. It all felt heavy.

High school feels heavy for a lot of kids. Maybe for most kids. Our self-esteem is so tied to our physical appearance during that time. We pursue such unrealistic standards of beauty. My problem, unfortunately, was that my fragile ego took a double hit. I didn't look anything like the cover models on magazines—not Elle Macpherson on *Vogue,* and also not Arnold Schwarzenegger on *Muscle.* Nothing about me looked or felt right, inside or out. I was completely miserable in my acne-covered skin.

Nevertheless, I was determined to go to college. I would find my place out in the world, travel, and write about other cultures, other beliefs. I set my sights on becoming a journalist. I imagined the flack-jacket androgyny of the international correspondent's uniform, hiking dusty hills into the highest, rockiest mountains, running for cover in the rubble of war-ravaged cities. I could prove I was brave and truthful, unselfishly caring about the people caught in the middle.

But I didn't make it that far. Even with a full-ride scholarship, I dropped out of college in my first semester. As I tried to step forward into the larger world, the small world of my childhood came crashing down around me: I had been a victim of long-term sexual abuse, and I couldn't keep it shoved away and locked down any longer. The memories, images, feelings, all swirled around me, and I felt like I was drowning.

My sexual abuse was an additional burden, not causal to my nonbinary identity, which was already established when I peeked into my sister's crib. Nonbinary kids without support seek connection and approval, like all children do, and when they cannot find that support, they make easy targets. I blamed myself, of course— my female body—that puppet costume the Blue Fairy couldn't see her way clear to upgrading into my real body.

It wouldn't have mattered; I didn't realize that boys are abused too. Which was the case for me: I was a sexually-abused boy, being violated in the body of a girl. By the very penis I needed to show that damn fairy I was real.

I imploded during that first semester of college. I just couldn't go on. I felt broken, defective. Unclean. Haunted. To save myself, I did what I'd been taught was right and good: I joined a church. A really big, really gregariously friendly, really over-the-top evangelical church. It was quite a spectacle, and I was wildly entertained, which felt so much better than confronting my trauma. Singing with the congregation, I was forgiven: for quitting college, for underachieving, for having been victimized. For being confused by my life. A clean slate. "Surely goodness and mercy shall follow me all the days of my life."

While I was singing, I so ached to believe. I yearned to feel whole and beautiful, so much so that I gave up and buried part of myself. I would try to be a good girl from now on, be what God and everybody else wanted me to be.

A nice young man sang next to me. I smiled at him. He smiled back. We started dating. I grew out my short hair. He was a person who never looked beneath the surface, and that was just what I needed, someone who'd give me a cursory glance and decide I checked all the boxes.

I'd found my man. We got married. He wore a jacket and tie, and I wore a dress.

He was the first of many husbands. Three, to be exact. For some reason, I just couldn't make a marriage to a man work, no matter how hard I tried. And I did try. I worked hard at them, not just for myself, but for my children.

That first sex with my first husband—that was a strange experience. It was vaguely similar to my childhood abuse but so different too. I wasn't too impressed in the moment, struggling as I was not to dissociate but to really try to feel what was happening. Over time, I learned to live deeply in the body I had, and it learned to respond. Sex was deep and powerful, and I loved it. I craved it. Here, I could bring forth the intensity of my true nature, joining male and female energies. I felt sane when I was having sex. I didn't realize what I was on to; it was only later I figured out that orgasm was a union within myself, as well as with my partner.

And then I found out I was pregnant.

Still living within the confines of my religious experiment, it seemed the next natural step for our marriage to become a family. Pregnancy had me puking nonstop at first, and very uneasy. But as my body grew with the baby inside, the morning sickness eased, and I confiscated my husband's child development textbooks, researching each developmental milestone of this tiny life. Who would this be? What if I messed up? What if I failed them? Science answered my questions so much better than religion had. I loved the poetry and mysticism of religion, that search for answers to unanswerable questions, but I relied on the math and measurement of biology to manage pregnancy.

The first time I heard my child's heartbeat from within me, I couldn't believe it. Such a miraculous noise, created by the science of Doppler ultrasound. Our shared blood flowing became a voice, calling to me. And just like that, I was hooked. One life pulsing inside the body of another made total sense to me. It was never weird after that. I laughed when their tiny elbows and knees stuck out, stretching my belly, saying hello. Again, I felt sane. Again, I felt united within myself.

Over the course of those three failed marriages, I had five spectacularly successful pregnancies and births. I was a natural at the fierce physicality of it all. I took on labor and delivery like a warrior, and my children came fast and furious, crying loudly, strong and healthy. I felt powerful. I felt lucky. And proud.

I felt like a proud dad.

As they were each born, I got to wrestle with what it means to be a mother. That word just never resonated with me. I'd had significant issues with my own mother, that was for sure. But this wasn't just about her. This arose from the core of me. As my milk came in to nurse each baby, I struggled again and again with my self-image. Usually lean and flat-chested, I watched in dismay as my breasts swelled substantially during pregnancy, and the foreign silhouette only became more pronounced as my body provided a bounty of nourishment for each hungry little mouth. While the big belly never bothered me, I found having huge breasts deeply disturbing, especially once the belly was gone. Men ogled them wherever I went, a predatory energy for which I was unprepared. Even as I felt exhausted relief that here was one thing I could do right for my baby, deep down, I didn't want to. And yet, I loved holding the babies that close, watching them drift off to sleep, cradled safely in my strong arms.

I felt like their parent, but not their mother. I'd always seen my father as my primary role model. We got along well because we were so similar. He was a good man, a good enough parent, reasonable, imperfect. I taught my kids the lessons he had taught me about responsibility, hard work, and honor. I realized I kept choosing partners who were more like my mother: moody, unpredictable, controlling, neglectful, averse to self-examination. I was a chip off the old block, all right, looking to marry someone just like the girl that married dear old Dad.

One of my marriages was particularly destructive. I fell for seductive charm, a sailor in the fog, not realizing the danger lurking under the siren's song. That relationship became so controlling that I nearly gave up for good, hearing my partner's words echoing in my mind, "You'll never be okay. You're going to need therapy for the rest of your life." Without knowledge of my inner self, he had still found the terror hidden in the secret place of my heart. In a desperate moment, I believed him. And alone with his words, I took a huge handful of pills.

Time often bends and slows in such extraordinary situations. I sat in my dining room, my hands flat on the table, waiting. And in the seconds between breaths, between life and death, I heard my own voice, from deep within: "I don't want my life to end. I want *this* life to end."

I knew what I had to do. While the house tilted and swayed around me, I staggered to the phone to call 9-1-1. Just as I picked up the phone, my husband walked in the front door. With my swollen tongue, I told him I had taken pills, and he rushed me to the hospital. They didn't let him into the emergency room with me. I relaxed my throat as they pushed in the tube to pump my stomach.

Resting under surveillance in the ICU, I knew it was time to make significant changes. I didn't belong there, surrounded by wires and nurses and beeping machines. I belonged in a larger world.

The next morning, the young psychiatry resident appeared nervous and fearful of any misstep as he checked in with me, the Suicide Attempt in Bed Four. I smiled at him, reassuring him that I would not make this same mistake again. I was no longer a threat to myself. I would be leaving my destructive relationship. He stammered, provided me with a referral for counseling, and left quickly.

Next, the hospital chaplain arrived. An older man with graying hair, he sat beside my bed and asked if I wanted to talk. I told him about the young psychiatrist and chuckled. "I'll take him up on the referral, though." I smiled, then took a breath and became more thoughtful. "I woke up this morning," I told the chaplain, "and I saw that blue, blue sky." I looked over toward the window. "And I realized: this day would have happened, with or without me." I turned back to the chaplain. "I never made a decision about living my life, before this. I was uncommitted, you know? But today, I decided: I want to be here, and live, every day, until I die."

He smiled and patted my hand resting on the white woven cotton blanket of the hospital bed. "You're going to be all right," he said, placing his hand over mine. "You're going to be all right."

I remembered his words, some twenty-five years later, as I took in the long view of the ocean from the mountains of Spain. Along the Camino, the pilgrimage route to Santiago de Compostela, I met many people, many friends who saw me for who I am: a human being. I wrote stories and songs along the way, and after forty days and forty nights, that classic time frame for one's passage through the dark night of the soul, I celebrated the journey with one dear friend in front of the great cathedral.

"Why the distance?" he asked me. "Why do you speak of your life as out here?" He stretched his arm out across the café table where we shared dinner.

"I think I learned this from studying Eastern religions," I began. "We're taught to bring an empty cup, like this wine glass, see?" I picked up my glass. "Life, experiences, these fill the cup. But we are not attached to our experiences. They come and go."

"Don't you see?" He smiled. "You are more than an empty cup. There is a *you*, inside, always. There is a *you*, in this cup."

I loved this man. I didn't understand how I could love him, yet not love him romantically. I wanted to kiss him. But I also didn't want to.

I thought my confusion was because I was learning to set new boundaries. I was such a work in progress. When I felt confident, my core male side came out, fearless, trekking across mountains and beaches and through forests. When I felt unconfident, I sometimes still retreated to my superficial female image and behaviors, sought the company of a man to prove I was okay.

But as I left Santiago and continued my journey onward, I gradually understood that men seek the company of men too. Men seek brothers, friends, confidantes. Love. Women are powerful, in their bodies, their resilience, their minds. We are all one.

When I reached Finisterra, literally "the end of the earth" and the 0.0 mile marker of the Camino, I sat with all the others on the high, rocky cliff of the lighthouse there, waiting to see the sunset far beyond us all. That night, the moon eclipsed the setting sun. We all cheered, so many small voices, as both lights in the sky were joined, passing one across the other.

Echoing Gloria Steinem, "I have become the man I always wanted to marry." I always was that man. And so much more. What a gift, to have experienced life growing inside my own body, to have given birth. I am reminded each year, when they call me on Father's Day, with love in their voices. I know I shouldn't brag; other dads will get uterus envy.

My grandkids call me Gorma. It is a play on the Celtic version of my given name. The name that means "wanderer, stranger, foreigner." The first name that, when joined with my middle name, translates as "wandering lightning." My true name, glimpses of understanding found in those unexpected flashes of insight and wonder, eclipsing the darkness.

I have many names. I am many people, all around you.

9
———

# ENVY

## MARY STRONG JACKSON

The dress with red elephants
green vines, yellow flowers, and black stripes
with a slit up one leg and fringe where it counts
the dress that got away
perfect for dancing on the plaza
and singing "I may be crazy"

the creamy caramel colored
French chair and ottoman
that exhaled when I sat in it
like it needed me to breathe,
held me like a baby cloud
with nimbus arms
and cumulus lap
I nearly cried from the comfort
a second-hand steal
that cost too much

once I got a chick dyed
pink for Easter then walked in morning cold
to the feed store hoping new food
would save it
saw my friend's bird weeks later

a living chicken
just blue tips now at the end of white feathers

it was the beginning of knowing
some things were never mine

# 10

## THE JACKET

### CRISTINA TRAPANI-SCOTT

Carolina pushed aside sweaters on a rack at the thrift store. She stopped at a ruby-colored one. Red suited her. It picked up the deep blue in her eyes and she loved that.

"You don't want that one," Carolina heard someone say. She scanned the store in search of who it might be but saw only the cashier at the checkout counter and one younger woman in her early thirties pushing a cart with a child in it. The woman wore a sleeve-less pink T-shirt a size too small. It rode up at her waistline, exposing a slightly paunchy midriff. A heart-shaped tattoo covered most of her pudgy upper arm just below her shoulder. The tattoo reminded Carolina of the one on her daughter's wrist, and she could feel a tear forming at the edge of her eye.

The woman gave Carolina a hesitant smile that bled pity but gave no indication she had said anything. The voice wasn't hers anyway. It was that of an older woman, Carolina guessed, though she couldn't be sure. She thought she detected a warble.

"Keep looking. Quick. Move the hangers. The hussy closes the store early. It'll be too late." The words came muted as if the voice were in a cave.

Carolina tried to remember the last time she'd heard the word "hussy." Her mother had said it once, the day Carolina turned fifteen. She'd bought some makeup with money her grandma had given her as an early birthday gift: blush, powder, mascara, and a deep cherry-colored lipstick. Her mother found the makeup in a box hidden in Carolina's closet. She confiscated it without a word. All but the lipstick. Carolina carried that in her handbag. The same day Carolina found her makeup gone, she painted her lips and sat for dinner that way. Her mother said nothing the entire time until Carolina cleared her place.

"Hussy," she had said as Carolina walked into the kitchen.

Carolina scanned the checkout counter searching for the voice, but the young cashier stood deep in boredom, glancing expectantly at the clock and biting her nails. Carolina bit her nails in response.

"Quit dillydallying and push those hangers," the voice said.

Carolina abandoned the ruby sweater and did as she was told. The metal hooks of the hangers squeaked on the bars of the rack in the way they do. The faint smell of must billowed as she moved the clothes.

"Hurry," the voice pressed again.

"Why so pushy?" Carolina whispered. She was afraid the woman with the child or the girl at the checkout counter might see her talking to the clothes rack. "That's not normal," she muttered under her breath.

Normal was a funny word, and it hovered in a distant, unreachable place sometimes. Carolina told her mother once that she wished she was normal. Her mother said normal was a made-up word. Carolina sifted through the rack slowly and methodically, in part to spite the insistent voice, and in part because she loved the feel of each piece: the wet silkiness of a satin blouse, the prickly scratch of a chunky wool knit sweater, the fuzzy softness of the occasional angora cardigan she found. She relished the way each piece held the shadows of the lives that once filled them, shadows of lives she wished she could fit into as easily as she fit into these clothes.

"C'mon. C'mon. That girl will shut those machines down, and one more night of this . . ."

The voice didn't finish the thought, and Carolina wondered what it meant as she moved each piece in a kind of dance, the swish of each piece creating a rhythm.

"Stop!" the voice said.

Carolina froze, as if the music had gone quiet in a game of musical chairs. She had played musical chairs often as a child, and she remembered twirling and dancing and running in a beautiful white eyelet dress as a piano clinked "Pop Goes the Weasel." Music played in the store now, old music from the 1950s that sounded surprisingly upbeat and happy with horns blasting in a way that made the fluorescent lights seem more stark and the old clothes and household items seem more worn.

Her hand had paused on a hanger that held a jacket her size. It looked like the double-breasted one worn by Jackie Kennedy the day her husband's life seeped away in her arms. But instead of a pink wool bouclé with the midnight blue collar and trim, the jacket on the rack was baby blue. The trim was just like the original. Carolina had seen her mother cry that day. Her mother never cried before or after.

Carolina touched one of the silk lapels. It felt cool like water, like the water from Lake Michigan that lapped over her feet in the summers when she and her parents spent time at their summer house. A few light brown stains trailed the front bodice to the right of one set of gold buttons. The tag inside read Chanl, like Chanel with no *e*, but the logo showed two overlapping *c*'s just like Chanel. A copy of a replica, Carolina thought. It had always been a replica, the one Jackie wore.

"Now, take me off the rack and let's get out of here," said the voice, which clearly belonged to the jacket.

"But the stains," Carolina murmured. "I never buy anything with stains. I mean, you know, and honestly. This jacket. With these stains." The stains were small and faint, but Carolina couldn't help but think of blood.

"They'll come off," the jacket said as it coughed slightly, "and what do you care about the stains anyway? I mean, look at you."

Carolina took the jacket off the rack and examined it closer. Other than the stains, the jacket looked almost new. She brushed the blue bouclé with her hand. It felt soft, soft like the sweaters her mother wore, the ones Carolina would bury her face in when she felt particularly bad about school. Her mother would sing and stroke her head, and Carolina would be lost in the soft sweater and the faint scent of citrus. Carolina knew her mother was lost, too, in her own field of sadness.

"Attention customers, uh, the store is closing in fifteen minutes. Bring your purchases to the checkout counter. The store is closing in fifteen minutes." The girl's voice came over the loudspeaker. It sounded like death.

Carolina had come in to get out of the rain. She thought she'd find some small items to add to her collections of figurines. Time had slipped away, as it does, and now she stood with only the stained jacket in hand. She had no need for a jacket. The rain had turned to drizzle outside. She looked around quickly, at the aisles of half-broken, random bric-a-brac and at the display of worn purses and handbags.

"Hurry. Get in line."

The checkout line was empty. The bored girl busied herself trying to ignore Carolina as she did other days. The woman with the tattoo and child had disappeared. Carolina couldn't remember seeing them leave. The empty store seemed vast and too fluorescent as she made her way to the counter. She placed the jacket in front of the girl. The stains looked darker and maybe bigger under the direct overhead lights that sat above the counter.

"I don't know," Carolina said.

"Don't," said the jacket.

Carolina looked quickly into the cashier's eyes, trying to discern if she had heard the voice. *Keep your mouth shut,* she remembered her mother saying. *People will think you're half crazy.* The cashier's eyes swam with emptiness. Carolina felt sure they were made of glass.

"Well, are you going to buy the jacket or not?" The cashier smacked her gum insistently. Her stringy bleached-blond hair was pulled in a tight ponytail that grabbed at her cheeks and the edges of her eyes, which were rimmed with thick eyeliner that contrasted heavily with her white hair and pale skin.

"Yes, of course I'm going to buy it." Carolina put her hand on the garment as if to claim it as hers.

"That'll be three dollars," the cashier said.

Carolina pulled the last few bills from her cracked leather wallet. It was a fine leather, from Greece or Italy. She couldn't remember. She handed the bills to the cashier. The cashier pinched them like she might a dirty napkin.

"Want a bag?" The cashier said in her flat, dead voice.

"No," the jacket protested. "I don't want to be stuffed in one of those things."

"But it's raining," Carolina said.

"What's that?" said the cashier.

"A bag. Yes, a bag."

The jacket moaned.

The cashier retrieved the hanger, stuffed the jacket in a bag, and held it as if she were trying to distance herself from it. Carolina took it and gave the cashier a side-eye look as she carefully hooked the handles of the bag on her arm and headed out the door. The lights flicked off before Carolina even exited.

Outside, she pulled the lapels of her coat up against the drizzle. The jacket was silent. Carolina would walk home. She had grown tired of the buses and the way the people would stare at her with pity. She'd never learned to drive, and even if she had, she would have hated concentrating on that one thing rather than looking at the world around her and noticing how the sun came through trees in small points of light.

At home, in her little efficiency apartment, she set the bag on a small table by the door as if it were any old item. It *was* an old item. The jacket had once belonged to someone else and possibly someone before that. Carolina wondered where it might have hung. Perhaps in a walk-in closet somewhere, one of those closets where one could lie on the floor, arms spread out wide, and get lost in the colors and textures that hung about. She couldn't spread her arms out on any part of the floor of her apartment. She wondered if the jacket would ever tell her the story. Carolina considered asking, but she wasn't sure she wanted to know right now.

"This is not where something like me is supposed to be, and it's getting kind of stuffy in here. I can't breathe." The jacket's muffled voice garbled through the bag.

"Hold your horses," Carolina barked back. "Let me get out of these wet clothes."

"I'm dying in here," the jacket huffed.

"Dying?" Carolina said. *How could a jacket know anything about death?* Carolina knew death. She knew what it felt like to hold her child's hand and watch life seep from her, watch the color seep out of her blue eyes, blue like the jacket.

The jacket fell silent. The drizzle had soaked Carolina through and through. She stripped off her wet clothes, threw them on a pile in a corner near her bed, and found some cotton pants and a T-shirt in another pile.

The walk home had made Carolina hungry, and she let the jacket be for a moment. She pulled a can of Campbell's chicken noodle soup out of a cupboard above the kitchen sink, cleaned the pot she'd used the night before for beans, and shoved aside a small skillet that sat dirty from her morning meal. The rain picked up and tapped at her window the way Carolina's mother used to tap on the table when she was angry with her.

Pictures hung on every bit of wall space in Carolina's apartment: some paintings, some old framed photographs—the sepia-toned ones of women in A-line skirts and form-fitting blouses, their lips painted dark, probably a deep red but Carolina couldn't tell. The men in them were in suits and fedora-like hats. No one smiled, but Carolina liked that. She took comfort in that. The pictures were of no one she knew. She'd just liked them when she saw them at an antique store. They made her feel like she had family, and Carolina liked the idea of claiming cast-off strangers in pictures as hers, just like she claimed cast-off clothing and cast-off books and cast-off kitsch. She felt like a cast-off herself.

She poured the soup into a bowl and set it down in the one small clear spot on the table. The heat radiated through the porcelain, warming her fingers. She sat with her hands wrapped around the bowl for a while before taking a spoonful. The salty liquid warmed her in a way that reminded her of being in the country, of being home in the big old house she had lived in as a child.

"Hey!" the voice from the bag called. The jacket. "Hey!"

Carolina set her soup spoon down. She had taken only a couple of mouthfuls. That was all she needed. Her skin looked thin like parchment paper. Blue veins poked through and snaked back and forth along her hands and up her wrists, but food had lost something it used to have. Carolina remembered the way her mother made cakes and casseroles and how the table was set perfectly, the bone china glowing under the crystal chandelier and Carolina making sure two forks sat to the left of the plate, the knife to the right, followed by two spoons. She couldn't ever remember using all of them except at holidays. She remembered, too, the slow and expressionless way her mother ate and how her mother expected Carolina to "eat like a lady." Carolina pushed the bowl of soup away.

The bag sat in a crumpled heap on the small table. The blue bouclé peaked out through the loop handles. The jacket looked more faded and worn than it had at the store. A wave of sadness coursed through Carolina. She pulled the jacket out and tossed the plastic bag aside as if the bag had caused the jacket to age.

"Oh, that's better. I really did feel I might die in there," it said.

"You can't die. You're a jacket," Carolina murmured.

"I know death, though."

"What's that?"

"Nothing. I mean, I know people die, you know."

Carolina did know. She knew well. She held the jacket up. The stains were shaped like tears, and Carolina swore they were darker than they had been at the store. She brushed at the stains with her hand. They looked set in, like they might not come out at all. They looked like small islands, dark islands in a sea of cool blue water.

"They really aren't what you think," the jacket said.

"How do you know what I think?" Carolina said.

"Well, your eyes. There's an ocean of . . ." the jacket paused. "Well, it doesn't matter."

*An ocean of what?* Carolina thought. She closed her eyes tight, in part to keep the jacket from looking in any further, and in part to see if the voice might just go away altogether.

"Perhaps you could put me somewhere I'm not cast off like the other things I see here." The voice wasn't gone, and it sounded more matter of fact than judgmental, but Carolina looked around her apartment anyway. Everything had spoken to her in some way—not like the jacket—but in some way everything had moved her. The piles of novels she thought she would read, the small chipped clay bowls with rustic sunflowers hand-painted on. Carolina loved sunflowers, and her daughter, Madeline, had loved them too. Carolina's mother told her they were chintzy. There were cookbooks with lavish cakes pictured on them that Carolina was never going to bake; scraps of fabric she thought she would craft into something; and clothes, piles of clothes she would never wear.

She must have heard their voices, their quiet murmurs that echoed *pick me*, but the more she looked now, the more she saw the layer of dust. It was thick in places, like the moss that grew on the damp forest floors up north where she used to take Madeline to see waterfalls.

*You're going to spoil that child,* her mother's voice echoed in her mind, always, but Carolina and Madeline had talked. The two of them had talked all the time, almost every day, even after Madeline moved out. And then they didn't and she was gone, completely gone, and the silence crashed in like the thundering of the water at those falls. Carolina could hardly breathe until she'd begun listening to the things.

"I could be propped up, in a closet, but not too far or too deep. I don't like the dark," said the jacket.

Carolina draped the jacket over her arm. "Why me?" she asked.

"Hmm. I don't know."

"I won't wear you."

"But you like my color. I know that."

"Yes, it was Madeline's favorite. But you knew that, didn't you?"

"Yes. I know."

Carolina stepped over a few piles to get to her closet—stacks of newspapers she hadn't read but meant to, some books, some clothes. She knew she should find places for things. She had in the beginning, just after Madeline died, but then all she heard in the empty spaces was her mother's voice blaming her. Carolina pulled a hanger from between the tight mass of shirts and pants and dresses, one of those padded silk hangers. Clothes pressed against each other, so it was hard to get fingers between them.

"I can't go in there," said the jacket. "You can't put me in there."

Carolina stared at the closet for a while. She wore virtually nothing in there anymore. Most of it was too big for her bony frame now. The black dress she'd worn at Madeline's funeral poked through the front.

It had been a small ceremony and few, if any, of Madeline's friends had come. They had all given up on her. Carolina hadn't. Even in her daughter's drug-weathered face, even through the gaunt pale skin and hazy eyes, she saw the child Madeline had been. The child Carolina fell in love with. Everyone, including her mother, told Carolina tough love was the answer, but love was layered and messy and painful. There was nothing Carolina could do to make it tough. It tore through her marriage, as if she and her husband were bits of thin crepe paper. And here Carolina was, amid all this stuff, holding this jacket.

She sat down on the couch and draped the jacket over her lap. The rain had passed. The sun streamed through the window overhead, flooding the apartment. It highlighted what Carolina saw, what perhaps hearing the jacket had made her see: the mildewed edges of books, the cracks that webbed porcelain, the yellow corners of old newspapers, most of which were from before Madeline's death. Carolina couldn't throw the papers away. All those living words. She thought Madeline might be swimming in them somewhere, but the paper was crumbling and turning to dust.

The clothes that stuffed her closet were the same, the lavender blouse she wore at Madeline's high school graduation, the jeans and T-shirts she wore making dinner for her daughter, or the sundress she wore in the afternoons in summer when she and her husband sat in lawn chairs and watched their daughter swing to her heart's content.

A tear fell on the jacket and the jacket sighed, not with contempt but with some kind of understanding. Carolina could tell that. Carolina had cried buckets of tears. The tough love was hers. She loved hard, maybe too hard, and she would always feel guilt over that. The stuff that filled every corner of her apartment was stuff that manifested because of the guilt, because for half a second when she touched those things, the guilt would be glossed over. She could feel almost like herself, like the way she felt on those days she had watched her daughter swinging. But that was temporary, and then the space around her would feel empty again.

"The sunlight feels good," said the jacket, and it sighed again. "It has been a long time."

Carolina felt for the jacket. "I know," she said.

The jacket felt heavy on her lap now, as if it carried the weight of everything it must have known and seen, as if it carried the weight of everything Carolina had felt. Carolina couldn't imagine where it had been or who it had belonged to. Maybe it had belonged to many different people. Carolina had belonged to many different people, and now she belonged to no one, but she carried the weight of all those people, of all those years.

"Carolina?" It was the first time the jacket had called her by her name. She wondered how the jacket knew.

"Yes?"

"You are good. You have always been good. I thought you should know."

No one had said anything near as beautiful as that to her in a long time.

"Thank you," she said.

Carolina thought, rather than stuff the jacket in the closet, she would hang it on the wall where the sun might reach it. She spread the jacket on the couch and stuffed the hanger carefully inside. As faded as it was, it had been something in its day. Carolina could tell that. She knew about things like that. She scrounged for a hook that would stick to the wall and found one. She placed the jacket on the hook.

"I'm sorry," Carolina said.

"Sorry for what?" asked the jacket.

Carolina shrugged her shoulders. She looked around at all the old and tired stuff crammed in every corner of her apartment.

"You have nothing to be sorry for," the jacket said in a tender way.

Carolina sighed. "I could have cleaned. I could . . . clean."

Both the jacket and Carolina were quiet for a time.

"We all have stains," the jacket finally said. "We all have stains that will never be washed away, no matter what we do."

Carolina understood. She wasn't sure she could wash the stains from the jacket or from herself. On the floor below the jacket sat one of those stacks of newspapers. The one on top read December 20, 2001. The picture above the fold was of a girl on a department store Santa's lap. She had brown curly hair, and she smiled in a kind of shy way. The girl in the picture could have been Madeline. She would have smiled like that. They were probably the same age in that picture.

Carolina picked up the stack of papers. She wondered how she had gotten from 2001 to here—to now—and how she hadn't seen in all this time that the paper was old and thin and just paper. The stack was heavy, heavy with time and lives and little girls on Santa laps.

She would have to take the papers a few at a time she realized, but she would, bit by bit, take them to the recycle bin. Then she would start on the chipped china and perhaps the mildewed books.

# 11

# THE SAINT OF DISCARDED ANIMALS
## LEW FORESTER

She moves through morning's purple air,
gnats swarming above her head like a halo.

Cats too many to count stay with her—
ruffles at the hem of her flowing gown.

An alpaca with a gimpy leg limps toward
her open palms. A blind dog lifts his head

at the sound of her footsteps. Animals once facing
starvation, euthanasia, live and thrive on her farm.

How many miracles are required for sainthood,
at least in the church of discarded beasts?

Miracles abound—she's declared of sound mind,
the humane society is satisfied. Dog chow, cat food

and sundry supplies materialize on her doorstep.
Veterinary interns volunteer. Clergy come,

they clearly don't know a saint when they see one.
They recoil at the sight of a cat that someone

once set on fire. What will become of the animals,
they ask, when in time her body fails?

Holding the cat, she says animals flow through
our lives like rivers, never dammed by time.

# 12

## MOLLIE

### JIM KROEPFL

**Shark Kills Research Pioneer at Florida Facility**

Sarasota, Florida. *A mako shark at the world-renowned Florida Institute of Shark Research killed Director William Serenby, who had raised the shark since she was born. Mollie, as the laboratory staff named her, is the only mako shark currently living in captivity, after her pregnant mother was caught in a fishing net. She is a popular specimen at the Ensiform Pharmaceuticals facility, and it is rumored the laboratory staff often interact with her. Mako sharks are among the smartest, but also most antisocial, of shark species. Mollie's domestication is a true phenomenon in itself, as no wild mako shark has stayed alive in captivity for more than five days.*

*Serenby was a pioneer in chemistry and marine biology, and his exploratory research involving marine life has led to groundbreaking advances in the reversal of cancer, dementia, and viral response. Dr. Jeremy Krepstein, current acting director of the Institute, has expressed the facility's condolences to the family of Dr. Serenby and vowed that his work would continue. Federal authori-*

*ties are investigating the matter, and the future of the shark is
undecided.*

---

I barge into the Institute looking for Krepstein. The facility is a
cross between a James Bond villain's lair and a second-rate tourism
trap. Lots of equipment. Lots of pools and tanks. Lots of fish. The
strong odor almost overpowers the smell of the Gulf only a hundred
yards away, which the tanks probably drain right into.

I find Krepstein dead asleep on a cot in the corner of one of the
abandoned laboratories. An empty bottle of Appleton rum lies on
the nearby stainless steel lab table, along with a small beaker half
filled with some similarly dark substance.

"Good morning," I offer.

He doesn't move.

"Doctor Krepstein!" I try again. More force this time.

The interim director pulls himself up and tries to focus. His face
is puckered, his lips dry. He is clearly not ready for confrontation,
which is too bad for him. I've only been here five minutes, and I
can tell you, I'm supersaturated with confrontation.

"Who are you?" he asks.

"I'm here to deal with your problem," I inform him.

Krepstein rubs his eyes. "Problem?"

I could be here for any number of reasons: The waste of
research funding, the absurd idea of letting sharks pool together for
the benefit of science, the insanity of harvesting their brain fluids to
create life-changing pharmaceuticals . . . a brilliant breakthrough.

It's also batshit crazy.

"The shark," I clarify, as if it's really necessary. Why else would
Corporate send me down? Everything has gone awry at this facility
in the last three months. The place had been a cash cow for Ensi-
form Pharma for five years. This shark ripped it all to pieces.

I pull up a chair and position myself just within Krepstein's personal space. "If someone gets careless out in the Gulf and they get killed by a shark, they just happen to be the wrong chunk of floating protein at the wrong time."

Krepstein scratches his head. Doesn't seem to be catching on.

I keep going. "But if a brilliant and valuable researcher catastrophically falls into a shark pool at an expensive research facility and gets killed by a mako . . . that's something entirely different. Don't you agree, Doctor?"

"I suppose so, um . . . Miss?" It's actually painful watching him speak.

"Maureen Windell. Marine Pharma division." I don't offer my hand.

"Corporate?" Krepstein coughs. "I thought you might be with the feds."

"We've been working to buffer this situation from those levels. You might be appreciative."

"Yes. Of course." Krepstein heaves himself up, goes over to the lab sink and splashes water on his face. "It's been pretty chaotic around here."

I don't respond. Why wouldn't it be chaotic? One of the world's leading pharma scientists is killed by a subject he's worked with for years, just before he was scheduled to present a major breakthrough. That's one reason we sent all the scientists home for a temporary sabbatical.

Krepstein wouldn't go.

The man looks at me. Blurry eyes. Unkempt hair. Lab clothes he's probably had on for days. "Well, then you probably want to see Mollie." He abruptly walks to the laboratory door and pulls it open for me.

I hesitate. Just for a moment, before I follow him.

"Know anything about makos, Miss Windell?" he asks without turning back toward me.

"Certainly," I answer. "I wouldn't be here if I wasn't well versed in all species of sharks." I'm used to scientists looking down on me since I lack that "doctor" before my name. But you don't need a PhD to be good at what I do.

We come to a door labeled *Pool A,* and he walks through it before me, this time not holding it open. "Then forget everything you learned, because you don't know squat."

Krepstein walks up to the edge of a large pool, one of the largest research tanks in Florida. No fish could want for more. State-of-the-art alkalization. Perfect light and temperature. All the gar it can eat. The shark in this pool is living well. But, more than that, I can smell the Gulf, and so can it.

"She's beautiful, isn't she?" he says, watching the mako circle the tank.

No doubt. It is quite the specimen. Young. Strong. It seems to move without effort, but certainly with purpose. I've read that it's quite receptive to others. Even humans. I get the feeling it knows I've come into the room, but its cadence doesn't glitch one bit. Krepstein can't seem to take his eyes off it.

"How do you feel about it being in a tank?" I need to evaluate if he's going to be a problem.

"Mollie shark is a pretty lucky princess," he says.

I give him a look. This isn't some well-bred Rhodesian Ridgeback. This is a predator. This shark is meant for the open ocean. The fact that it's even existing in a man-made pool is incredible. No other mako has been kept alive in captivity, but this one is adapting. Better than I would. Better than any human. A shame I have to do what I've come to do.

"Do you want to meet her?" Krepstein kneels next to the pool. He doesn't put his hand in the water. He doesn't splash, but the shark swims right up to him. It's been watching us.

Krepstein puts his hands on it and I catch my breath.

The shark just sort of hovers there. Swishing its tail in the calmest manner. They've made a connection.

"Come on," he says. "Mollie won't bite."

Tell that to the late great Dr. Serenby. Still, I tentatively walk to the edge of the pool, keeping my limbs on dry land. "Is it receptive to other sharks?"

"Like ice cream and root beer. We've tried her with all varieties of shark species. Sand. Nurse. Hammerhead. Of course, not mako." He smiles at it like a proud parent. "Eventually, they just sort of calm down. Get slow. Glide along at her pace. Until Ernest." He coughs. "You know what happened there, don't you?"

Of course I do. Ernest was the second-most-promising subject in shark research. They thought it would be productive to put him in a tank with this bitch, and it ripped him apart—a male twice its size. No one knows why.

"And there've been no other incidents?" I ask.

He looks down at the magnificent creature circling below us. Smiles. This shark has become a bit of a celebrity for the Institute over the last few years. Not many sharks let you feed them by hand, or pet them like a puppy. A man-eating puppy.

"None," he says. "We're thinking it might have been a territorial response."

I watch the shark . . . Mollie . . . gliding easily around the edge of the pool. If any species is driven by instinct, it's sharks. An instinct to prey. An instinct to kill. An instinct that resonates with me.

I shudder. Until two days ago, they were letting children pet her.

Mollie skims the edge of the pool right in front of me. She's beautiful. Long and sleek and powerful. Evolved over millennia to survive.

What would she be if she were out there in the Gulf where she belongs? She can certainly smell the open water from here. Being so close to home but not able to touch it would drive me insane. But she's calm.

Krepstein strips off his lab clothes, revealing a swimsuit. He drops into the pool and calls for her. He's either a fool or the bravest man I've ever met. Hopefully the latter.

She swims up against him, and he wraps his arms around her in a macabre embrace. Then she playfully nudges his side before darting away.

I let out the breath I didn't know I was holding. "You can't act like that display of affection was nothing."

"She's sweet. But you're right. A shark's home is out in the water, on her own. Fending for herself. Being what she was meant to be."

If it weren't for humans—their fishing nets and labs and experiments—getting in the way, that's where she would be. "And yet, you're hugging her." *When did I start calling Mollie* her *instead of* it?

Krepstein just looks at the shark longingly. "I don't think you exactly understand what it's like to befriend a shark. Granted, there are risks, but the reward . . ." He shakes his head. "Beyond belief."

His reverent tone almost makes me wish I knew. Sharks are like no other marine species. Streamlined body. Streamlined intentions. Millions of years of evolution that aren't going to be reversed with a little food and attention.

Which brings me to the reason I'm here.

"I appreciate the facility's potential, Doctor, and the company certainly recognizes the Institute's contribution to society, but that contribution is a risk, and I'm here to protect the company's ability to move our world forward."

Krepstein glares at me. "And what happens to Mollie?"

"What happens to the subject is the same thing that was going to happen to it before any of this crazy bullshit ever happened. Shark fin soup." I start to shrug but catch Mollie's eyes on me. I look away. My attempts to keep emotionally distant from the subject are failing.

"Destroy her?" Krepstein moves to the edge of the pool and pulls himself out quicker than I might have thought possible. For the first time I notice his wiry build. A body type more like mine than that of most scientists I've met. "You can't kill Mollie. She's been the keystone of everything we've discovered here. She deserves better."

Part of me agrees, but the higher ups gave strict orders. Still, I can't help asking, "What do you suggest, Doctor?"

"Let her loose." Krepstein says it so matter of fact, I know he's already been thinking about it. I wonder why he hasn't already and claimed that he put her down.

But thinking of them in the pool together answers my question.

I shake my head slowly. "That's insane, Doctor. You can't let a shark like this loose. She's an alpha. There's a reason they never let bullfighters practice with the bulls destined for the ring."

Krepstein is in my face now, voice intense. "Mollie came into the world in a pool. She's never known anything else, and she's given us more than any scientist or subject in history. Let her have the ocean. You'll never need to think about her again."

"It's not going to happen," I say. "A number of patents have been developed from this facility, and it's a valuable part of the company. I'm not going to let a fish threaten that."

He shakes off the water clinging to him, splashing me. "Let me ask you something, Miss Windell. Ensiform Pharma probably kills a thousand sharks a month. For drugs. For profit. And Mollie made a lot of that happen. What would you do if she were a scientist ready to retire?"

I frown. "They'd probably offer a golden parachute and a non-compete agreement. But this isn't a human scientist we're talking

about, it's a shark. A shark that has committed interspecies murder."
I'm being melodramatic, but I have to seal this up.

"You might want to revisit your thoughts on that." Krepstein
stares at me like he knows everything I've worked for. Everything I
really believe in. "Then you might just figure out why Dr. Milo
Serenby died in a tank he designed for a shark he loved."

The realization hits me like dynamic fission. Could there be
more to Serenby's death than an accidental shark attack? Krepstein
is certifiable. But could he be right?

"You think you can sharpen everything down to the bottom
line," he continues. "Well, let me tell you something. People don't
just build state-of-the-art shark sanctuaries because they like sharks.
And most of the time, the feeling is mutual. They do it because
there is an amazing opportunity. For them."

"Doctor, what you're suggesting is both baseless and
dangerous."

"Yes, Maureen." Krepstein says my name with an emphasis I
don't care for. "Which is because you don't know everything you
could know. But I'm going to answer your question."

Krepstein's boldness makes me take a step back. "I'm not sure
I've asked one."

"That's because you're a million miles away from what you
should be asking."

"Which is?"

"Why are you really here?"

He holds my gaze, and my mind reels. How did Serenby keep a
shark species alive for three years that nobody has been able to keep
in captivity for more than five days? How did a mako shark, the
most antisocial fish in the ocean, learn to interact with, and even
control, other shark species? And how on God's beautiful earth was
this crazy doctor just hugging her?

The answer comes to me.

"What did Serenby develop?"

Krepstein doesn't hesitate. He's been waiting for me to ask. He goes over to the wall, lifts off a whiteboard, and reveals a safe with an electronic lock. His right thumb presses the sensor, while his left hand punches in at least six numbers. The door pops open. He pulls something out, comes back to me, and extends his hand holding a simple atomizer. A light brown liquid glistens in the tube.

"What is that?" The liquid is mesmerizing, and I can't look away.

"*This* is why we're here. Shark essence taken directly from their brains. Developed under very specific conditions. Serenby was working on it even before Mollie was born. It's used for drugs that can help people. Just, not everybody."

I tear my gaze from the tube and frown at him. "What do you mean?"

"Boutique pharma. Manufactured scarcity. A very unique drug for very unique people. A substance that can help certain people. Help them know they're special. Help them know how to proceed in the world. And Mollie is a big part of it."

"I'm not sure I understand," I say, although I'm pretty sure I do.

"What do you think it's like to respond like a shark? Instinctually?" He extends the atomizer. "You'll never understand what they want. You'll never even know why they want it—until you actually experience it." He spritzes the substance into the air in front us. Brown droplets glisten in suspension. "Don't you want to know, for one night, what it feels like to be one of them? One of the true predators? The real sharks?"

He closes his eyes as the cloud passes over his face. I can tell he doesn't want to breathe it in. Doesn't want to go there again. Doesn't want to have to come back. But he does. He has no choice. He spritzes the atomizer again and breathes in the mist. Then he holds it out to me.

I take it.

Am I really going to do this? Feel what it's like to be a true predator? Feel the clean discipline of a shark's instincts?

Haven't I already started?

I push the button and breathe in the mist. There's no smell. No taste. No sense of giving in to something. Just an acceptance of the way things really could be.

Then it comes on.

The feeling of strong breath, strong propulsion, and absolute purpose. The feeling of being awake. The feeling of being ready. For whatever. Whenever. Being on.

Being.

The world sharpens and narrows. I see what's before me—and only what's before me. I am strong in my skin. I know the sense of moving through everything around me with quickness and force. I see what moves. What's holding me back. I see a world terrified. A world that needs ferocity. Sharpness.

---

I don't know how long it's been since I've taken the essence. I only know that I can have the life I want. I can be the person I want to be. I can be a predator with a purpose.

I can be a shark.

I don't think about the company. I don't think about the research.

I think about Mollie. In the pool. Surrounded by concrete. Fed dead fish.

Swimming in circles. Around and around.

And I can smell the Gulf.

Open water. I feel a need.

I know what I have to do.

I go to her pool.

She looks at me. Mollie. She knows that I came here to kill her.

That by that same token, I'm the only one with the right mindset to set her free. And I know in that moment that no other choice makes sense.

Krepstein watches as I place my hands on the gate to the salt water intake that brings in the water from the Gulf and lets it back out. The doctor may have been friends with her longer, but a scientist could never understand her the way I could. The way I do now. He watches as I open the gate.

A huge pipe connects the pools to the Gulf of Mexico. A few valves. A few gates. But the water flows free between the two when the gates are open. And you can bet a shark will notice something like that.

Mollie does.

She swims through the series of pipes without hesitation. She knows the Gulf. She's never seen it, but she's smelled it all her life. The world she belongs in.

She's going to experience it now.

She's going to be free.

And so am I.

### Wave-Surfing Championship Cancelled after Massive Shark Attack on Florida Coast

Sarasota, Florida. *The Wave-Surfing World Championship, sponsored by Ensiform Pharmaceuticals, to be held in Sarasota, was called off today after two competitors were attacked by sharks during training runs. The governor has issued an executive order closing the beaches in Manatee, Sarasota, and Charlotte counties indefinitely. Shark attacks have been reported up and down Florida's southwest coast from Boca Grande to Tampa Bay. The attacks all took place between noon and 2:00 p.m., which is unusual for sharks, who typically feed at night. Unfortunately, this is also when the beaches are most populated. Witnesses suggested that the sharks were actually working together, waiting for the wave-surfing contestants to be in the most vulnerable situations before they attacked. Ken Moriarty, the reigning gold medalist, noted, "It's like they knew what we were doing. We were in their world. And we were at their mercy."*

# 13

# BUCKET OF BLUE

CELIA TURNER

We might think
the worst already here
but for our inability
to imagine gaping chasms.
Ignore it we must,
to survive mayhem,
strictly as a species.
Too little too late.

A storm is coming.
Where is the blue?
Everywhere and nowhere.
Some days I lift
the lid on the sky.
Others, I sit drenched
in it, like a wet cat
left out in the rain.

We are the oyster
opening our house
just enough to feed—
or the barnacle
who sucks back
its feathery furl
at lightning speed
as if burned.

If we start now
is there a chance
for us or do we
go down
as humanoids
have, awash in a
bucket of noble blood
of our own creation?

# 14

# RARE EARTHS

## ANNE MACDONALD

Harold treasured the purples, browns, beiges, coppers, golds, and gray-greens of the New Mexico landscape. The sweet dry air. The sky a sapphire blue. The clay as golden as the ancient rocks supporting the bluffs. He rode his '72 Schwinn across the dirt road. To think they'd destroy all this beauty for spark plugs, lasers, stainless steel, polishing powder, glass, camera lenses, and cell phones.

*Lanthanum, Cerium, Praseodymium: Lately Complete Poopheads* . . . As he rode, Harold recited his rare earth mnemonics. *Samarium, Europium, Gadolinium: Steal European Gold* . . . The rare earths did not belong to Frost Mining, the BLM, or LithiCorp. New Mexico's rare earths belonged to the earth.

Harold tied his red Schwinn to the wooden pole outside the mobile office he shared with his colleague, Jackson Reid. The browns and greens, brush and pinion pines of Magdalena Ridge loomed in the distance.

"What did they say?" Jackson asked as Harold stepped through the office door.

"'We're retiring you, Harold.' That's what they said. 'You're done. We're test-blasting tomorrow, old man.' That was it. You're next." He handed Jackson an envelope. "The Frost Mining suits were not happy with our questioning the upcoming auction. Office of Surface Mining went along. Couple of BLMs sat in the room."

The midafternoon heat followed Harold into the trailer. September 30, the end of the government's fiscal year—the witching hour for new budgets and government layoffs. Harold plopped into the office chair. The air smelled dusty, clay-like, a scent as sweet as rain on dry asphalt.

Harold and Jackson's thirty-year career as government geologists had produced over two hundred reports for oil and gas drilling, gold mining, lithium mining, extraction of molybdenum and other lanthanides. They'd experienced the evolution of rare earth mining. They'd also witnessed government bureaucrats secretly auctioning off mineral rights to please one senator's donor or another. They watched crooked deals between oil companies and various government agencies approved for the cost of a weekend in Las Vegas. Land disemboweled, chopped up, cut open, killed off, for what? Enrichment of a few already-prosperous companies? For rare earth metals to make a magnet, an X-ray, junk electronics to satisfy some dumb-ass teen? Each time his bosses suppressed a report, each time they sneaked around public hearings, each time the mineral rights were surreptitiously auctioned off to cronies with inside information, Harold fumed. Harold argued. He pleaded. He raged. Then Harold blew up.

His bosses treated Harold just as his wife had treated him—one more irritating oddity in the course of maintaining universal power. Day after day, month after month, year after year, his wife picked at him—his thrift store shirts, his red '72 Schwinn, his name. *Calling yourself "Harry" would at least say to the world that you're secure in yourself. That life is made of choices and being born a Harold can be easily remedied by calling yourself Harry. But no, you insist on being called "Harold."* His refusal to own a television, his insistence on living below the radar, his hatred for convenience, they all drove her crazy. Well, she'd paid for those nags.

"Blasting starts tomorrow," he said to Jackson. "They're testing the site."

Jackson took his envelope. "Told you whistleblowing never pays. They get you in the end."

"Not on my watch, they don't."

Ten years before, Harold's boss had illegally forwarded his and Jackson's Piñon Field report to Frost Mining, who'd made a mint. The purchase had eviscerated over two thousand acres of rich New Mexico land on the cheap, making a few insiders rich. Of course, his boss had never admitted to rigging the mineral rights sale, but no matter to Harold.

"Frost Mining won't get away with it, not this time." A ball of red, orange, and blue flames grew in Harold's mind. *Neodymium, Promethium: Never Produce . . . Gadolinium, Terbium, Dysprosium, Holmium: Gilded Treasure Discovered Honestly . . .*

Jackson dug through his bag and pulled out a block of steel gray ore mounted on a polished piece of wood. "Here. This is for you. I knew our days were numbered. New world, Harold, and corporate is king now." He handed the mounted ore to Harold. "For old time's sake. Our first rare earth find. Remember? 1985. Right here in New Mexico. We wrote the book on rare earths. Go out with that accomplishment."

Jackson had retirement plans—vacations in Bermuda, a house in Hawaii, trips to European capitals, kids, grandkids. His wife loved him. He looked as healthy as his name. Who wouldn't respect a Jackson?

Harold? Harold's entire life could be written on a postcard, as his wife had often reminded him. *Oh my God, Harold, get rid of the red Schwinn. Get a cell phone. Join the world.* She may as well have added *you overweight balding glass-eyed government bureaucrat.* He'd showed her.

Of course, it was an accident—if a brick to the head can be called an accident—but in the end, he'd showed her. Which was why Jackson was really the only person left in Harold's life. Jackson never showed disdain for Harold . . . for anyone, in fact. Neither did Jackson's family, on those numerous holiday dinners since Harold's wife "left."

"It's illegal to disclose the draft reports to outside bodies," Harold snapped. "But those company men were sitting in that room with inside information. It's wrong. No one is following the rules. The government bureaucrats are actually buying stock in Frost. When no one follows the rules, anarchy prevails."

Jackson set the mounted rare earth ore on the desk and pulled up a box. He began packing his files. "Special rules for special people."

Harold glanced over to the large cabinet on his right, the one with the padlock and the red warning sign.

Jackson followed his gaze. "What are you going to do, Harold? Blow the place up? Over a draft report a first-year geologist could have produced?"

But Jackson's words were lost within the rage of Harold Smith. The rare earths were *his* finds. They were beautiful sections of ore that needed coaxing to expose. They'd remained in the earth for millions of years—away from human interference, rare and beautiful ore in the ground covered by a land of enchantment.

"Don't even think about it," Jackson added. "We'll get good severance pay. We keep our mouths shut and they hire us as consultants."

"We need to figure a way to reveal this to the world."

"What's this *we?*" Jackson packed in more files and closed up the box. "They retire me. I slouch quietly into old age."

A star-filled sky. The soothing mantle of the Milky Way. That evening, Harold Smith rode the red Schwinn up to the next day's blast site. The fading twilight captured the muted brown and red, gray, green, and gold of the landscape as magnificent as the holmium, promethium, and ytterbium hidden within the ore within the earth. Bluffs shot into the sky, casting shadows along the line of the road before him.

He and Jackson had found nine spots in New Mexico that held rare earths—terbium, holmium, erbium, gadolinium—as far south as Wind Mountain and Red Hill, as far north as Petaca and Laughlin Peak, as far west as Lemitar and Gold Hill. They'd withheld the draft report until public hearings, hoping a time would come when everyone stopped the junk electronics and the land could remain safe. But the draft report had been secretly handed off.

Harold placed his red Schwinn against the lone bush on the top of the bluff. If he didn't stop this land deal, in two years' time the brilliant reds and somber browns, the spotty gray-green brush and pines atop the high mesa would be gone, replaced by a deep cyclone of a mine, a vortex of wide dusty road winding its way to the bottom of the earth, exposing the reds and browns and burnt-oranges of its insides. Constant blasts would remove the guts of his land, black oxides exposed to the outside world, inner life drained of its last breath. Miles and miles and miles of his land turned inside out, his rare earths dug up until the landscape resembled nothing but a whirlpool of black, red, and brown bowels.

Harold crawled across the soft dirt, leading with his elbows, just like his years as an Army blaster. He didn't blame Jackson. Jackson was a good guy. He went along to get along. That was all right, in Harold's estimation. Harold's role in life was to protect the Jacksons of this world. *If you don't follow rules, anarchy prevails.*

After inching fifty feet over a small hill, Harold located the first of the six blast-bore flags that marked each of the square-hole points for the next morning's blast. The explosion, the blast, would test the ore content of the bluff and confirm the presence of the rare earths.

Anything can happen at a blast site. Premature discharges go off all the time. Test blasting causes fatalities when workers stand too close to the blast. Blasted rock hurls much farther than predicted. Unexpected lightning sets off explosions. Explosives drop down a dry borehole. Careless handling of the blasting caps; misreading of a discharge protocol; unnecessary, inconvenient, unscheduled use of a cell phone could set off the detonation site. Anything could ignite the *dy-no-mite.*

All through the night, Harold scooted across the top of the blast site bluff. He removed each of the flags that marked a true blast hole and moved them one mile east of the blast site—where he knew there were no rare earths—creating six fake boreholes, each two feet apart. He knew exactly where the suits would stand during the next day's test-blast, looking up and east, greedily discussing the rich potential of the find. The Frost Mining bosses and the BLM bureaucrats would be looking at the flags over the fake boreholes, while the real blasting boreholes directly above them would fill the air with dirt and rocks, burying them with the very earth they would despoil.

When he finished moving the flags, Harold hopped on his red Schwinn. The mine would never be built. The company would be in litigation for twenty years. The *suits* would be identified. Questions would arise. Why were they at this blast site? Why a blast site when the final report hadn't been released? Why were government employees present with Frost bosses? Investigators would find mineral rights illegally auctioned off. Harold would be called to testify. *Closure,* his wife used to say. *You've got to bring this divorce to a closure, Harold.*

*Closure*, he now sniffed. She saw closure, all right.

He took off into the night, reciting his and Jackson's rare earth mnemonic: *Lately Complete Poopheads . . .*

The next afternoon, Harold lay flat on his stomach, watching the action down in the ravine. His red Schwinn leaned haphazardly against the tallest bush on the bluff. Harold no longer owned a car, not since he'd disposed of his wife's car down by the Mexican border, the car that had carried her to her burial ground. Burying a body in the desert was amazingly easy. No one had ever checked on her disappearance. The lazy bureaucrats couldn't even follow up on the disappearance of a nagging wife.

Across the ravine, five men stood, all suited up and ready to deal. He recognized two government yahoos by their khakis and polo shirts. The two men in shiny suits and alligator boots must be Frost Mining bosses—fashionable boots that never stepped into anything resembling dirt or mud or bullshit. The fifth man must be their mining engineer. Harold cursed himself for not bringing his binoculars. He'd like to name every one of those men out loud.

One of the bureaucrats pointed up to the blasting flags, obviously indicating the site of the upcoming detonation. He would be telling them that once the blast hit, the seam of ore would be exposed. They could then take a sample back to their people and examine it for the rare earths inside . . .

The mountain's breathing suddenly erupted. The rocks began their disturbing and building ruckus—grumbling, groaning, wreaking havoc through progressive seismic waves. Finally, the rocks screeched, so otherworldly, so ethereal that they seemed to scream themselves loose. A piercing blast of hot air, an explosion— bigger than the atomic blasts Harold had watched as a child—blew the entire side of the bluff to smithereens. Dirt and rock rained down like filaments of fireworks, cramming the west side of the ravine with rocks and clay and dirt and sand, a shower of asteroids flying toward the earth.

Seconds later, an avalanche of earth cascaded down to where the men stood.

Harold scooted himself up from his hiding place, unleashed his red Schwinn, and made a beeline for the trailer.

---

Harold sat alone in the bare trailer, the draft report a crumbled mass of paper in the bin. His heart beat rhythmically. The smell of explosives inched its way into the stifling hot room; the sound of sirens blared in the raw desert air. As he packed up his computer, he hoped no one had seen him on the bluff, or that his red Schwinn had not left a trail. No, he'd covered all the bases, down to creating a fake blasting protocol.

He hummed "The Revolution Will Not Be Televised" as he put together a government-issued archive box and started packing up his desk. He looked around for Jackson's stuff. Jackson was always in the trailer before Harold. Thirty years they'd been colleagues; through the discovery of oil, coal seams, gold, silver, and his rare earths; through the disappearance of his wife, the unaccounted-for death of their Piñon Field boss. Jackson had never ridiculed Harold, never rolled his eyes. Jackson had sat there each morning, boots up on the desk, satisfyingly sipping Harold's coffee. He was a good guy. Harold envisioned him and Jackson high-fiving, hugging. They had finally gotten the suits. Of course, he could never tell Jackson what actually happened.

Harold picked up the mounted rare earth ore Jackson had given him the day before. He looked it over, wondered how deeply set the cerium might be. He pictured how, with his help, the yttrium iron garnet would remain in the earth, never to be used for such trivialities as a spark plug or a microwave filter, or a computer chip.

He should have thanked Jackson for the gift. Jackson was a good partner; he'd enjoy retirement. Oh well, Harold would thank him another time.

A note sat under the mounted ore: a note in Jackson's handwriting. *Going to the blast site. A beer tonight?*

# 15

# ADVANCED CIVILIZATIONS 101
## MELISSA HUFF

Today's lesson:

Trees really do communicate
with each other. With scent.
With underground networks of
tiny fungal filaments. Dense
intertwining root systems pulse
with electrical messages.
Chemical dispatches. The
talking has begun. Don't
misunderstand—you'll get no
gossip from these gracious
creatures. No backbiting. No
passive-aggressive language.
Far from it. In fact, they send
water and nutrients to nurture
ailing companions. Emit gases
to signal danger. Disperse
pheromones throughout the

air—scent signals that summon good insects to attack the bad. So next time you find yourself in an ancient grove, consider it a classroom for learning kindness.

And don't forget to take notes.

# 16

# A JOB UNFINISHED

## JOHN BLAIR

You wanted oranges
sweet, succulent
out-of-season oranges

        I tried to persuade you
        implored, yet determined

knowing your penchant
I stowed them in
your refrigerator.

        You pulled carpet tacks, *work for*
        *a younger man?* I asked.

That was the last time
except
in the hospital after

        you explained, *painters arrive*
        *on Monday* and I wondered why

the stroke felled you
I stroked
your forehead

                              or perhaps you
                              sensed a transition

you
whimpered
like my hand was hot

                              hating to leave
                              a job unfinished.

# 17

# A GARDEN OF LESSONS

## MICHAEL HAGER

This midsummer Sunday morning arrived not unlike most days in our mob-scene-of-a-household. My mother was losing the battle against the chaos of infighting between my brothers and me as to who would be the first to face the cleansing wrath of our twice-weekly baths.

"Eddie, stop fooling around and get ready!" Mother bellowed down the hallway as she struggled to reach the fastener on the back of her yellow cotton dress.

I relished watching her slightly overweight frame chase down my youngest brother, Wesley, as he raced down the hallway, attempting to escape the greasing down of his unruly hair with a sloppy portion of Vaseline. It was a miracle—amid the frenetic scrubbing of bodies, brushing of teeth, and screeches of resistance —that somehow, we would all be ready for our weekly family outing at eleven o'clock sharp.

With our mother and father in the lead, we marched single file the twelve blocks to my grandparents' house on the outskirts of Venice, California. My two younger brothers and I, in our unbounded enthusiasm for twisting the truth to match our imagination, christened our grandparents' white-clapboard Victorian home perched on a half-acre the "frontier manor." Any environment other than the blacktop world of inner-city Venice where we lived just had to be what the dime-store western novelists meant in describing "the untamed life beyond the concrete jungle."

As our family approached my grandparents' back-porch door, the heavy aroma of boiling chicken fat and oven-fresh biscuits drifted from my grandmother's kitchen window, filling up our senses with warm anticipation. My grandmother always prepared her standard fare of chicken and dumplings for our traditional afternoon gatherings. A small, but not insignificant, reminder that our family's roots were furrowed deep in the Midwestern plains of Kansas.

Gigi—whom my youngest brother dubbed while struggling to pronounce her first name of Geraldine—was incapable of cooking a bad meal. After all, she was the matriarch of the family tradition, caretaker of a revered down-home cooking mythology she dutifully protected for future generations. Unfortunately, my parents had only graced her with three grandsons, who showed little-to-no promise of carrying on her culinary wisdom. I often wondered whether we would simply disappear from Gigi's consciousness if she had ever been so lucky as to be blessed with a granddaughter. I say *lucky,* and yet we all had serious doubts a sister could've survived the relentless torture we would've heaped upon her. My mother often joked in private that her older sister, Doris, would have to be the bearer of such welcome news to Gigi. There was no way Mother would bring a daughter into this world only to have her face the burden of trying to survive three cantankerous brothers.

Our Sunday dinner always began promptly at two o'clock with Pops' stirring rendition of the Lord's Prayer. He wasn't necessarily the best example of a bible-toting churchgoer, but his fervor for this particular spiritual practice was unmatched by even the most ardent of Baptist preachers. He always began his prayer with "If you don't have time for the good Lord, then he won't have time for you."

As I bowed my head in silent reverence, I often wondered if Pops actually believed our family gathering warranted the undivided attention of the good Lord, and if so, what about all the other families who were vying for his attention at the same time? Was there some universal order as to when dinner prayers commenced and thus were acknowledged by this all-knowing Being? What recourse did we have if God were too busy with the more critical issues of the world? Would we have to simply wait before raising our well-worn silver-plated forks to spear one of Gigi's fluffy white dumplings while God tried to solve world peace?

Fortunately for our ravenous appetites, Pops was just as anxious to partake of his wife's cooking as the rest of us. Having finished communing with the Lord, and somehow receiving the go-ahead from the heavens above, Pops raised his hands to the sky and clapped twice, thereby giving us the signal it was time to dive into Gigi's culinary handiwork.

Observing Pops as he meticulously ladled out each steaming helping onto our plates was like watching a jewelry-maker pour hot molten silver into an earring mold. Even the thought of letting one drop of gravy fall onto Gigi's handmade lace tablecloth was unthinkable. It was not only the responsibility of the *spooner* but the *recipient* to make sure this act was performed with the utmost care. As he often notably offered before lifting the ladle, "A steady hand and a steady heart make for a sure-handed man." Pops definitely had a flair for homespun adages. Not a lesson easily ignored as I anxiously held my plate under the unwavering hand of Pops.

Prayers offered—and plates filled—signaled the beginning of our dinner conversation. These Sabbath confabulations always seemed to begin with cautious consideration but inescapably ended with full-blown indignation. My father was a devout liberal and defender of the downtrodden, whereas Pops was a rightwing, ultraconservative John Bircher. If words were bullets, they both would've been dead before the gravy cooled on our dumplings.

"What would you have us do? Let the commies take over the country?" Pops shot across my father's bow.

"No, but McCarthy is running a witch hunt, and you know it."

"Hell, as far as I'm concerned, they can put all those commies in jail."

"Does that include me, if I were of that persuasion?" demanded my defiant father.

"Well, if I have to pick sides—"

"Gentlemen," Gigi broke in politely but firmly, having had her fill of uninterrupted bickering, "that will be enough arguing at my table. I refuse to sit here and be insulted by your total disregard for my efforts in the kitchen." It was awe-inspiring to watch two head-strong men cower in the presence of this mild-mannered homemaker.

Fortunately for me, her condemnation offered my one chance of escaping the bitterly fought tête-à-tête. After devouring my share of dumplings and having been totally confused by the difference between socialism and communism, I slithered from my chair and made my way to the screened-in back porch. Having escaped, I boldly leapt over the three wooden steps, landing at the portal of Pops' backyard garden.

There among the young cabbages and the lush filigree of carrot tops, I felt safe from the turmoil of the adult world Pops and Father vociferously professed. Here in the cool shade between the furrowed rows of blooming sweet peas, I learned the true value of "two bits" and hard work. Every Sunday afternoon I picked up my designated hoe and began the task of gouging and digging at the weeds invading Pops' garden. I was at best clumsy, and at worst useless, in helping Pops grow the most bountiful garden this side of his Midwestern farming relatives. My ineptitude was mostly due to the fact that the hoe handle was twice as long as I was tall. Very often after ten minutes, my arms were so cramped I could barely raise my hand to tip back my soiled Dodgers baseball cap.

Pops, having abandoned the battle with my father and been appropriately scolded by Gigi, soon joined me in fending off a relentless encroachment of crabgrass and dandelions. Although I treasured these interludes with Pops, I knew it wouldn't be long before he found a suitable example to lay bare one of his elegant truths of life. Most were spoken, but some were simply learned by his straightforward example. I can still hear the slow drone of his voice: "Patience is not only a virtue . . . it's a requirement of the avid cultivator."

Of course, his words not only applied to the wisdom of growing a vegetable garden but also to the rearing of his grandson. I can't count how many times I fell victim to his backyard yarns told solely for the purpose of affirming his sage advice. On one occasion, he actually convinced me there was such a thing as *snipes*, and how he'd gladly teach me to hunt them. Only after a long night of sitting in the crotch of a pear tree did I learn this was just another one of Pops' ploys aimed at teaching me a lesson in the art of persistence.

Aside from his stealth words of insight, just watching Pops tend to his garden was lesson enough. Working alongside this descendant of Thor, I watched as Pops hunched over to whisper words of encouragement to his favorite tomato plants. He would gently cup his hand around a bright red orb and caress it as if it were a baby's face. I often wondered why he performed this strange ritual, and what value his tomatoes gained from such a one-sided conversation. Later in life when I first held the soft cheeks of Brenda Morgan before our first kiss, I understood the importance of a "gentle touch," of taking my time to sense the full extent of this sensuous textural experience. I almost wanted to whisper in her ear sweet words of appreciation, not unlike how Pops whispered to his prized tomatoes.

As tempted as I am to raise my grandfather onto a pedestal of total admiration, that would be folly on my part.  Pops was not the most beloved man outside his private world of chickpeas and cornstalks. To many he was a cold, distant Swede; his emotions were buried deep in the crevices of his antisocial life. I heard stories about his fits of anger and how he ignored his children to the point of tears. My mother, on more than one occasion, shared with me how she and her sister purposely instigated trouble just to break the cycle of his blatant disregard for their existence. Having only heard him raise his voice in anger on one occasion—which was after my younger brother foolishly threw a rock at his beloved Dachshund, Tammy—I couldn't possibly fathom how Pops could be a *cruel* man. But, not unlike with all beloved idols, I soon learned there was a darker side to my grandfather.

Along with his beloved hobby of gardening, Pops also raised rabbits. A good portion of his garden was bordered by every size and shape of wire and wooden cages. Though he sold a few rabbits for meat to friends and neighbors, his primary interest in these lovable furry creatures was the income he received from selling their fur. During the 1950s, rabbit fur was in high demand, from glove liners to blankets to full-length fur coats. On any given day, one could open the old creaky doors of Pops' cluttered barn and see the efforts of his endeavor as a low-income furrier. From the rafters hung as many as a hundred skins stretched tight across wire frames.

My first viewing of this eerie scene remains firmly etched in my childhood memory, as if branded by a hot iron, permanently leaving its mark on my psyche. One warm April afternoon when my curiosity got the best of me, I unsuspectingly wandered into Pops' musty, half-lit barn to experience his lethal handiwork. Seeing the evidence of the fresh carnage, I ran outside screaming at Pops that headless rabbits were flying all around his barn in a ghostly parade of blood and guts.

The horror of seeing those murdered heroes of my bedtime stories was shocking enough, but to have Pops proudly admit he had actually butchered them all, one by one, left me frightened of being in his presence for several days. The thought of Pops holding his favorite Buck knife against their outstretched necks, and imagining his finely pressed white shirt spattered with Thumper's blood, was just too much for my innocent mind to grasp.

Not long after this ghastly awakening, I devised a plan to free the poor whiskered creatures imprisoned by Pops—which, by the way, were mostly females. Their lives spared only as long as *his ladies* remained part of the breeding stock. Once they stopped producing, they were fair game for the stretching racks in the barn. This, of course, gave even more credence to my forthcoming heroic deed. *Kill mother rabbits, how dare he?*

Having hatched my rescue plan over the weekend, I decided to put it into action the following Monday morning before heading off to school. On my way to catch the school bus I made a detour down the side alley that ran behind my grandparents' backyard. As I crept along the jigsaw fence searching for the least risky place to climb over it, a vision of William Holden from my favorite World War II movie, *Stalag 17*, materialized. The hours being glued to the movie screen and watching my hero leap over barbed-wire barricades into muddy trenches under the blanket of 50mm gunfire gave me the instant fortitude to go ahead with my mission. Not unlike my mythical war hero, I knew one mistake would lead to disaster. When I finally located the ideal spot to breach the garden fence, I easily scaled it and was ready to assume my role of freedom fighter.

Slowly, I made my way from cage to cage, unlocking each wooden latch, gently lifting the rabbits and placing them onto terra firma for the first time in their lives. I proudly gave each one a firm pat on its rear haunches, and off they scampered to the inner sanctum of Pops' garden. When I had unhooked the last cage door and turned to view the results of my efforts, more than forty-five rabbits frolicked about Pops' garden.

After a moment of fleeting pride, sickening panic washed over me. I reached down in my chest for my next breath, but it was smothered by the terror of seeing a kaleidoscope of fur scrambling around me. I watched in paralyzing fear as the newly freed escapees munched furiously on the fresh red-leaf lettuce and carrot tops. I was stunned by the pure savagery of how fast they consumed the dark green spinach leaves Pops had so dutifully nourished for the past eight weeks. Leaping from plant to plant with the same voracious appetite as a horde of locusts, they devoured everything in sight.

A sense of deep dread ensued, of complete helplessness. I felt as if I had dropped a bag of marbles on a polished tile floor and had to scramble to pick them all up before a burning house collapsed around me. I started running away as fast as my wobbly legs could carry me. When I reached the fence I had so easily soared over but thirty minutes earlier, I felt as though I was standing under the shadow of an unscalable obstacle. *Who could expect a boy of my size to climb such a looming precipice?*

Glancing over my shoulder at the chaos in Pops' garden, I was instantly provided with the only inspiration I needed to attempt this physical feat. It took every bit of energy I could muster to lift myself up and over the fence and into the safety of the deserted alley. Of all the times I had strolled down this twenty-foot-wide dusty path, I had never truly appreciated the separation and protection it provided from my grandparents' backyard.

For days after my rebellious act, I expected to get the inevitable call from Pops requesting my presence behind the barn for a good ole switching—but it never arrived. I had only once before felt the stinging swat of a birch tree branch, but rest assured, it left a lasting impression on something other than my bruised pride. After what seemed an interminable amount of time (actually only two days), I decided my best strategy was to confess my ill deed to Pops and accept the predicted consequences. I remember cautiously sneaking up on him as he futilely attempted to save what little was left of his beloved radicchio and butter leaf lettuce.

"Where you been, boy? Can't you see there's work to be done here?" Pops barked, never looking up at me.

"Pops, I have—"

"Somehow the rabbits got loose a couple of days ago," he said before I could finish my confession. "Can you imagine who could have done such a thing?  Well . . . whoever it was, I'm sure by now he's realized the error of his ways." He turned in my direction with a steady glare. "Don't you think?"

I stood frozen in the mantle of my shame, knowing this was his peculiar way of forgiving me. Tears welled up in my eyes as I tried to sort through the real meaning of his consoling words. Just before I was about to offer another attempt at confessing my ill-fated actions, Pops said, "Are you going to just stand there all day, or are you going help me?" He turned his garden spade over in the freshly tilled dirt.

With that, I knelt down next to Pops and started forming small mounds of earth around each frayed lettuce plant.

Though most of my grandfather's lessons were unmistakably stated in his soft but gruff voice, this particular lesson was purposely left unspoken. Like most of his skillful tutoring, the full measure of its impact wouldn't be fully realized until I was old enough to truly understand the secrets of his wisdom.

It wasn't until the day I peered into Pops' coffin during his memorial service on the eve of my sixteenth birthday that I fully appreciated the depth of his lessons. Kneeling before his finely carved cherry wood coffin, I could barely force myself to look at his corpse.

When I finally did work up the courage to look down at his ashen face, I noticed a small yellow moth had landed on his freshly pressed blue suit. I thought how unfortunate for this poor creature to be unknowingly buried alive with Pops for eternity, and how Pops' best suit would soon be chewed to a tattered mess by the moth's appetite to survive.

As I reached down to remove the moth, with my heart pounding against my chest, I could see my hand visibly shaking. I hesitated, unsure if I had the fortitude to remove the moth from Pops' breast coat pocket. But just as I was about to lose my nerve, I felt a soothing calm come over me as I remembered one of his favorite mottos: "A steady hand and a steady heart make for a sure-handed man." Almost instantly, my quivering hand steadied, and I gently plucked the moth from his coat pocket. Glancing down at Pops one last time, I was left with knowing that he would look his Sunday best for the rest of eternity and that his lessons had not been lost on my youthful ignorance.

Living by myself as I approach my late seventies (and yes, I did eventually marry Brenda Morgan, but sadly she passed away a year ago), I am probably more like Pops than I'd like to admit. Maybe not as hardened or as cold as some described him, but for sure I value the solitude of my own company. And not unlike him and his daily habit of tending to his garden, I stroll out every morning onto a small plot of earth reserved for *my* vegetable garden. This is as much a spiritual journey for me as a means for nourishing my body.

As I bend over my plump-ripe tomato plants, I can hear the soft echo of his voice curling through my mind, encouraging me to flourish, to stretch out my branches beyond the boundaries of living an ordinary existence. Challenging me not to be a common garden-variety tomato but to be a Blue-Ribbon winner. Yes, Pops is still teaching me lessons that I have yet to learn, especially about losing something or someone you deeply care about. If I think about them long enough, every lesson from his garden has been, and hopefully will continue to be, a trustworthy compass for living out the waning days of my life with integrity, kindness, and a *sure-handed* purpose.

# HOLLYHOCKS
## MEGAN E. FREEMAN

The prairie rises and falls south toward the road
and down into the ditch that's mowed monthly
by the sun-burned old man on the county's tractor.

He cuts swaths through the grass, cropping both sides of the trench
and only altering his course to avoid standing water,
speed limit signs, and the occasional culvert.

Yet just past the mile marker, surrounded by short, sharp grass,
hollyhocks stand over six feet tall,
shocking pink in a sea of burnt sienna and yellow-green.

We wonder why he doesn't mow them too, like the hapless grass
for miles in each direction. Perhaps his late wife loved hollyhocks.
Perhaps each time he comes this way, he thinks of her.

# PRIDE AND PECKISHNESS
## LYNETTE MOYER

Maggie scanned the array of party food. She nixed the pickled herring. She decided to save her top choice—the Swedish meatballs —for a second plate. For an appetizer, she plucked two large Sicilian olives onto her tiny paper plate, along with three crackers slathered in basil and garlic goat cheese. Satisfied with her choices, she glanced up from the table and saw a man approaching, all confidence and speed. He startled her with his sudden proximity.

He was shorter than she and wore a multi-colored, long-sleeved tunic with a stand-up collar over skinny jeans. The design seemed vaguely Polynesian. He had chalky skin and a couple days' growth of red beard. His spiked black hair stood at attention. He stared at her through gigantic pure white frames, scanning her face with no attempt at subtlety. Black eyes darted behind the thick lenses. "You're Maggie, aren't you? Gerald's wife?"

"That's right."

Proud of his guesswork, he turned to the table, speared a large red grape with a toothpick, and popped the grape into his mouth. Chewing, he asked, "So, what have you two been up to?"

Maggie knew who Drake was, and he clearly assumed as much.

The dean's third husband—fresh from England or Australia or somewhere, rumored to be ten years younger than his wife—didn't bother to identify himself. He looked about fifty, only a few years older than Gerald. Drake's advent at English Department parties had stirred things up, with people gushing about his intelligence, eccentricity, blah, blah. She wished she'd paid better attention to the exact data. All she could remember at the moment was her husband's admonition to "behave herself" if she ran into him—Gerald was up for promotion to full professor. She assumed that "behaving well" meant bland small talk without casual cursing. She'd also assumed she wouldn't run into him.

"We've just bought a house," Maggie said, swirling the red wine in her glass and watching it glimmer. She hoped to avoid eye contact.

Gerald's admonishments added stress to the challenge of navigating his department parties. She'd only recently learned how to answer questions about her own profession—having settled on "software architect"—mumbled in a sort of gargle that ended the inquiry. She felt on solid ground, however, talking about their new house.

"You bought a house? Tell me all about it!"

"It's in Lumpton. It's a nice design."

"Oh, a *nice* house? Lumpton, yes, east of here, where all the houses are done in a sort of rakish postmodernist Tudor." He turned to survey the food, wrinkling his nose at a platter heaped with barbecued chicken wings.

"No, actually Lumpton is to the west, about twelve miles from downtown. Just south of the interstate, and the houses are, well, hardly Tudor. Brick fronts, the rest siding."

Was Drake an architect? A real estate agent? She started to ask, but he cut her off.

"Yes! I know that area with the brick. All those two-story Colonials with working shutters. It has the historic designation, doesn't it? Charming little nook, the winding brick streets, the linden trees, tidy gardens in the commons. What's the monthly HOA?" He said the words while also managing to fish, with a red wooden toothpick, a Swedish meatball from a tub of gravy that bubbled in the warming stand next to him. He wiped a drip of gravy from his lip with the edge of a paper napkin.

Watching him chew and fighting her own fierce desire for meatballs, Maggie replied, "Uh, the HOA isn't too steep. And the streets are a grid. Perfectly square. I like a grid." She pictured the grid. "Can't get lost, right? The avenues run east and west, and the streets run north and south. Streets are named after Civil War generals. We're on Stonewall."

With this announcement, Maggie raised her chin, readying for a lecture on the crimes of the Confederacy. She'd heard it from Gerald, and almost everyone who had visited. She shouldn't have volunteered the name of the street. Hoping to avoid a debate, she continued rambling. "It's closer to work. Cuts the commute by ten minutes. No, fifteen."

"I remember now. The grand oaks!" Drake pointed at her with the gravy-stained napkin. "Not historic, but it's an older neighborhood filled with foursquares, am I right?" He was still munching on a meatball. "Just east of the old part of Lumpton, stately and quiet. The downtown is still walkable from there, with dozens of little gourmet shops and boutiques. That'll be lovely for Gerald. I know how much he likes cooking." Drake's eyes closed under raised eyebrows, perhaps imagining the quaint boutiques.

Maggie frowned. They'd already established that the neighborhood was to the west. "I *suppose* there are shops. There's that big shopping center, the Crest Ridge Mall, I think that's the name, or the Crest View? It's nearby . . . you'd have to cross the interstate." She paused, remembering Gerald's knee replacement surgery scheduled for next month. They were both too young, she felt, for such surgeries, but the doctor attributed it to all the hiking they'd done.

Truth be told, they'd be happy in a mountain cabin. She smiled, picturing her husband darting across six lanes of interstate. "There's a new Walmart," she said, offering a rueful smile. Why was she feeling apologetic?

"The mall with elegant restaurants and that new auditorium for the symphony."

"Um . . ." She looked upward, as if she could find the missing piece of their small talk dangling off the chandelier. "I hadn't noticed there was an auditorium, unless it's behind the Walmart."

"Oh, yes, it's magnificent." Drake's gaze veered off the right edge of her shoulder. She wondered what he squinted at. Then, with a quick motion, he speared another meatball and chewed with vigor. As if given permission, she started to reach for the meatballs too, but that required reaching behind him for the toothpicks.

He stood firm, blocking her path to the meatballs. "But tell me about the house. The inside must be lovely." He studied whatever was going on behind her. Her annoyance at his apparent indifference overshadowed her need for meatballs.

All the same, Maggie was glad to skip the phantom auditorium. "It's a two-story, with a great big master bedroom and one of those five-piece bathrooms, you know, with a jacuzzi tub."

He nodded knowingly. "Built by that architect, Richard Samuels." His eyes fixed on her.

"The bathroom?"

"The new auditorium. It's especially nice for, say, string quartets, but not perhaps big enough for the full chamber orchestra. Okay, a small one, I suppose. Cellos get muddled somehow. Don't you agree? Too bad, really. All the money they raised. But never quite enough, right?" He signaled a waiter, accepted a refill of wine, and drank half of it.

String quartets? "Well . . ."

"Five-piece, did you say?"

At a loss for answers, Maggie looked around for her husband.

There. Was that Gerald, standing near Dean Stapleton? He appeared deep in conversation. Not ready to leave the party. He had hoped to catch the dean alone. Discuss his recent article.

"The bath." Drake said it as if speaking to someone slightly deaf.

Maggie blinked. "What?"

"You said the bath is a five-piece and features a jacuzzi?"

Hiding her irritation, Maggie said, "Yes, I can't wait to use it. Maybe even with Gerald!" She chuckled mirthlessly.

"Candlelight and chocolates, champagne cooling on ice nearby." Drake raised his glass.

"Right." She held her empty wine glass in one hand and her paper plate languishing with three olive pits in the other. Maggie had never mastered the art of eating party food while carrying on small talk. She'd never mastered small talk, period. She wanted those meatballs. But there seemed no hope of getting Drake to move on before he emptied the tub himself.

Drake chomped away at his fifth meatball. "I can see it now. Mirrors reflecting the candlelight. A skylight twinkling with a million stars overhead." Drake raised a hand, fingers like so many feathers, to indicate the stars.

"I prefer beer," she said. Maybe she could bore him into wandering off, without actually offending him. "The cool thing is we installed a big-screen TV. We can watch Broncos games almost as if we were in the stadium."

"Gerald likes football?" Drake asked, raising his eyebrows. He stacked a slice of salami atop a smear of stinky cheese and covered it with another cracker. Balancing this tiny sandwich, he went on, with no attempt to hide his disdain, "I guess there's a certain attraction. The roar of the crowd. The thrill of the scrum!" He winked, holding the tiny sandwich in midair like a small artifact. Was he going to eat that bite, or was he offering it to her?

Wait. He winked at her?

She cleared her throat. "Scrum?"

"You know, where grown men in shorts get all cozied up, head to hip, and grab one another's thighs and push and shove, straining to reach some sort of inscrutable climactic understanding." He tightened his shoulders, wiggling them. "Then the football pops out and away they go!"

Maggie exploded with laughter. He kept a straight face, cocking one eyebrow.

"You're thinking of rugby!"

A sneer crossed his lips. "Similar deal. Neither game makes the least bit of sense." He popped the cracker sandwich into his mouth.

"But they do! Rugby's, like, so different! Rugby is played—" she halted, overwhelmed with the need to point out the key distinctions between two unique sports, albeit with similar roots. Yet, there she stood, paralyzed between competing desires—the desire to instruct and the desire for meatballs. Wait, hadn't she planned to bore him? Yearning for a stronger drink than red wine, her stomach turned. Her heart pounded. "Excuse me, I see Gerald over there signaling to me. It's been so nice chatting . . ."

"But you haven't really begun to tell me about the house, Maggie. And Gerald is hardly signaling, unless picking out the largest smoked oyster is your secret signal." He barreled on. "Quickly, how many rooms?"

Maggie held her breath. She counted to ten. What game was this? She'd met plenty of snobby academics at her husband's department parties, but Drake was well on his way to taking the prize.

She would simply state facts. "How many rooms?" She drew in and exhaled a loud breath. "Let's see, it has the usual three bedrooms, a family room, a living room, a gourmet kitchen, and—most important of all—my private study. I'm going to decorate it with my collection of Chinese tea mugs, add a comfy couch, maybe hang the rainbow trout I caught last summer. I had it stuffed!"

"You must hang the lion head in the den!"

"There's no den."

"Very Hemingway, that lion's head." He winked at her again.

She was supposed to trade smug literary allusions here. "I never read Hemingway."

"Elizabeth Bishop, then?"

She stared blankly.

"Her fish went free, of course."

"Gerald's the poetry professor in the family. I design software. Back to the house, it's just a suburban house, exactly like all the others, though we have a nicer porch and a hot tub in the back . . ."

"And a deck overlooking the sunny gardens below the fountain."

"It's a flat yard, easy to mow."

"The deer park nearby, behind the hedgerows."

"Hedgerows?" In the twenty-first century? Her mind went to a documentary she'd seen about World War II. German Panzers. "It's a smallish yard, with a concrete birdbath that can't be moved."

"How romantic!"

"You don't seem to be hearing me."

"On the contrary, I'm caught on the wings of your description! I can see the conservatory, the bird sanctuary, the light filtering in, the exotic butterflies . . ."

Maggie planted her feet and peered directly into Drake's giant lenses. "Okay, yes. We've moved to a manor house. It has turrets, a moat, a widow's walk done in marble and gold, *and* a grand reception hall that doubles as a ballroom for the annual harvest festival when we invite in the local peasantry. It came with a head butler, a housekeeper, a staff of twenty, a dozen or so hunting dogs, and a chauffeur to take us to the mall whenever we shop at the Walmart. The furnishings are all eighteenth century, restored for modern use, and the kitchen is located below ground level, with room for seven scullery maids, though Gerald plans to indulge himself with all the cooking. I plan to read to Gerald while he adds pinches of saffron to his Persian duck stew, perhaps from the original edition of Jane Austen's *Emma* that, remarkably, was left in the library by the previous owner. The grounds stretch for miles. I can't wait to invite you and Sarah for a weekend of foxhunting."

She parked her empty wine glass and her plate with its forlorn olive pits on the table, grabbed a larger plate, reached around Drake for toothpicks, and loaded her plate with meatballs. She stuffed the meatballs into her mouth, two at a time.

The white-framed eyes, black and blinking, the spiked hair—he resembled a magpie.

Something chirped out a tune.

"Well!" He pulled a phone from his jeans pocket, glanced at a text. "What do you know? Sarah is ready to retreat homeward and have a decent glass of port. Goodnight, Maggie. I'm so happy for you and Gerald. You'll be quite contented in your little house in the suburbs. The picket fence and Happily Ever After! Ta-ta! Cheerio!"

He turned and walked off, poised, his back straight. He strode directly to Dean Stapleton and offered his arm in an old-fashioned, gallant way. She smiled and took it in spite of being bigger and sturdier than her new husband. Her other hand grabbed a coat. Then they walked arm in arm toward the door, skirting near enough to Maggie that she could hear his words.

"Lumpton! Of all places! I'm delighted to discover that the younger faculty feel a need to impress me, but she insisted on bragging she's a wealthy computer geek who could afford a *nice* house. It's a typical suburban tract house, but you'd think it was a manor in the countryside! I have to say, the woman sounded delusional. And she hardly ate a thing. Poor Gerald! One wonders about his judgment."

# 20

# CORN SEASON

### MARILYN K. MOODY

we set the battered pots on the stove
got the water boiling and bubbling
steam circling around the kitchen
steam in the already hot and humid room

we ran out to the garden
ran down the rows of corn
snapped the ears off the green stalks
crack, crack, pulled down the husks

we made a green trail of torn husks
piled the naked ears in a steel pan
cut off the tops and ends
with a red-handled butcher knife

we rubbed a soft faded washrag
over and over across yellow
milky rows, pulled every strand
of corn silk off, threw it down

we balanced the heavy pans
in our arms, carried the
full load back to the house
slammed the screen door

we made splashes as we
slid the ears into the furiously
roaring water, hot water spilled
over the sides onto the stove

we watched and waited seven minutes
tongs in our hands, ready, ready
steam hitting us, pulling ears
out, piling high on china platters

we slathered butter and salt
pierced the kernels with our teeth
greedily bit through rows and rows
without stopping until an ear was done

we ate and ate, how many ears of corn?
could you stand them end to end until
they matched your height? could you
devour eight, nine, ten ears of corn?

we finally finished eating
we thought our stomachs might explode
we couldn't imagine anything more
we lived like kings in corn season.

# 21

# HANDS-ON EXPERIENCE

## CAROLENA ROMEE

Have you ever just touched your own hands, your fingertips steepled so your left thumb meets right, right pinkie meets left? Doesn't matter if your hands are lotioned and moist or rough and cracked, because the point isn't about calluses or whorls—just this essential need to feel something.

I was always a tactile kid. Yes, I plopped everything into my mouth as a baby, but it was about the touch. Squares and triangles and circles, stars and moons made of plastic all tasted the same—like China, I guess, or Taiwan. But touching them, shoving those shapes through their matching receptacles, then fishing them back out from the Fisher-Price belly, waiting for my mom to wash them, then doing it all again—it was about touch.

By the time I was four, Mom let me sort and fold the socks for our family of—back then—five. I mostly knew my colors, but I could feel which socks went together, the pairs that were equally knubby and worn, whose heels were thickest and who had a third toe longer than the second. I'm not claiming I knew all of that at age four—no. I was just having fun sorting socks, helping Mom. Watching her work, her arms wiry and muscled, already freckled.

By the time Jimmy was born and everybody wanted to hold the newest baby, I was a bat boy, busy at the ballpark, a talented and employed ten-year-old, but after patting Jimmy's tousled curls once, it was Mom I wanted to caress. She, with lumps under her freckles. Like I said, I was ten. Not a dermatologist. But I felt the lumps, along with a flushed sense of overpowering anxiety that filled me from ball cap to sneakers: Maybe I should run to the garage and grab the box cutter, cut those hard spots out myself? Though my panic subsided, our overall anxiety levels did not. Mom had to have big patches of herself removed before Jimmy was two. Melanoma and, later on, Merkel cell carcinoma.

She lived long enough to give me several more brothers and sisters and constantly told me she had me to thank. I mean, it wasn't rocket science. People should pay attention to changes in skin texture. My real thanks was I got to do tick checks on my siblings when we came back in from playing in the woods. Though, to her credit, Mom was the one who burned them off with match heads or tweezed them out, dropping their disgusting blood-bloated bodies into a cup of rubbing alcohol. If one of the twins was sick and Mom didn't have the mercury thermometer close by, she'd grab my hand and press it to a warm forehead, heedless that I didn't want to catch what they had. At that point, I didn't think of my "gift" as a curse.

I was thinking about bats and batting gloves back then. Well, gum and Gatorade, too. Free handfuls of the former and endless refills of the latter from the five-gallon container in the dugout. It was my job to pick up the tossed Dixie cups and spit-out gum, scrape wet sunflower seeds off the home and away team's benches, and yeah, this meant I was baptized in baseball players' spit. I volunteered for these things when I realized the groundskeepers hated this part and brought grouchy energy into the dugout. Their muttering somehow seemed wrong, like they were dropping the bibs of their overalls and emotionally pissing into our sacred space. Whereas the players—the players tousled my hair with sweaty hands and, when they won, now and then they showered me in Gatorade. Sometimes, I thought of myself as their good luck charm. They let me know I was more than a bat boy, for damn sure.

Here's the thing. I wasn't the leanest or the fastest kid, but I knew Joey Martinez from Stephen Dady by their batting gloves. You could've put me in a cave and I'd know Martinez's bat was a Marucci and Dady's was a Louisville Slugger. The players said the entire operation flowed less smoothly when they were on the road because those older bat boys, who could miss school for away games in Cleveland or Kansas City, they weren't as reliable as me. Couldn't tell the sticks of wood by the sweat stains and skin cells of the players, which wasn't that hard, to be honest.

Bat boy days were my best days. I was kind of a legend. The ball players brought me back slabs of ribs from St. Louis and Boston Baked Beans from Chicago, not the kind out of a can but the little red sugar-coated peanuts. I'd listen to a Sox game and cram my mouth full.

Ten years of eating went by, and then Mom found lumps in her breasts—I had no reason to touch those and I wasn't an oncologist. Jimmy was probably ten and had been followed by Sammy, Jillian, Patsy, and Lee. There were nine or ten of us by then. I'd lost count. Okay, that's not accurate, but suffice to say I'd lost interest in the chaotic and noisy household that was my family. I was nearing twenty and struggling with my weight. College hadn't worked out so well. I was back at the ballpark but as a peanut salesman, hawking Planters by the packet, carrying trays up and down the stands. Got to handle fives and tens and twenties, but mostly folded-up ones and warm dimes and quarters, passed down the line of fans to me on the stairs, where I made change and gave out the goods. Later, I lost that gig to someone with seniority, and that's when I got to hot dog days instead.

Have you ever worked at a ballpark? No? What about a hockey

arena? Ever fundraised for your kid by spending five hours in a stand, running the cash registers or making hot dogs so you can pay your daughter's softball dues or for ice hockey lessons? The point is, have you ever seen how the hot dogs come frozen in bags of seventy-five, how hands have to count them at the start and end of every shift? You are trusting total strangers to get the food safety and handling right. Trusting that the frozen dogs haven't slipped out of the bag onto the floor where numerous feet have trod, or been turned, turned on the grease-caked auto turner but maybe not for the minimum seven minutes. Still raw and pink and partially frozen inside, or worse yet, thawed just enough for the juice of pig parts to wet the bun.

I don't know. Most people don't want to think about hot dogs. But they sure do eat them. Sold me a lot of hot dogs at the park. Carrying hot dogs is a lot heavier than peanuts, I tell you.

And that was trouble, because I had Grandpa Berl's genetics. Not lean like Mom, even before the cancer ate her away from the inside, one cell after another, organs eviscerating, despite all those kids and accumulated "baby fat" in her abdomen. Not a smoker like Dad, who never weighed more than 185, not even after a rainstorm when he was soaking wet, sitting in the cheap seats to cheer on the home team while the grounds crew was covering up the sacred baseball field for a two-hour rain delay. By then, I was pushing 225, which isn't ideal when you're barely five foot seven, sweating it out, hauling a tray of dogs plus condiments up and down stairs.

What, they don't sell hot dogs at your stadium? Yeah, I get it. Times change. Twenty years ago, now, those were the days. Slick mustard running over your fingers, salted grit and oil on peanuts that tasted like summer, candy bars they don't even sell anymore that I used to eat two or three at a time while waiting for Mom to come out of surgery or one of her radiation appointments. Meanwhile, my siblings sat there and read books or put together puzzles, hardly bothered while Mom died a day at a time. While I, I picked up each hair that fell from her head onto the seat of my lousy beaten-up car. A car as beaten down by life as the rest of us, rusted near the wheel wells. It smelled of the cigarette smoke of the previous occupant; cancer sticks were the aroma of my life when I wasn't at work, driving Mom back and forth. I picked up each hair of Mom's and tucked it inside a Ziploc bag, kept that in my glovebox, each hair parallel so it looked like a bag of very thin, fine spaghetti. Each follicle I collected was a prayer that Mom would recover. A bag full of failed faith, stashed mere feet away from my heart.

But we were talking about the ballpark. My hot dog days. I was huffing and puffing up and down those stands, carrying my tray of dogs and an array of condiments. Nobody cared or remembered that I used to be a legend, a bat boy in this very place, the one who knew if the bat was going to crack from heat or overuse. Players trusted me to warn them about things like that because my hands were never wrong. I could feel it in the wood, the grain thinking of separating before the inning was through.

What does any of this have to do with anything? Well, I asked you, way back at the beginning, if you knew what it was—this sense of touch—steepling your fingertips, touching the pads of flesh. If you didn't do it before, it's okay. You can do it now if you want. Take a good look. But imagine your fingers are fatter. Part of the 250-pound you. The 300-plus-pound you. Okay, you might not be able to see it—I get it. Maybe you're thin like Dad. Or you've had a kid or two, you're heavier, packing on a little extra weight around the middle—but not in the hands.

Do you have them pianist hands? Pretty, tapered beauties, nimble digits that can tumble around an organ and play "Take Me Out to the Ballgame" or rally people to shout "Charge!"?

Yeah, not me. Life had got to me. So much so that I stopped taking care of my body. Refused to brush my teeth for days at a stretch—didn't feel like smiling. There was honestly nothing to smile about, and I sure didn't want to see myself naked. Went weeks without bathing sometimes. Chewed my nails to the quick until my cuticles bled and I had to hide my hands in my pockets. As I said, life got to me.

By the time I was thirty, Mom was gone and Dad gave up smoking—not because he was worried about cancer, but because he still had all those kids to at least get through high school. Dad wasted away to brittle bones, but every one of my brothers and sisters did all right. None of them were anything super special, but they're doing good. Not fat, like me. You could practically pick any three at random, add up their weights, and yeah, they might equal one of me on a bathroom scale. Well, not a bathroom scale, because those suckers don't go high enough.

In here, they do. We got special scales. Scales of justice, the nurses like to call them. The "care team" thinks it's pretty funny that we fat-farm dropouts need to be locked away from the Boston Baked Beans and racks of ribs. As if some of us might bust outta here and become cannibals. While there certainly were some oddballs stuck in here with me, I don't think any of them looked like good candidates for bludgeoners or serial killers. There was a guy once, Fat Johnny people called him, which wasn't very clever, seeing how all of us looked in a mirror, but anyhow, Johnny Blubber broke into the nurses' station. That was straight out of *One Flew Over the Cuckoo's Nest*, I tell you, and we did have our share of Nurse Ratcheds, we did. So Johnny broke in and stole all the nurses' junk food, their Tab sodas and Mike and Ikes, their Slim Jims—which made us laugh, to be honest, as Johnny told the story —and somehow, he came across a box of Boston Baked Beans. I lived for a long while on listening to Johnny describe the taste and texture. If you don't know what those are, run out and buy some. You don't know what you're missing.

Except my weight is down some now. Ten fingers' worth.

Because, you know? Those fingers looked a damn sight like ballpark hot dogs. And I'm locked up in here, a place with smooth walls that all feel the same. Same as the floors, the ceiling, and trust me I know because I crawled the floors, clawed at the imitation skylights. It's all fabricated material, designed to give a little under impact. Each tile is *exactly* the same, even for me, who could feel the skin and sweat of ballplayers on a piece of wood. These tiles are . . . all the same. The pills, all the same too. Every one of us eventually loses our appetite. For food, for drink, for life. We feel no pain, dumbed down, the ridges in our brain smoothed by chemical reagents called prescription drugs, the only things dispensed by the handful in this cold and heartless institution.

They got me in here and it's hard, being on a two-thousand-calories-a-day liquid diet, no texture, just swallowing gruel, really. I miss the ballpark, and they never even show baseball around here, where most of the people are old with frazzled white hair. And me not even forty-five. Me and the new baseball manager, we're the same age. Even have the same birthday.

The nurses wouldn't give me cake for my birthday—not even an ice cream sandwich.

So I ate my fingers.

Not all at once, mind you. Over several hours. A night shift, because that nurse on duty was playing games on his phone. He was our favorite. At least, he was my favorite. Sometimes he could be bribed to slip us a fountain drink from 7-Eleven, or give us a pull of the tequila he kept in a flask, tucked in the same pocket where he kept his cell phone. That night, I traded him one of my rarest and most collectible baseball cards—it'll break me to tell you who because that can never be replaced. Let me just say it was the best of the best players, one who will go down in history as a blessed saint. In return, the nurse handed over the freshly filled flask. That was the last thing I grasped in my fingers, the metal cool and smooth like the walls and floors of this place. The tequila numbed my lips, my tongue, but my heart and soul were long deadened not by alcohol, but the absolute loss of everything I once held dear.

My fingers were the texture of hot dogs, except not cooked the full seven minutes. I did spit out the fingernails. Laughed a little bit, envisioning overalled groundskeepers grumbling about having to clean up my spit-coated digits, wishing some bat boy would do the job on their behalf. Wrapped my stumps in the last thing Mom ever gave me—a pair of thick knubby socks she wore in hospice, with rubber bumps on the bottom meant to give her traction and keep her from slipping on equally smooth linoleum floors. At one time, these cotton bundles used to smell like her, so much so that I kept these balled-up in my underwear drawer, to remind me of the person who gave birth to me and would have loved me no matter what my size and shape, be I an overstretched shirt or a pair of thin leggings. Rather than the triple-XL son I turned out to be. Mom was ever sweet, her font of loving generosity unstoppered by cancer and a slow, demoralizing death and disintegration.

I staunched the bleeding with those socks, and Mom saved me from bleeding out, as God is my witness. Even toes can smell like love, if you can believe it. But smells fade, and people disappear. They get thinner and thinner until they're entirely gone. *Vamoose.* Mom faded from my life, followed by Dad. And along the way, everyone who once knew me as the "bat boy with a gift," yeah, they all forgot that I was real. Real! The bat boy with some sort of extra-sensory touch. A bat boy who maybe was a good luck charm, knew which bat and gloves to pick at any given moment. The kid who scraped up sunflower seeds and Bazooka Joe gum, Big Red and Doublemint, Juicy Fruit, oh how I remember them all. Those were the days. My best days.

No, I didn't write any of this, you paying attention? I ain't got any fingers left. That night nurse who used to play games on his phone wants to be a writer and is setting all this down for me in exchange for fountain drinks and Boston Baked Beans. He says I'm a prime example of gluttony. Such a craving for my lost youth that I turned my fingers into stadium fare.

But he's missing the point.

I just couldn't stand having nothing left to touch.

# MRS. GONZALES' DIFFICULT CLASS
## EMILY RODGERS-RAMOS

She's called parents. Sent
some to the principal.
Laid them at the feet
of Jesus.

Now, before class
she pictures each of them
chewing. Everyone chews, she thinks. If you watch
a person eating, you can't stay mad

        like her husband,
      quietly chewing, with an endearing

                tilt of the head.

# A THANK YOU LETTER TO THE GUY I USED TO SIT NEXT TO IN CHEM CLASS

## KARI REDMOND

Thank you for having the vices that I appreciate and that we share, which might have something to do with why I appreciate them. Thank you for not having the virtues that mostly only annoy me and for having such virtues as 'sharing is caring'—those notes surely got me through a quiz or two, and 'calligraphy'—I was always happy to sign your name when that attendance sheet came 'round and you weren't there, too (maybe that also falls under 'sharing is caring . . . '), and 'chivalry'—I remember you at that one party at that one frat that one night at the beginning of freshman year and you pushed that guy away from me when it was clear I wanted nothing to do with him but he wasn't getting that, and finally for your 'easygoingness'—that first day in class, I kind of knocked you out with my giant backpack as I took the seat next to you and you were so cool about it and that's not at all how I thought you'd be when I turned around and saw you for the first time. You kind of looked like one of those preppy guys that my brother warned me about that would probably be in a frat with your sandy blond hair in a surfer style even though we went to school in New York. You were surprisingly nothing like what you looked like. So thank you and I'm not just writing this because it's an assignment for comp class and I might even send it if I knew where you were anymore.

Love, the girl you used to sit next to in chem class. (God that class was rough.)

# 24

# SORRY NOT SORRY
## MONTEREY BUCHANAN

Ruby never would have come to her tenth high school reunion—with a Wild West theme, of all things—if she weren't looking for George. They'd reconnected over the alumni app. But now, as she searched the sea of cowboy hats, she realized coming here without a plan was amateurish. She should have asked for a video chat, or at least a more current photo than the one in the yearbook, before agreeing to meet.

The reason she wanted to meet George was he was one of the few people on the app who was excited to chat with her. Ruby was a recovering high school mean girl, so joining the alumni connections app meant confronting the parts of her school career that made her cringe. *Sorry* was the word her predictive text suggested most when talking to someone new on the app.

A shiver of unease rippled through her body. She had apologized for all the bullying she could remember, but there always seemed to be more—memories long suppressed out of adult shame that bubbled back to the surface with each disgruntled classmate. A cruel nickname here, making fun of a girl's outfit there. Why should meeting George again be any different?

She must have said or done *something* to him back in school. Had she used him to do her homework? Cruelly turned down his invitation to prom? She hadn't been entirely honest with George now either, but then again, she hadn't been honest with anyone about the reason she'd taken a semester off back in high school.

The guilt spurred her hunger. She found herself at the buffet table, assembling a cheeseburger and trying to grab something to drink from the pyramid of soda cans someone from the alumni committee had stacked to one side. Still no sign of George. Perhaps he'd figured it out, done just enough internet stalking to decide she had too much baggage and wasn't worth the trouble.

But then the crowd parted and there was George. "Well, that was an odyssey." His volume drew almost as much attention as his wheelchair as he glided over to the buffet table beside her. "Sorry I'm late. Traffic was hell. Ruby . . . wow, you haven't changed a bit." He leaned forward with eager interest and the excited glint in his eye Ruby had seen in many men before.

Ruby found herself weak at the knees, and not just because of George's good looks—though he certainly had those: dark hair, deep brown eyes, muscular arms—but because her unreliable feet were starting to hurt from the dull pain of standing too long. She should have done the smart thing and brought her cane so she could last longer, but she didn't want to give suspicious former classmates more reasons to whisper about her. She could blame her odd stride on foot blisters from her pink cowgirl boots for now, but George would eventually start asking questions.

"Great to see you again, George!" Ruby said, hearing her voice spike up too high. Partial memories were starting to come back now: the two of them sitting together at lunch, George trying to get her into Tim Burton movies. But George was nothing like Ruby's usual popular crowd. Why had they been sitting together? Was it too late to ask him this without sounding rude? It probably was, and besides, if she started asking questions about his disability, it was only a matter of time before he returned the favor.

George was still gazing at her with interest. "Penny for your thoughts."

"It's just been such a long time," Ruby answered, shifting into a weird giggly voice she didn't like. "What have you been up to?"

In Ruby's experience, if you needed thinking time on a date, it was best to get the guy talking about himself. Meanwhile, she mined her memories for the start of their friendship and whatever she needed to apologize for this time.

"I went up to California after graduation, did a little computer programming and web design for my dad's store, then got my degree. Hoping to start my own media company someday. In fact . . ." He rummaged in his pocket and pulled out a business card, glancing at Ruby's legs as he did so. "Are you ok?" he said, frowning with concern.

Ruby's legs were shaking now. How much was due to the stress of standing too long and how much to nerves, she didn't know.

"Oh, yeah," Ruby said, tossing her hair automatically and trying to rest her chin on her hand at an angle, but the shaking threw her off. She should do the smart thing and issue a blanket apology for whatever she had done to him in high school, then go home and soak her legs in a hot bath.

"Maybe we should get a table," George offered. Ruby accepted, glad he had been the one to say it.

George found them a table draped with the school colors, and as he made his plate at the buffet, a new fear crept in: Ruby had never actually dated a disabled person before—or was it a person with disabilities? Considering she was one, she should have decided which term to use by now. In the months after her in-patient recovery, Ruby had gone to events and social groups for people with disabilities, but she'd always felt out of place. She didn't "look disabled" after all. And why should she be limited to friends and boyfriends with disabilities? Not to mention dating someone like that in high school would have killed any chance of reclaiming her Queen Bee title, already in a precarious position after her being absent half the year. Oh no. That was it, wasn't it? She had probably made fun of his chair in a desperate attempt to hold on to her popularity. No wonder they'd lost touch after graduation.

She sat with George, grateful for the full plate of food that allowed her to avoid talking. George must have felt the same way since their meal passed in silence. When it was clear that someone had to say *something*, Ruby mentioned a day at work where someone had reordered custom rainbow tutus from her website six times by mistake. She'd panicked trying to make them all by the deadline. George chuckled politely, but suddenly his smile no longer reached his eyes. Silence settled over them again.

"Hey, Ruby, if this isn't working, I get it. Apps aren't the same as real life."

Judging by the feeling in her cheeks, Ruby's face was going as red as her hair. George thought *he* was the problem.

"Look," she said, taking a deep breath. "I just want to say that if I ever, you know, made fun of your chair back in high school, I'm really sorry."

Instead of accepting the apology, George's eyes narrowed in confusion. "What?"

"It's just that . . . I never really got used to having a disability in high school, and I was a bit of a bully back then too, so if I ever . . . you know . . ." She ended with a bit of a whimper.

"You never . . . oh." George's eyes widened, then he smiled again. "Well of course the chair is going to throw some people off, but like you said, 'Sorry not sorry.'" George shrugged and drank from his soda.

"What?" Ruby said, giggling at his imitation of a girlish voice.

This made George go serious for a moment. "You really don't remember, do you?"

"Remember what?"

"The first time I met you, you were coming into the disability accommodation office at school . . ."

Oh no, here came the real horror story to apologize for . . .

"And everyone in there was looking at you. They saw *me* there all the time, but no one knew what to think of the popular girl who'd gotten in a car wreck and then disappeared. So, there you were, filling out all the paperwork, chewing the end of this sparkly pencil, and finally this jock in a football jersey straight up asked you why you walked all 'funky' now, and you just flipped your hair, glared at him, and said, 'Sorry not sorry.' The guy bolted and was afraid of you for weeks." George threw his head back and slapped the table, laughing and smiling wide. His laughter was contagious, and now Ruby could feel the smile on her own face.

"It was a cheesy comeback," Ruby admitted, the relief making her feel lighter as the memory returned. "You had better ones."

George shrugged. "Yeah, but I've had a lifetime of practice. For a disability newbie, you did great."

Now the memories were coming back. Their friendship had been brief, but essential. They sat together during those awkward lunch periods, trading physical therapy stories along with movie and music preferences while everyone else stared and whispered.

A weight lifted off of Ruby; she hadn't done anything to hurt him after all. And now that they were only an arm's length apart, Ruby noticed a detail that made his glow-up even more considerable: He had a tattoo peeking out from under one of his shirt sleeves.

George was looking at the tablecloth now, and it took a moment for him to meet Ruby's eye again. "Is it weird for me to admit I had a thing for you back then?"

"I'm flattered," Ruby said. "I'm just sorry we never—"

George reached across the table and took Ruby's hand. His felt warm and protective over hers.

"It's okay. You don't have to apologize for *everything*."

# 25

# CONFESSION

AMY IRISH

Forgive me, Father. The first boy I kissed is dead.

After months of stalking (with intimate threats
hissed alongside my new, four-letter name: *slut*)
I began to believe. In evil, visible as a leer.

I believed in good, too, in angels wearing human
garb. Father, with my full body, I believed
in evil always drawn to good, hell-bent to tempt
and hungry to corrupt. To feed. Too late.

I knew I'd been this full, Father, this filled
with light. And like a beacon I'd brought him
and his slithering need. But when I broke his hold,

I couldn't get back my holiness, couldn't sense
the sacred. Because every day he taunted me
with his kissing (and more) corruption. Took pleasure
in my terror and torment. Sullied me anew. Father,

Can you forgive? How I lit a bitter candle, prayed
with tears and rage electric-charged, on fire
with Old Testament faith? I prayed for him to die.

But not simply. I wanted the sword. I prayed hard
for pillar-of-salt destruction, for righteous wrath.
And Father, the next day, his family said
he was gone. No one knew where.

I believed he was dead, then. Truly coffin cold.
And I pictured his bereft mother, his funeral,
his silent body descending into crumbling soil.

I felt his erasure, his complete absence. A world
without. I lived it in my mind and believed
I had completely destroyed a life (however vile)
with my need for fiery, eternal vengeance.

Then the runaway returned, and my white-hot fury
faded. I was sated, but also a little scared. I decided
such calls for death were not a sign of good. But

I was actually good—*so good*—at belief.
In a power, higher or otherwise. At conjuring
thought to flesh. So Father, I released that vivid death.
Instead, I believed that this sadistic, spoiled boy

Did vanish—from my life. I imagined him unmade,
disappearing molecule by molecule. So he did.
From then on, Father, he was invisible at school, deflated,

Defanged. A specter without substance, a shadow forever
mute. I had faith that his every malicious deed made him

more powerless, more alone. So years later, when he took
drugs and (already forgotten) made his own choice to die—

Forgive me, Father.  I wasn't surprised.

# 26

# DIGGING MYSELF A HOLE

## LYNN KINCANON

I was digging a hole for a pond
in the heat of the Virginia summer
Into the sandy, loamy soil.
I had read about it in *Southern Living*.
They said I could do it in a weekend.

So I began, shovel by shovel,
inch by inch. Digging a six-foot hole
In the shape of a perfect rectangle,
Ten foot by five foot under scrub oaks
and wisteria, and beside six-foot-high
azaleas and camellias.

It took me days and days of hauling out dirt
and carrying in stones, mortar and cement.
I did this alone.
I always worked alone, despite
the presence or absence really
of a husband who was married

to his drink and his broken computer mind.
In isolation he would live,
in his room he would stay.
And sometimes he would leave for days.

That is when the neighbors
began to question the innocent
backyard project, that to all appearances
looked like the perfect grave—
Which sometimes I secretly wished
it could fulfill both promises.
The beautiful fish that would keep my company,
and my perfect life of living alone
high up in the trees.

As I wondered why this hole in the ground
was swallowing me up, I remembered
the photograph of the perfect people
on the page creating their pond.
The holy trinity. Husband, wife,
dutiful child which I would accept
was not my life.
That continuing to dig and dig and dig
to find the truth, and the words to say it
was what that long weekend taught me
staring six feet down
into the earthen crystal ball.

# 27

# FIREPLACE MANTEL

## JONATHAN ARENA

My husband's business trip lasts all week. They usually do. He expects me to stay home, alone, except for groceries and errands. He expects the chores to be done, the house to be without dust, and the laundry to be washed and dried and folded away.

I expect I'll do it all too. I always do.

I locate the feather duster exactly where I left it. I wonder if the duster is made from real feathers. A bird was slaughtered, bled, and plucked so we can dust our material goods and impress guests with a clean home. I pour a gin and tonic.

Perhaps multiple birds died for this duster. I take a long sip.

I work my way around the house and eventually to the fireplace mantel. It's the easiest part to dust because it's empty. I never noticed until this exact moment how much of an eyesore it is. It looks barren, unused, forgotten.

Morning sun shines onto the emptiness of the mantel.

My mother had all sorts of items atop hers. She cherished the fireplace mantel. She said it was like a display of the family. The centerpiece of values, traditions, and memories. It was her favorite part of the whole house.

I remember the mantel so well. An old clock sat at the center. Its tick was loud and distracting. You could almost feel time passing you by. Family photos, flowers, candles, and a small basket of pine cones were there too. Even the wooden butterfly I painted when I was six years old made the grade of the prestigious mantel. I painted it purple and pink and yellow and blue. My mother said it was beautiful, like me.

But our mantel is empty.

I pour a second glass. More gin than tonic this time, but I savor the taste of London Dry. He's a warm friend that accompanies me downstairs into the basement. We may not have an ornate clock to sit at the center, but we do have a cuckoo clock. I bought it at a thrift store early in our marriage. I loved birds, still do. But my husband hated it, still does, so down in the basement it survived for years.

Blood feathers from the duster give the clock new life. I wind the mechanism in the back and place it on the mantel. It fits perfectly.

I search for family photos, but we don't have many. My husband never likes to smile and it's only the two of us. No kids. No pets.

I find an old photo of our honeymoon. The sandy beaches of Mexico. I look so happy. We look so happy. I didn't drink back then. Time passes fast but slow at the same time. I position the photo next to the clock and wipe away a single tear.

Now flowers. I remember we don't have any. I gaze out into the backyard. Yellow dots are scattered in the browning grass. Dandelions.

My husband hates them, insists I buy poison at the store this week to kill them. He wants to kill them all. He always wants to kill things.

A third glass of gin and tonic. Almost no tonic.

I add dirt to my husband's two favorite coffee mugs. I carefully dig out two dandelions and place them inside and pack the dirt until my fingers stain with soil. The flowers slump a little but look beautiful. I add water and allow them a chance.

I arrange two blue candles on either side of the pots. Ocean Blue Mist. I light them and take in the aroma. It feels like I'm on the beach. The sandy beaches of Mexico with a wide, ignorant smile.

The mantel looks almost complete, but there's still room. I need to add something that a member of the family has created, like the butterfly.

I wander from room to room with my eyes alert. I make my way to the closet and open the door and there it is. Stashed behind some clutter but poking out as if it wanted to be seen in this very moment. I don't think I've laid eyes on it for years.

A ceramic bluebird.

I crafted it in a ceramics class early in our marriage. I loved birds, still do. It's not perfect, but nothing ever is. My husband was quick to point out its flaws when I brought it home. The left side droops, and one of the eyes is bigger than the other. Its fat legs look a bit awkward too. But I created it with my own hands. Painted it with my own hands.

I place it opposite the honeymoon photo and take a couple steps back. I admire the mantel. The cuckoo clock, the photo of happiness, the potted dandelions, the burning candles, and the glorious bluebird. It looks full now.

It looks like home. No, it *feels* like home.

I drink from my glass and a few drops escape the edges of my lips and spill onto the hardwood floor. I hesitate to wipe the mess up. Maybe I'll leave it for my husband to clean. He'll search for hours where we keep the towels, perhaps days, all while tonic seeps into the wood and stains deeply. I smile. I spill a little more on the floor. I laugh. I spill a lot more. He'll have to clean it all up. The rest slides down my throat.

I step forward to delicately shift the position of the ceramic bird.

I think I'm satisfied with the adjustment. Everything looks perfectly spaced now.

The sun no longer stares directly into the window.

My smile strengthens but another tear rolls down my cheek and collects under my chin where it hangs for a moment until falling. I want to cry more, but I don't, I hold it in. I hold it all in, like I've always done.

The clock strikes noon. The wooden bird jumps out of the tiny door and breaks from its mount. The detached model flies and hits me on the nose.

I stumble back and slip on the spilled gin and tonic, mostly gin.

My arms wave frantically until my balance is inevitably lost. My head smacks against the mantel with a resounding impact but I feel no pain. The empty glass smashes on the floor, and the cuckoo lands next to the broken pieces as if it belongs. I love birds, always have. Blood rushes down my face. More for my husband to clean. I feel woozy, dizzy.

I close my eyes and dream my old dreams.

# 28

# INFIDELITY—A VILLANELLE
## KAREN BETSTADT

I learn to bed myself each night
pillows to puff covers to turn
alone in the dark I see the light

My wallpaper's striped pink, black and white
my black barred bed-boards form my urn
I learn to bed myself each night

From all I've known none to invite
to hold me close as I turn
alone in the dark I see the light

Despite my rage I am contrite
too late now to dodge your spurn
I learn to bed myself each night

Bold infidelities indict
surely you'll choke and slowly churn
alone in the dark I see the light

Sure as your lies became my plight
Dante's betrayers in hell will burn
I learn to bed myself each night
Alone in the dark I see the light

# 29

# YOUR SOCK

### KARI REDMOND

I found it,
two years later.
You had moved.
My turn now.

The washer and dryer
loaded on the truck—
the last thing to go.

One final look
before leaving.
There it was, your sock.

Lonely and spider web covered
I picked it up,
loose between two fingers.

Two years and a day ago
Perhaps it was on your foot
Inside your shoe.
When I still knew you.

I bet you have new shoes now
And socks
I do not know you anymore.

What remains of us now?
But an abandoned sock
You didn't know you were missing.

# 30

# THE FIVE-DOLLAR DIFFERENCE
## KRISTINE OTERO

Humiliated, tears welling up, Glory stomped out of the store. New to this level of poverty, she cursed the broken system, her ex-husband, and her own ignorance. She had thought their problems were solved the day she finally got approved. They would have real food in their bellies, but Glory's daughter now had a fever and a cough. "'Food stamps, they have a name, they can only be used to buy food,'" she mumbled.

*The cashier didn't have to be rude*, Glory thought, loading the bags into the car. *She didn't have to humiliate me. The system is broken. I can feed my daughter, but I can't buy medicine?*

"Shit!" she yelled. "I forgot the application." A requirement of having food stamps was that Glory had to prove she was looking for work. A challenge, as she didn't have any experience.

The wind picked up; snow swirled around the dark empty lot. Glory ran to the cart return—only monsters left their carts in the lot. As she pushed it into the corral, the blowing snow revealed something wedged in another cart. Two five-dollar bills. One stamped with the word "Lucky."

Glory thanked the cold night sky. She might find faith, but it would take time. For now, she could buy cold medicine and get some gas. Shivering as her car warmed up, she planned to stop at the mini-mart down the street.

At the stoplight near the mini-mart, a woman stood on the corner with a sign that read, *Need coins, please help!*

The sentiment strange, the woman familiar, with her eye swollen shut and her arm in a sling.

---

Faith was about to give up when a car stopped at the light and rolled down the window. The cold wind and snow mixed with the pain of her bruises made the few steps difficult. Keeping a safe distance, she leaned down to peek in. *Sixteen more nickels.*

In the glow of the interior, a woman—her kin—offered her one of the two bills in her hand. Ashamed to need it, Faith shivered a nod. The woman nodded back, a smile curled up on one side of her mouth. A sisterhood of secrets.

Faith was surprised to realize the woman had handed her a five-dollar bill. It was stamped with the word "Lucky." A sign. Faith went into the mini-mart and asked to trade the bill for nickels.

"That's two and a half rolls of nickels, lady," the cashier said.

"I know; can I have them in the rolls?" she asked.

Rolls of coins were no substitute for strength, but Faith knew they would get the job done. Jack had promised to beat her silly if she ever talked back again. Faith had tolerated years of Jack's abuse, but now she had a secret—someone else to think about. Two nights prior, when dinner was late and no explanation would satisfy Jack, he had kept his promise. Faith, in turn, promised herself she would leave, but not before getting her own revenge.

Faith went over her plan as she walked home. Failing was not an option. Sitting on the stoop, she took off a shoe and sock. She put the rolls of nickels inside the sock, then the loose change, before tying the end. After a few good practice swings, she snuck in.

In a flash, Faith beat Jack as he slept—prison style. Catching him off guard. As he tried to stand, she realized *she* had beaten *him* silly. With one more swing she broke his jaw and knocked him out. A moment of glory, and Faith knew hope was on the horizon. She cradled her belly and grabbed the bag she had hidden.

Hope had already begun to feel sick when she got to the mini-mart for her overnight shift. To keep her restlessness and nausea at bay, she listened to an audiobook called *Grace through Faith* about common sense and human decency. It only added to the agitation of withdrawal. Nothing would solve the problem of the night, or the year, she was having.

Before her shift ended, she opened the register and took out a five-dollar bill. She giggled to see it said "Lucky." She promised herself she would pay it back.

The morning was cold, but the sun shining off the fresh night's snow gave an illusion of warmth. Hope craved the warmth of heroin spreading through her veins, but the morning sun had become a welcome yet weak substitute. She had stopped shooting up eight months ago, but the cravings never stopped. Instead of the subway, she walked to the clinic. Every morning, same routine. Pay Nurse Ratched the $5 co-pay, get the methadone.

Hope felt better immediately. The illusion of levelling out was almost as powerful as the medicine.

Grace had a pep in her step on the last winter morning she would have to walk into the methadone clinic. The voices inside her head were especially loud today. All of them at the microphone at once; they knew how the day would end and fought amongst themselves. Grace wouldn't be dissuaded.

Apologetically, she told the nurse she only had a ten-dollar bill.

"Just this once. You know we aren't supposed to give change," the nurse said, handing her a five-dollar bill.

The bill returned to Grace had the word "Lucky" stamped on it. It was fate.

Thanking the nurse, she put the methadone and five-dollar bill in her pocket.

When Grace got back to the shelter, Lucky was still sleeping. She kissed his head, promising a better tomorrow.

Grace put the methadone with the other thirty in the Altoids box. Relieved at reaching the magic number, her brain screamed over and over.

The five she slipped into the hidden pocket of Lucky's teddy bear. Everything she could save, in the bear—for the baby.

When night fell, she bundled Lucky up, placing the teddy bear in her bag. Grace was determined to carry Lucky one more time.

The fire station had a special door with a special bell. She kissed Lucky's head, and breathed him in one last time before placing him, the teddy bear, and a note inside. Lucky's life would be better. She rang the special bell, letting tears freeze on her cheeks.

The letter she left explained why. She wasn't an addict. She was schizophrenic. Unable to afford treatment or her medicine, she didn't trust herself. A quiet exit felt like her best option. The system had failed her, as it had many other women. A cycle of poverty, abuse, and inequity. Grace knew there was no glory in death, but she had faith—and above all, hope—that Lucky would live up to his name.

# 31

# GEORGE FLOYD AND ME
## EMILY RODGERS-RAMOS

Once I handed a cashier a twenty-dollar bill.
*It looks suspicious,* she said, and held
it up to the light. She summoned the security guard
standing nearby. He threw me to the ground,
and killed me. Just kidding. I'm a white woman.
She handed me back the twenty.
I paid with a card.
I ate my salad.

# LAND OF OPPORTUNITY

AMY IRISH

My father likes to brag he counted cards.
Best grifter in a rigged system, got a kick
out of getting kicked out, that blacklist
for every casino like red carpet special treatment.

Then he switched to stocks, sought a payoff
to set him up. Just wanted the minimum, really,
just a million so he'd make the Who's Who list.

He lost a family fortune on the way but claims
that made him a player. Able to fast-talk his way
back in, connected and buying on the sly,
then selling on executive speculation for a big win.

He proudly calls this *resilience, rugged independence,*
*grit*. Because all's fair in that Wild West tradition
of poxed-up blankets and treaties tricked away.

At least he admits it's a con man's world.
Freedom to fleece in this land of taking advantage.
With ample opportunity to pull yourself up,
always by someone else's bootstraps.

# 33

# A THOUSAND FINGERS

## JOHN CHRISTENSON

*Whatever I will become will be what God has chosen for me.*
—*Elvis Presley*

When my brother Ray banged on the trailer door and shouted, "Hey, Travis, it's time to get the old band together," I knew he meant to drag our family skeleton back into the daylight. And I couldn't let him do that. I couldn't go against Momma's dying wishes.

Ray crammed himself into the trailer's tiny kitchen and caught me in a bear hug. We were twins who'd looked identical at birth, but now I looked ten years older. My braids had turned gray, but his short-cropped hair was still jet black. There were only a few lines in his face, but grooves tracked across my cheeks like runnels carved in the desert by a spring cloudburst. And damned if I wasn't an inch shorter than Ray. When had that happened?

"We have to talk, Travis," Ray said in that clipped tone he used when he wanted something. "You and I are going to do the rain dance again."

Just like I thought—he'd let that skeleton rest for almost thirty years, but something big must've happened. I tried to change the subject. "I'm shocked that Wall Street let you take time off to see me, since you were too busy for Momma's funeral."

Ray ignored that and squinted at the picture on the wall of the two of us, taken by Momma the day we turned fifteen, the day we learned how to control the weather.

I tried again. "You haven't returned my calls. You must be awful busy these days."

He frowned and rubbed his chin for a moment. "Yeah, busy. Got anything to drink around here?"

I gave him a cola, hoping he wouldn't want anything stronger. To my relief, he said it was fine. "So," I prompted, "how's that fancy investment bank treating you?"

Ray took a long pull from the soft drink and shrugged. "You know how it is. They need a fall guy whenever the market crashes, so this time they blamed the Indian."

"You mean they fired you? They can't do that! It's illegal, it's discrimination, it's—"

"You haven't heard the half of it. My firm spread the word around and now no one will hire me. So, I'm out of a job and a career. I lodged a protest, even tried a lawsuit. No dice." Ray nodded at the door. "Show me around the ranch, Trav."

Even under these circumstances, I was still happy to see my brother. My wife left last year, said she'd finally had it with ranch life after the latest drought had wiped out most of our stock. And then Momma died two months ago. Now I was alone. Sure, Ray and I had our differences, and he was probably here because of a scheme he'd hatched, but I still wanted more than anything for the two of us to be a family again.

We took the rusted Jeep to the sparse north pasture, where a couple dozen head of cattle with their ribs showing were trying their best to forage on parched clover and fescue. I introduced Ray to the two remaining hands, who were filling troughs from a watering truck. I told Ray the ranch wouldn't survive much longer, that this was the worst dry spell since Father's liver gave out twenty years ago.

"We could fix this," Ray said. "We could make it rain, you and me. That's why I'm here."

I squinted at the cloudless blue sky. "Since you didn't come to the funeral, I never had a chance to tell you what Momma said about the thousand fingers, about why we can't do the rain dance anymore."

Ray gave a snort. "What are you talking about? The whole thing was her doing in the first place."

"I'm telling you, she wouldn't like it."

"Hey, Trav, I know you still live by the seven virtues Momma drilled into us, and I know you look down on me because—"

I waved my hand to cut him off. "No, that's not it. We're just different people. We went our separate ways a long time ago."

"It's okay, Travis." Ray gave me a lopsided grin. "The truth is, I look down on me too. The drinking, the endless cycle of greed on Wall Street. No matter how much I had, it was never enough. Hell, I can probably tick off all the vices Momma disapproved of and then some. But I want to make amends. I really do."

I shook my head. "I don't know. I've seen this before, a smoke-screen to make people think you've turned over a new leaf, but it turns out to be just another scam."

Ray threw back his head and laughed. "See? You do look down on me. But I've changed, bro, that's the point. For me, it used to be all about, 'I have rights.' Now I'm trying to live by, 'I have obliga-tions.' That's what I feel for the tribe, Travis. A sense of obligation. They need our help, and they need it now."

"Yes, they do," I agreed. "And no one else is going to help them, that's for sure. I'm just not sure I can trust you."

Ray shaded his eyes and stared across a dry arroyo at Black Rider Mesa, its flat top rising above the late-afternoon haze, floating like an apparition. The place where it all began. "If the tribe is going to survive, it's up to us," he said. "Our rain dance is the only hope they've got."

"But Momma—"

"It's time to stop hiding behind her apron, Travis, now that she's gone. I'm staying in Farmington for a couple of nights. You've got that long to come to your senses. You know I can't do this without you."

I told him I'd sleep on it, but I didn't get any sleep for two days. Instead, I thought about how Momma had renamed the ranch from the Bar C to The Finger of God when she'd realized what her sons could do. "The Finger of God has touched my sons," she'd told everyone.

At the end of the second sleepless night, I walked out to the porch on the front of the trailer to watch the sunrise and let that long-ago day wash over me. It had all started on the afternoon of our fifteenth birthday. Dark clouds loomed on the horizon, and rising wind brought the eye-watering smell of sagebrush and the tang of ozone. Our father had given us our first real saddles that morning, hand-tooled, silver-chased—took all the money he had. Momma was furious. She left us standing in the trailer, the same one I still lived in, and stomped off toward Black Rider Mesa. Legend said that one could speak to the old gods atop the mesa, but Momma went there to think and meditate. Father told us to let her go, but Ray and I followed, hoping to bring her back before the storm reached us.

At first, she wouldn't talk to us after we'd clambered up one of the rocky sides of the mesa. When I promised her that Ray and I would get jobs to earn back the money for the saddles, she pushed her face close to mine, her teeth clenched, nostrils flared. An old lech at the BIA once told Momma she was the only pretty squaw he'd ever seen. She didn't look pretty now. "It's not about the money," she said in a voice boiling over with anger. "It's about ranching. He wants to keep you here, to trap you." She hugged me with one arm and put the other around Ray.

I looked into Momma's eyes and saw that she was the one who felt trapped. And deep in my heart, I knew why. Years ago, a Hollywood talent scout had wanted to give Momma a bit part in an Elvis Presley picture, *Fun in Acapulco*, because he thought she could pass as a beautiful Mexican woman. The prospect of being in a movie with her idol had thrilled Momma, and something in her died when Father forbade her to do it, accusing her of trying to run out on him.

Before Ray and I could convince her to come down off the mesa, a sheet of water slammed into us, rain so hard you couldn't see your hand before your face. Then came hail, hard as shotgun pellets. The three of us had to crawl to the edge of the mesa, but the sides had turned into waterfalls so we couldn't climb down. I took deep, gasping breaths and felt like I was drowning.

That was when Momma did a crazy thing. She raised a finger to the sky and said, "God, I'm asking you now, give my sons a special destiny." Momma had been raised in a church orphanage and believed in the Christian god.

And just like in one of those biblical epics Momma and I watched on late-night TV, a bolt of lightning hit nearby, knocking us flat. My lungs wouldn't work, and before I knew it, Ray was pounding me on the back. Why couldn't Momma have just asked her god to save us from the storm? I lay with my face in the mud and shivered uncontrollably. But then something began to grow inside me, something that drove out the terror, something that hummed and vibrated from my toes to my eyeballs. I looked into Ray's eyes and knew he felt it too. We nodded at each other, then pointed at the storm and screamed, "Stop it!"

And the thing was, it did. Just like that. The wind and lightning quit, the clouds dissolved into wisps like dandelion seeds and drifted away.

Ray gave a low whistle. "Sheee-it, bro."

The short of it was, I could control the weather and so could Ray. We were Stormtalkers. That was Momma's word for it. Oh sure, it took a few weeks to convince ourselves this was for real. At first, we thought it was a fluke because Ray and I tried several times to stop the rain on our own and failed. Then one afternoon when a thunderstorm was brewing in the west, we shouted at the rain together, and the clouds disappeared like smoke on the wind.

But we had no luck in our attempts to make it rain. That is, until Ray decided we should do a traditional dance like the People did at spring powwows. To our amazement a respectable cloud appeared overhead after we'd finished and gave us a lovely, soaking shower. A few more successful rain dances convinced us we'd earned the title of Stormtalkers.

Folks made the dusty trip from all over the Four Corners area to see a couple of teenaged kids give them something far more precious than gold or silver. They scaled Black Rider Mesa to watch us do ceremonial dances and conjure up rain clouds. The clouds grew larger each time we performed, rumbling out over the arid plateau and providing moisture to ranches and homesteads.

Momma loved all the attention, all the excitement we created. One day, maybe to get back at Father for not letting her go to Holly-wood, or maybe because she loved the King so much, she decided we'd do Elvis numbers in addition to the traditional dances. She dressed me in black like the young pre-Hollywood Elvis. Ray, to his embarrassment, had to portray the latter-day Las Vegas Elvis, complete with white-sequined suit and cape. We even learned to play guitar and sing a little. As time went on, we dropped the tradi-tional dances and just did the Elvis act. We could still make it rain, which was all that mattered.

At least, we thought it was all that mattered. But the tribal elders were furious and boycotted our performances. An elder named Jim Hustito came to our trailer to confront Momma. Jim was a huge man with a nose that had been flattened by a wild mustang or his ex-wife, take your pick. There wasn't enough room for all of us to sit down, so Ray and I watched from the trailer's cramped hallway while Momma and Jim faced each other across the kitchen table.

"I don't get it," he said as he banged a fist on the table. "Why Elvis of all things? Are you snubbing the People? Are you making fun of us?"

Momma fixed him with her enormous dark eyes. "Of course not. It's just that . . . my sons have a destiny given to them by God, don't you see? They're too special to just—"

"To just act like Indians?" Jim shouted at Momma. "Is that what you're trying to say? I'll tell you how special your boys are. They're so special you've gone and turned them into a cheap lounge act. First you cut off their braids, then you cut them off from the tribe. You talk about Christian virtues all the time, but you're a hypocrite. This is nothing but the sin of pride. Don't you see that? Pride and arrogance."

Momma pointed at the door. Her hand was shaking, and I could tell it was all she could do to contain her temper. "How dare you," she said in a low voice that sounded like distant thunder. "No one talks to me like that. Now get out. You don't understand. Nobody does."

Jim rose to his feet. "It's you that don't understand. And I hope you do before it's too late."

Partly to escape the wrath of the elders, and partly because we were heading into a bad drought, we took our act on the road. We cooked up some fair-sized cloudbursts in Colorado, New Mexico, Utah, and Arizona that might have made the difference between life and death for ranches and farms. But we couldn't save everything. After all, the southwest is a vast place. Still, we tried our best to help the People.

After a couple years, our rain dances grew few and far between because the drought had eased up, and because the real Elvis had died. From then on, we only did the Stormtalking on our birthdays, mostly to please Momma, who never got over Elvis's death. Ray tried to keep up the tradition after he moved to New York, but then he started missing birthdays, and finally he stopped coming at all.

That was a long time ago. I had to admit that seeing him again made me realize how much I missed the excitement of our rock 'n' roll rain dances. An intense longing swirled inside me, sucking me down into the past. Finally, I called my brother and said I'd do it.

When he arrived the next morning, I told him, "Before we do this, I need to tell you what Momma said about the thousand fingers."

Ray waved me off. "Later, bro. Are you in or not?"

"I said I was, didn't I?"

Ray grinned. "Where are the guitars? You didn't throw them out, did you?"

I backed away. "Oh no, not the Elvis shtick. Look at us, we're fat old men! We're older than Elvis was when he died. Can't we just do the ceremonial dance?"

"It'll work, Travis. Trust me."

I'd come too far to say no at this point, so we rummaged through a storage shed and found our moldering guitars. Ray thought we should don our Elvis togs, just like in the old days. But the old days were also skinnier days. We hauled the guitars up the mesa and plugged them into portable amps Ray had brought with him. He stretched out his arms and gave a war cry that made me jump. Then he winked at me. "You ain't seen nothin' yet." He launched into a cover of "Burning Love" that was pretty good despite the out-of-tune guitar, and I backed him. The song ended none too soon. Ray's face was dangerously red, and mine was probably the same. It felt like it was pushing a hundred degrees, and I could definitely feel my temperature rising. Ray belted out the last line, and we stared at the sky. The clear, cloudless sky.

"Okay, Travis." Ray stopped and wheezed. "Now it's your turn."

I shook my head. "Nothing doing." But he kept pleading, so I launched into "Heartbreak Hotel" and wasn't half bad. For a moment, it felt like we were kids again, with cheering fans and adoring looks from Momma. But I kept hearing her weak, raspy voice whispering about the thousand fingers and the sin of pride. I hit the last chord, and we looked up to see a small cloud. I held my breath as it grew larger and darker.

A raindrop sizzled on a hot amp. Another. Then the cloud let loose and drenched us. We screamed and ran around the top of the mesa like idiots.

I told Ray he could stay in Momma's bedroom that night, but he returned to Farmington. A terrible feeling took root inside me and began to grow as I sat on the trailer's rickety porch, watching the moon set behind the silhouette of Black Rider Mesa. Despite Ray's talk about a sense of obligation, the rain dances were wrong, just like Momma had said, and now I knew how to prove it.

It took all night, checking websites for historical weather data, but by sunrise I had what I needed and called Ray. He was grumpy because I'd woken him up so early, but I told him to get back out here pronto. I pointed at a stack of printouts on the kitchen table when he arrived.

We sat down and he flipped through them. "Looks like a bunch of weather logs. So what?"

"We did Stormtalking on our birthdays, from the year we turned fifteen until you moved away. Then a few more times after that, whenever you could get away from your job."

"Get to the point, Travis."

"Every year, there was a major weather disaster right after we made it rain. Hurricane on the Gulf Coast after our sixteenth, one of the largest on record. Rains and flooding in the Mississippi River valley following our seventeenth. A typhoon in Malaysia, right after we turned eighteen. That was the pattern until we started skipping years. When that happened, there were no big weather events after a missed birthday."

Ray blew out a long breath. "Okay, I get it. You think there's a connection, that we somehow disrupted global weather patterns. The butterfly effect and all that. Two stupid kids do a rain dance in New Mexico and storms happen halfway around the world. Interesting idea, but not very likely."

"We did this, Ray, you and me."

He stared out the window a long time before responding. "Yeah, maybe you're right. But the thing is, there are always winners and losers in life. When I made a killing on Wall Street, someone else lost his shirt. And vice versa. When we make it rain, that puts us in the winners' column."

"Winners . . ." It finally clicked. "Ray, this whole thing was just a get-rich-quick scheme, wasn't it? Tell me, how much were you going to charge for our rain dances?"

Anger flared in Ray's eyes, but then he slumped in his chair and nodded. "Yes, that was the plan. We weren't going to come cheap, I can tell you that. But you have to believe me, I was never going to ask the tribe for money. For them, it really was all about obligation."

I studied the person across the table from me and wondered who he really was. "People may have died because of our rain dances. Do you really want to make a buck off that?"

Ray banged the table just like Jim Hustito had done all those years ago. "You were as much a part of this as I was. I'm not going to sit here while some high-and-mighty hypocrite living in a crappy trailer tells me what's what."

Hypocrite. That's what Jim had called Momma. Told her she was claiming to be virtuous while embracing the sin of pride. Pride in her sons had seemed like a good thing when we were making it rain, but now I understood the terrible consequences. I put my head in my hands. "All I wanted was to be a family again," I said. "But now I feel more alone than ever."

Ray reached over and touched my arm. "Hey, Trav . . . that was a stupid thing to say, and I didn't mean it. I'm sorry about the rain dance, sorry about everything. Maybe we can start over."

I lifted my head and met his gaze. I wanted desperately to believe him. "You really mean it?"

"I do. It's you and me, bro, from now on." He gave me a smile like the sun coming out after a storm, and then he started to laugh.

I laughed with him, happy I'd gotten my brother back. "What's so funny?" I finally asked him.

"You, that's what. And me. What the heck were we doing up on the mesa?"

"Hey, don't knock it. You were pretty good. Maybe Elvis Impersonator will be your next gig."

"Geriatric Elvis, that's me."

I shrugged. "Gotta say, it beats investment banker."

Ray laughed again. "That's a low bar."

I grabbed a couple of colas from the fridge, and we drank in silence for a while. When I asked Ray what he was thinking, he gave me a somber look, like the sun had disappeared again. "Travis, I want you to tell me about Momma's last words, about the thousand fingers."

"You really want to know?"

"More than anything."

I took a deep breath. "All right. Momma wanted to climb the mesa one last time, but the cancer had eaten her up, so I carried her to the top. Carrying her was the hardest thing I'd ever done." My throat tightened, and I had to stop and compose myself.

"I understand," said Ray. "A lot of weight to carry up that steep slope."

"No, that wasn't it. She was light as a feather by then. It was the weight of knowing this was the last time we'd be together in that holy place, the last time I'd see the sky and the endless flocks of clouds reflected in her eyes."

Ray massaged his temples. "I should have been there with you. No one should have to bear a weight like that alone."

"It was tough, but it was also wonderful. I felt like I was really one of the People for the first time in my life."

Ray's eyes were shining. "You've always been one of the People, Travis."

"Thank you for that. I wish you'd been there with us. When I laid Momma down, she looked at the sky for a long time. Then she told me, 'It was madness, wanting you and Ray to be special above all others. I did it out of pride, just like Jim Hustito said, and there will be a terrible price to pay.'

"I asked her what she meant. She took my hand and said, 'I know now, God has a thousand fingers, touching all things, just like drops of rain. Fingers like drops of rain.'"

Ray bowed his head, and we sat in silence for a long while. Finally, I rose to my feet. "My weather-making days are over."

I braced myself for an argument, but Ray stood up and said, "Sure, Travis. We'll find some other way to help the People." I was surprised to see I had somehow regained that inch and could look him straight in the eye. "Thank you for telling me about the thousand fingers," he added. "I'm glad you were there for Momma."

I walked out to the porch to get some air. And then I saw it: the face of madness. A towering mass of clouds, darker than any I'd ever seen, blotting out the sun. A lightning-flecked monster turning the sky green, crawling toward me from the east, where storms never come from in the high desert. If you saw something like this in the Midwest, you'd head for the nearest storm shelter.

The wind whipped up, pelting me with cold rain and hail. A bolt of blood-red lightning cracked above me, a sure sign that this storm was unnatural, an abomination. The pitch-black clouds swirled and pulsed like they were alive. I shivered, and not just because of the rain. The screen door banged behind me. "Our pride and arrogance have come home to roost, brother," I said to Ray without taking my eyes off the thing. Dozens of tornadoes began to form, spinning down from the clouds and probing like delicate fingers, not yet touching the earth.

"Is that even real?" Ray had to shout to be heard over the storm.

I pulled my gaze away from this creeping horror and saw the stricken look on my brother's face. I leaned toward him and said, "As real as we could make it."

Ray put a hand on my shoulder. "I'm glad Momma didn't live to see this."

I started singing, "Can't Help Falling in Love," Momma's favorite Elvis song. Ray joined in, and we sang louder as the wind picked up. *We should run for our lives*, I told myself, but we kept singing, kept watching as the fingers approached, and waited to be touched.

# 34

## PRETENDING
### SUNNY BRIDGE

*after Ada Limón*

I used to pretend. I used to pretend my life was perfect. Or maybe I used to *almost believe* my life was perfect. And in fact it was pretty great. Not now, of course. And I used to pretend I could understand anything if I cared enough to try. No. *I did* believe that. I actually believed that. I admit it. Maybe not quantum physics, though I still sort of think I just never really cared enough. And I used to pretend I'd be fine without my beloved, but I never believed that one. I used to pretend, though, for his sake, maybe even for mine. Two years gone and I'm still not sure I believe that. What does *fine* even mean? *Fine* sounds too much like, *whatever, I'm good either way*, when grief is more like a cosmic game of Go Fish, rigged so you can't win. You keep asking for things no one can give you. *Go Fish*. But I never wanted to play in the first place. And no, I don't understand. I don't understand how I'm supposed to go on. I don't understand how I'm supposed to quit feeling sorry for myself. I don't understand. I don't. And I don't have the energy to pretend anymore. So no pretense. I'm okay. I'm not good. I'm not fine. I'm certainly not perfect and neither is my life. But I *am* okay. And I'm not pretending.

# 35

# IT WAS ALL FOR HER

## JENNIFER ROBINSON

I now know what it's like to have your life pass before your eyes in the hour of death. Only some live to tell such a thing, of course.

I'm not going to survive. I've never been so aware of the beating of my heart and the passing of air through my lungs. My soul feels heavy somewhere beneath my ribs. I'm more conscious of it than I ever have been before, knowing it will soon disappear. I suppose memories of a life like mine can do that.

I wouldn't say that my existence was pleasant. I didn't know until later in childhood that other people didn't have families like mine, that parents are supposed to feed you properly, to teach you how to bathe and dress. Other kids always looked at me funny for my ratty hair and clothes, and I smelled terrible. I was skinnier than a drinking straw because Daddy made me skip meals for punishment, and I was in trouble with him for simply existing. And Mama? Who knows. The one time I asked Daddy, he told me he'd make me regret it if I brought her up ever again. I didn't.

But the memories I cherish? They are all of the one woman who taught me to smile.

The first time I saw her was in seventh grade, March of 1951. The world was muddy and strange as the ice from deep winter melted in the afternoon and froze back overnight. Existing in two seasons day after day—not an ideal time to start at a new school.

I couldn't help but notice she didn't look like any other kids in class. Her hair wasn't brushed, stains marred her misfitting skirt, and one of her shoes had a hole in the toe. I'd never seen another child who looked like that. I'd only ever seen one in the mirror.

Her name was Scarlet. I'd never seen someone so beautiful in my life, and never would again.

She kept herself distanced, head down toward the ground as if she wanted to sink right through it and disappear. At lunch, she ate like she hadn't eaten in days. We both sat by our lonesome. She was terrified of everyone; any comfort she had in fellow humans had long since evaporated. I knew the feeling, but I wanted to trust in her. At the very least, I knew my own kind and believed we needed each other.

That day as I waited for the bus, I watched as she climbed into an old Chrysler with all the paint peeling off and spots of rust like hives. The woman behind the steering wheel was young, with a skeletal face, and didn't look at the girl when she climbed into the passenger's seat. She barely waited until her daughter closed the door to press the gas and speed away.

The next morning, while standing under a naked tree waiting for the school bell to ring, I noticed Scarlet had a fresh bruise on her arm. I had one to match on my lower back. We were connected. I approached her and lifted up my too-small coat to show her my mark.

"Spilled my Cream of Wheat this morning," I offered.

She simply blinked at it and met my eyes for only a moment. I think she saw something in me, because she didn't say a word but also didn't pull away.

It went on like that for a while. She kept near, and I talked. When there was a new mark on her skin, tucked away enough under her clothes that the teachers wouldn't notice, I'd tug down my sock or unbutton my shirt a bit to show her a new one of mine.

"I didn't pick up my crayons." I showed her a bruise on my arm one day.

Another day, another mark. "I forgot to feed the chickens yesterday before school. Daddy would've hit me either way. If I fed them, I would've missed the bus."

Spring had become warm and constant the day Scarlet lifted the hem of her skirt a little, showing me an angry black bruise on her thigh. "I dunno what I did . . ."

We became inseparable. It turned out that she only had a mama, and I only had a daddy, and both of them would rather not have us. There was barely food in either of our houses, and unlike the other kids whose parents bought them clothes and food and new toys, our parents bought liquor and drugs. Scarlet and me? For years our only reliable meals were school lunches. The rest of the time we'd steal what we could from the corner grocer and the bakery, milk from porches in the early mornings, and vegetables from gardens in summertime.

When we moved to high school, things got worse for Scarlet. Her mama saw that her daughter was still thin but becoming pretty as her figure filled out. She wasn't awkward in her childish body anymore, instead transforming into a young woman. Scarlet's mama was ugly, her looks warped by booze, little sleep, and the drugs she got with the weekly check she earned from cleaning motel rooms out by the highway. Scarlet was gorgeous and popular with everyone, boys and girls alike. The jealousy in her mama made Scarlet's life hell.

When Scarlet didn't show up for class one day, my gut ached. I knew something was horribly wrong. I skipped school, giving up my one guaranteed meal of the day, and ran off to find her.

To my relief she was in the first place I looked: at the park, crouched under a tree. She wore a stocking cap over her head despite the sweltering September weather.

"What happened?" I asked her, out of breath. "Why weren't you at school?"

She pulled her cap off, and I bit back a gasp of horror. Where long black hair had once graced her lovely head, now matted and singed locks showed clear signs of being haphazardly chopped by dull scissors. Her scalp was burning red where hair had been burned clean off.

Fury ignited in my chest. "She can't do this to you."

"Joe," she folded her arms around her knees and held them close to her chest, "yes she can . . . nothing ever stops her."

I had never been so angry in my life. Fury burned white hot and made my muscles squeeze in a way that left me unable to talk or even breathe. We sat for a long time under that tree, until the sun was gone and the sky was all stars. Scarlet's pain couldn't go on; it would destroy her.

Two nights later, that shitty Chrysler was found by a farmer upside down in the middle of a field, but Scarlet's mama wasn't inside. Police found her body fifty feet from the car, bloody and shredded from going straight through the windshield when she crashed. They guessed she was going too fast for the speed limit and lost control on her way to the motel. No doubt in their minds she was drunk when it happened.

I couldn't understand why Scarlet was heartbroken about it. The abuse from her mama was over, and it wasn't coming back. But she still cried as she packed all their belongings into one old suitcase, and she cried as she got into a cop car and was driven across town to her mama's only surviving relative—a cousin once removed who was kind and gentle. Scarlet was given enough to eat there, and she didn't get hit.

One morning soon after, the police found Daddy dead on the kitchen floor, his head split open from where he smacked it against the corner of the table. They said it must have been an accident, just another person in town who drank themselves to death. The coroner covered his body in a white sheet and took it away. I never claimed his ashes, and neither did anyone else.

Scarlet and I dropped out of high school to leave for Denver, hoping it would offer us more than the miserable town we grew up in. She found a job waitressing, and I was able to get on at a manufacturing plant making huge glass panes for skyscraper windows. Scarlet smiled a lot in those days. We rented the basement in a widow's house near both our jobs. Scarlet often told me, "Joe, I've never been so happy in my whole life."

It didn't last long—she found a boyfriend fast. Considering the feelings I'd developed for her, and the bruises that began showing up on her skin, it made me sick. She knew she couldn't hide her wounds from me. "Joe, it's just what men do." We both knew better, despite our past.

His name was Brian. He and Scarlet showed up at home together the nights he would pick her up from her shift at the diner. He was nice enough when we washed dishes together after Scarlet cooked supper. After a few rounds of blackjack, they would retire to her room. I would listen to records to try to ignore the animalistic noises of their lovemaking.

One night, I couldn't. She screamed in terror behind the closed door before a sickening crash reverberated through the night. When I yanked the door open, a naked Brian loomed over her. Scarlet laid in diamonds and blood, her bedroom mirror demolished. She bled from the cuts of thousands of shards.

He met my eyes and saw the deep hatred inside. Without any attempt at explanation or a single word in his own defense, he picked his jeans up off the bedroom floor and left. At least he was smart in that way; he would have regretted staying in that basement even a single second longer.

I found towels to press on Scarlet's cuts and wrapped her in a bathrobe before driving her to the hospital. After she was stitched up, the police came and took a report while I held her against my side.

Two months passed, and even with all the evidence, they never contacted us again. Scarlet lived in fear until we read in the newspaper one morning that Brian had died of a heart attack the week prior, after leaving a bar not far from the glass factory. He was thirty-six, according to the report. He'd told Scarlet he was twenty-five. "Asshole," she whispered under her breath. I turned the page, and we managed to laugh with Blondie and Dagwood for a moment. Brian would never darken a day in her life again.

Scarlet stayed single a long time after that. I'm not sure why she wouldn't let it go on for eternity, just her and me, Joe and Scarlet. She must have known how I felt about her, but neither of us brought it up. Maybe she just wanted me to be her friend forever, a sibling she never had. There was always this distance she kept between us, an arm's length away, and I could never quite reach her.

I would have been okay with that if nothing changed, but things always do.

Scarlet became fed up with the guys who teased her every shift and left shitty tips, so she decided to take a job as the secretary at Collins Insurance Agency. Mr. Marvin Collins was charming and swept Scarlet straight off her feet. His courtship was like a whirlwind through both Scarlet's life and mine, and they married one drizzly day in June a year later.

I was alone. My soul missed her. I would always love her, and that's why I fought to be content for her. At least she seemed to be safe with him.

Though she belonged to someone else, I couldn't stop thinking of her constantly. I'd had her by my side for twenty years, and suddenly she was gone. She was a wife and then became a mama as time marched on. She kept in touch, though it was clear I had become much less important in her life than she still was in mine. I was just an old childhood friend to her. To me, she would always be the sun everything revolved around.

I saw her again one April afternoon for lunch. She blew into the restaurant with a gust of wind. Motherhood had plumped her and made a few of her roots silver, but somehow she still swept me up with her presence and beauty. "Sorry, Joe," she said, collapsing into the booth across from me, "things were crazy this morning. Marv forgot his papers on the kitchen table, then I had to take the girls to dance class—"

As she panted and carried on, I fought not to make a face. I hoped the people she chose to keep closest appreciated her as much as I always would . . . Why couldn't she see how much I could give her? Why was she always just far enough away that I couldn't reach?

I'd become lost in my thoughts and pulled myself back to reality. "So, everything is still going good with you and Marvin?"

"Oh yeah," she smiled, wiggling out of her coat and tossing it on the vinyl seat beside her, "things are really good." Scarlet placed her chin on her palms and leaned closer across the table, smiling with bright-red lips. "What about you? Find someone special yet?"

A long time ago I had. "No," I told her. "You know me, I'm not that kind of person."

She sighed in frustration. "I do know you, Joe, and I think you need to find someone to love and care for. You always took such good care of me. You would enjoy settling down with a family of your own."

She was the only person I'd ever cared for; the only family I wanted. It had been so long since I had even been that close to another person, someone I actually desired to talk to instead of push away. "That's all good for you, but not for me."

"But you've never tried dating, have you?" Her smile was yellowed from coffee and cigarettes, but no less bright. "You know, at work, there's someone I can introduce you—"

My palm hit the table louder than I meant, clashing silverware against the linoleum. "I said it's not for me." I saw her flinch, caught a glimpse of what I recognized as fear in her eyes and pulled back. "I'm sorry. I—"

The conversation ended abruptly with a shake of her head as the waitress approached. Scarlet ordered the same thing as always, a BLT with mashed potatoes on the side. At least some parts of her didn't change.

During our meal, her arm moved to expose a small sliver of skin above her elbow, revealing a bruise violet as wine, rimmed in a jaundiced yellow. I grabbed her wrist to keep her still while I looked. Her fork dropped with a clatter to the table and she tried to pull away. I held tighter.

"He did this," I said. It wasn't a question—I knew he did.

"W-what?" she stammered out. She followed my gaze to her elbow where she forced a laugh. "That? Goodness no! There's a sharp corner on our staircase handrail that gets me every time! I'm still trying to get used to the new house."

I didn't believe her. How could I, when she'd been hurt count-less times before? I was her sole protector, the only one who could ensure her safety. I was stupid to leave her to her own devices and think she could keep herself out of harm's way.

"Joe, seriously, I'm fine," Scarlet told me quietly, voice so low only I could hear. "Marv is a good father and a good husband. He would never, ever hurt me. I feel safe with him." She turned her hand to clasp my wrist in return. "I promise."

I knew better. That night I drove to their pretty little brick house on the edge of the city, turned my headlights off, and parked across the street. I could see the Collins family inside the front window. Two twin daughters seated at the dining room table with their breathtakingly beautiful mother as she assisted them with their homework, Marvin in the background of the picturesque scene, cleaning up from dinner.

I watched them do the same thing nearly every night for weeks.

I noted every time the lights were on when I drove by. Scarlet was absent on Thursday nights when the twins and their father ate on TV trays in the living room, illuminated by the blue glow of the television.

I called Scarlet one of the final weeks I surveilled the house, and she seemed caught off guard by my call and teased me that I must miss her. She reported that on the first Monday of each month she and Marvin had dance class and dinner out while the girls spent time at their grandparents' house. When I asked her what she had planned for the rest of the week, she said just her book club on Thursday. She and Marvin had signed the girls up for music lessons, and they would be starting that night too. "Marv will finally have an evening to himself." Scarlet chuckled. "He must be tired of being around females all the time. He could probably use some time alone."

Just as Scarlet said, that Thursday the house was empty save for Marvin. I watched him across the street in my parked car, shrouded in darkness. He brought home a bag of fast food that he ate while watching TV—some sort of movie that Scarlet would never enjoy, with explosions and car chases. I'll never understand what she saw in him. She came home with the twins around eight and pressed a kiss to his lips at the front door. Fire burned in my throat.

I was confident that next Thursday Marvin and I would have plenty of time to discuss the matter of Scarlet and her well-being.

That week was the longest of my life, waiting, watching through that window. One night Marvin exited the house alone with the garbage to put into the bin at the curb. He paused, looking at my car. I was confident he couldn't see me, but I nearly got out to discuss the matter at hand with him then. I talked myself down, promising that my patience would be rewarded.

The anticipated evening finally came, and after Marvin had eaten his bag of fast food and put down the TV Guide, I approached the house. It felt surreal being in the place I had stared at for weeks, a lucid dream.

I pressed the doorbell, and he answered. "Joe?" I can't say he looked happy to see me on his front steps. "Sorry, Scarlet's not here," he told me, hand still on the door knob, "but I'll let her know you dropped by."

"I actually came to see you," I replied with a forced grin.

"Me?"

"May I come in?"

Marvin hesitated, but stepped aside to invite me in. "If you don't mind taking your shoes off," he said, gesturing to the gleaming white carpet, "Scarlet breaks her back keeping it clean."

"I understand." I slipped them off. Out of the corner of my eye, I saw the staircase. A corner stuck out on the railing, wrapped in a towel and secured with rubber bands.

He caught me looking. "I know it's an eyesore, but Scar catches her elbow on it all the time." He patted the towel.

"I see."

"Well, Joe, what's on your mind?"

Our discussion went as I expected it would. He was not easily persuaded to leave her. I did what I had to for Scarlet, and I'll never be sorry for how the conversation ended.

Afterward I waited on the front steps. A little before eight, Scarlet pulled into the driveway with her girls. She gave me a look as she got out of the driver's seat of her car, simultaneously locking the doors to secure the twins inside. "Joe? What are you doing here?"

"He won't hurt you anymore."

A pause, and we stared at each other through the suburban darkness. She was still, frozen like a terrified doe before a hunter, ready to bolt. "What are you talking about?"

"Let me take care of you." I reached for her, but she pulled away and rushed toward the house. She called for her husband by name and yanked the front door open.

I'll never forget her scream.

At least I left the white carpet unscathed. Nobody, not even Scarlet, would be able to get those stains out.

---

"Wright," I hear a voice say, and I lift my head from my pillow. Nobody calls me Joe anymore, not around here. "Time to follow me."

I have no reason not to obey. The warden has always treated me with as much respect as I give him. Through the portal in the cell wall, my hands are bound in cuffs before the guards open the door and bind my ankles. They flank me, and the pastor I talked to earlier gives me a gentle nod. Together, the four of us follow the warden.

I'm deeply aware that this is the last time my feet will touch the ground to propel me forward. Air is cool through my nostrils as it passes into my hot lungs. A perfectly working body, even though it aged some since I was locked up. A waste, but I accepted my fate long ago. I feel like I've been dead for years, ever since Scarlet refused to speak to me again. All my letters to her went unanswered. I've wondered every hour of every day if she's even still alive. The world wouldn't be as beautiful if she wasn't in it anymore, but I haven't been outside barbed-wire fences and prison walls in years. I couldn't tell you if the world was still beautiful if you asked me.

The guards guide me into the next room: my final passage. Fear isn't something I've felt since I was a child, but the stirring in my chest at the sight of the seafoam-green gas chamber comes close to the forgotten emotion. It looks like it's from both the distant past and sickening future, a submarine and a UFO designed to kill those who go inside. A death machine. A singular chair in the middle is surrounded by windows. My throne, with portals for witnesses to peer through.

I'm seated, and the guards strap me in. Wrists, ankles, thighs, waist, biceps. The curtains in front of the chamber open. Dozens of people are seated in the audience, but I only see one.

Scarlet.

She's aged, years etched around her eyes and mouth. I hope it's from smiling and not from the pain I've apparently caused her.

"Joelene Wright," I hear the warden's voice echo against the cold hard walls, "you have been sentenced to death for the murder of Mildred Anderson on October 17, 1956; the murder of Daniel Wright on November 2, 1956; the murder of Brian Scott on January 29, 1960; and the murder of Marvin Collins on May 21, 1972. Do you wish to make a final statement before your sentence is carried out?"

I stare at Scarlet, and she stares right back. Those eyes are unreadable, glistening the same way I saw in the seemingly endless days in that courtroom all those years ago. Hatred, betrayal, sadness; each are possibilities of what she feels, and I can't understand a single one.

I just want to see her smile one last time. A selfish wish from a woman sick with love. Will she never understand I was protecting her? She would if she only took my calls or read my letters.

But if she never listened before, why would she listen now? "No, sir," I say. I don't take my eyes away from Scarlet, not until a leather mask is put over my eyes.

She's the last thing I will ever see, and I savor her behind my eyelids as I hear the iron door creak shut and seal.

The world is still beautiful, because she's here.

Silver and black hair, red lipstick as bright as her name. Brown eyes warm like an autumn afternoon.

I hear hissing from behind my feet, and the air smells strange. My nostrils sting.

The way she laughed when we read the morning paper together as young women over coffee.

It hurts to breathe.

Two children sitting under a tree, sharing snack cakes and apples we'd stolen together back when we had nothing. I've always had nothing but her.

I hear a woman scream.

I think she's me.

# 36

# INCANTATION

## MEGAN E. FREEMAN

(he calls) and my amygdala
bursts into hot pink flames
lighting every neon match
in the tinder box of fight or flight

dear cup of tea
dear candle
dear pen and postcard waiting for my hand

buy me time while my pre-frontal cortex
recovers her wits

guide me through this gray matter battlefield
of synaptic triggers

temper this violent urge to flee

extinguish the flames of panic and history
and bring to bear the breath of calm and truth
and sanity

(amen)

# 37

# PRELUDE

LYNDA LA ROCCA

Car door slamming
engine revving
yelling on front stoop so
all the neighborhood can hear.

Back inside,
glass breaking
floorboards creaking
bare feet slapping up the stairs,
pounding on another door
rattling the doorknob
locked
pretending to be sleeping.

Later
creeping
to the kitchen
drinking sour cup of milk
still dark outside,
in other room
shouting starting up again,
face slapping, lamp tipping,
hiding underneath the table
with the dog
shaking
licking
spilled milk
from one small hand.

# 38

# BETTER PLACES
ANONYMOUS

There must be
better rooms
for a little girl to remember
than those in a small gray house
a baby brother asleep in his crib
and a babysitter tugging
her to the basement

There must be
better places
for a little girl to remember
than a dark storage room
cracked ceiling tiles
shag carpet rubbing her shoulders
nightgown bunched under her armpits

There must be
better words
for a little girl to remember
than lies from his mouth
big girls like this
if you tell
you'll be in trouble

There must be
better places

# 39

# THE FORMULA FOR FORGIVENESS
## HEATHER HEIN

*For Andrea*

F=A+A+C. The formula for forgiveness I've learned in therapy.

This is my first thought as I open my eyes, the alarm on my phone squawking at me. It takes a minute for me to orient myself to this hotel room where the sheets are crisp and the furniture looks the same as it does in any other hotel room in America. This one has a floral pattern on the coverlet and southwestern prints on the wall, but otherwise they're all the same.

I'm due at the hospital in ninety minutes. That's enough time to shower off the recurring nightmare, get some free breakfast from the impersonal lobby, and make it across town to the hospital.

The water pressure is strong, good for scouring away the megrims. My recurring dream replays in my head as I soap up with the complimentary lavender body wash, trying to rid my flesh of the lingering sensations of violation. I reflect upon sex education in junior high. In the eighties, no one really talked about sex of any kind. We were separated so boys wouldn't have to contemplate the horrors of menstruation and we girls wouldn't have to imagine what a wet dream was like. Back then, no one talked about sexual abuse. That was a family matter and was not something discussed in polite circles. Or any circles for that matter. In fact, the only concept presented in that class was abstinence, and nothing more needed to be said.

I had always felt dirty and soiled. I wore frumpy clothes to hide the fact that my body was turning into a woman's body. Camouflage was my favorite color, but it never seemed to hide me from the wandering eyes. The lather slides down my naked skin, and I can still feel their gaze crawling across my skin, stopping at my breasts, which grew much faster than the rest of me. By the time I was fifteen, I was wearing a size D and experiencing the back pain associated with being well-endowed. I wore tight-fitting sports bras so my breasts wouldn't be as obvious.

I never dressed "like that," so I was confused as to why I was being sought out as a sexual outlet by a woman who could, and did, have any man she wanted.

Tears fall freely here behind the generic white shower curtain that never really seems to keep the floor from getting soaked. The scalding water washes them down the drain with the hospital smells from the day before. But nothing can wash away the thoughts that race through my head. I mentally prepare myself to seize this day and try to get through the emotional turmoil it holds. As I dry off, I think about my twisted childhood.

Those were terrible years for me. Divorce had afforded her the privacy she needed to victimize me when she didn't have someone spending the night. God, I loved all those gentlemen and the respite they afforded me. A night of peace. A night when the smell of whiskey wasn't wafting across my cheek while the woman who gave birth to me slid into my bed and spooned against me. Sharp breaths that came faster and faster, then finally subsided. I would keep my eyes squeezed shut until the door clicked softly behind her and I was alone again. Only then did I open them and let the tears spill silently down my cheeks as I clutched Wabbit to my chest, wondering why it had happened and when it would finally stop.

From the age of fourteen until I left the house the day of high school graduation, I'd often contemplated ways to get out of my predicament. In the end, I remained mute, just waiting for the day I could get away and celebrate my freedom. Suicide, running away, going to the police all seemed too difficult. As a child I was informally trained to be the peacekeeper, to avoid conflict, and to be a "nice girl." So I kept the peace, avoided conflict, and remained respectful. Inside, I was seething: a kettle that threatened to boil over if the heat wasn't turned down.

I rummage through my suitcase to find a pair of jeans, T-shirt, and a sweater. The hospital is always cold, and nothing seems to keep that chill from settling into my marrow as I sit through twelve hours of purgatory until my brother arrives to take over the quiet vigil. We take turns waiting for the relief that will follow when she finally gives herself over to the end-stage liver failure that's reduced her to a husk of her previous self.

I tell myself I should be feeling sorrow, sadness about saying that final goodbye. I tell myself I should feel guilty. But I don't. I feel like it's exactly the kind of ending she deserves: slow and painful. It's karma.

As I've grown into a confident adult woman, I understand I did nothing wrong. At the time it seemed normal. I figured most of my friends were experiencing the same thing and no one ever talked about it. Now I understand how absolutely abnormal it was. My mother eventually remarried a man about half her age, and although I never cared about him, I thought I'd finally have the respite I so needed. It didn't last long, since he picked up and split the scene when she got sick. What I do care about is that he had two daughters when they got together. I've never asked them if they had midnight visits from the woman who slept with their father, but I hope my silence didn't make them into victims themselves. Thanks to therapy, I've absolved myself of any blame, because I know that only one person is responsible for what happened. My mother.

In my sessions, we talk about forgiveness. Dr. Offenberg tells me forgiveness is a formula and forgetting is not really an option. Her reasoning is Forgiveness equals Acknowledgement, Apology, and a Commitment to do better, which I think of as an algebraic formula: F=A+A+C. As a research scientist, I like logic, math, and concepts boiled down to their basic atomic principles, so this is an idea I can wrap my head around. In order to be able to forgive, all three elements must be present. And because of this, I still haven't forgiven my mother for her "indiscretions." That's the word we use in therapy because it's the one I can use without feeling filthy or victimized. Our goals in therapy aren't to help me get over my feelings of anger, hurt, and betrayal. They're to help me live with these feelings until the day I can come to forgive. *When will that day come?* I often wonder. It may never come. And time is running out.

As I drive to the hospital again for my turn to watch over my mother's decaying body, thoughts swirl around in my head. Like flipping through an old photo album that will never be shared with others, I mentally gaze at those images with a heart filled with fear and rage. The question of "why" tries to rise up, but I squash it down. That line of thinking is no longer productive. I already know why. She's an offender, and I am the offended. I don't own her behavior or her mistakes and shortcomings. I am still the dutiful daughter, and I still show up to keep her company, to get her fresh water, to change the TV channel, and to alert the nurses when she needs something.

I don't know why I agreed to this, but it's not because I'm waiting for her to keep up her end of the bargain in fulfilling the formula. I know that's probably not going to happen. There's never even been the first "A"—Acknowledgement. I only show up to watch my mother die in order to share the burden of her slow march toward death with the only one who has ever loved me for myself. My brother, Ben.

The mammoth hospital is looming ahead, and I pull into the parking garage, find a space, and take five deep breaths just like I was taught to do. I close my eyes and ground myself. Name five things you can hear: The thump-thump of wheels on the level above me, the thump-thump of my heart in my ears that keeps the same beat, the low talk on the public radio station I can't make out. Birds swooping through the parking structure, scolding the cars for interrupting their peaceful way of life. Murmured conversations of people walking toward the elevators. Four things I can feel: My jeans against my unshaven legs, my hands gripping the steering wheel as I will them to relax, the slight breeze coming in through my open window, the pinching in my toes from my new red Converse high tops that haven't been broken in yet.

I open my eyes. Three things I can see: The giant number three painted on the wall in front of the rental car, my phone to provide me with distraction while I sit alone and angry, and the scar across my wrist from the time I felt too much at once and tried to shut things off. Three. Three elements necessary for forgiveness.

I sigh with resignation, roll up the window and shut off the car, clenching the steering wheel one last time for strength before I climb out and make my way toward my mother's sickroom.

The hospital doors whoosh open, and everywhere people are masked. I remember my own mask and walk back outside to put it on, per state regulations in the time of pandemic. Masks are uncomfortable, but they have one nice feature: my mother can't see my mouth twist into an expression of distaste when her skin comes in contact with mine. Or the teeth clenched in rage when she complains I'm not helping fast enough. I've found myself wishing more than once for that old My Little Pony costume mask I had the Halloween before my family fell apart. Then she wouldn't be able to see me at all.

I should feel lucky they've granted hospice patients one visitor at a time, but I don't. Part of me wishes she could die alone. It would serve her right.

My older brother will be waiting anxiously for my arrival. Although he never had to cope with childhood trauma as I have, he's as fatigued by this hell as I am. He's warned me about letting things go unresolved, especially now with the truth of mortality looming ever closer. But he doesn't understand, because he was the favored one. The boy child who was wanted and revered. The football star, the handsome boy who looks just like my mother. Tall, slender, dark haired, chiseled jaw structure; he's an All-American Ken Doll. I take after my dad—short, stocky, uncoordinated. I'm a thinker and my brother is a doer. I was a disappointment in so many ways. But I refuse to be a disappointment to myself.

I've never confronted my mother. She needs to be the one to initiate the process. Maybe I am stubborn, like my brother believes. But I'm not the one who needs forgiveness because, as my therapist has taught me, I haven't done anything wrong. There's never been that crucial A for Acknowledgement from her that something happened all those years ago when my father left. A fourteen-year-old girl can't take a lover's place. I wonder if it would have happened if he hadn't left us, but I imagine it would have. There would have been an opportunity at some point, and she would have taken it, and having taken it once, would have taken it over and over again.

The icy chill in the hospital raises goosebumps on my skin as I make my way to the main elevators and the fifth floor where I will sit for the next twelve hours. It matches the chill in my heart, which I keep in an iron box with a lock when I'm here. That box keeps me safe.

It's funny, I think as the elevator rises, people never consider that women can sexually abuse children just as men can. Women aren't considered sex offenders the same way men are. Maybe that's another reason I never said anything. Maybe that's why it didn't seem like a crime all those years ago.

The nurse almost bumps into me in the doorway as I enter the dim confines of my mother's room. I let out a little shriek and jump back. The nurse apologizes with her eyes as she whisks away toward the nurse's station. I take a moment to collect myself before entering the dungeon and assuming my place.

Ben emerges from the bathroom and smiles when he sees me. He gives me a brief kiss on the cheek. "I'll be back at ten o'clock tonight," he says, then evaporates, anxious to escape the antiseptic smell of the dying.

The TV is turned on to *The Price is Right*. Some things never change. Except the show's host, that is. There's really no substitute for Bob Barker. As I sink into the uncomfortable beige recliner, listening to the familiar fart sound of the faux leather, I remember my mother and me watching this show every day, both of us trying to come up with the right bids and jeering at contestants. We would have done better. We kept a tally of our own points, and the one who would have won the Showcase Showdown made lunch that day.

Not all memories are bad, and that's what makes this so hard. I remember her teaching me how to knit, and all the misshapen sweaters she would make for me. I wore them with pride because my mother made them. I remember the long evening walks we took in the summer. The deafening noise of the cicadas in the trees and the crickets singing their sleepy evening songs. Stopping by mulberry trees along the way and eating until our fingers were purple. The relief when the summer heat began to subside for the day and breathing was a little bit easier. That incessant whirring sound of cicadas still calms my heart and makes me yearn for those summer evenings when it was just the two of us enjoying the simple pleasures.

She wasn't a complete monster. I understand as an adult that she had internal conflict, and that alcoholism contributed to the situation. But understanding does not equal forgiveness. That's not a part of the formula.

I hear a scrabbling noise beside me and am snapped back to the present time and place. She's reaching pathetically for the bedside table where the little pink mouth swabs and a Styrofoam cup of cold water sit. Obediently, I rise from my chair and help her moisten her mouth. Her wrinkled lips look like a sphincter as she sucks the moisture off the little pink sponge. She opens her mouth to release the swab, and I set the sponge back in the little pink kidney-shaped basin on the bedside table.

Her eyes regard me from deep in their sockets; dark purplish circles under them look like bruises. Is there regret in those eyes somewhere? I find myself looking for a glimmer of the remorse that I realize I so badly need. I know our time is limited now, but what I search for cannot be found in those glittering black diamonds, the scleras around them yellowing from chronic liver disease brought on by years of alcohol abuse.

I return to my chair and dig the paperback novel out of my bag. On the TV, the Showcase Showdown has begun, and it makes me think about those lunches of long ago. Today I will be feeding her lunch regardless of which one of us would have guessed the closest retail price without going over.

My heart lurches with brief anguish inside its protective case, and I press a hand to my chest to keep it from escaping and flying around the room like one of those trapped birds in the parking ramp. I don't want her to know I have any feelings left. I want to be as cold and detached as the nursing staff as I set about caring for her needs in this sterile room with its pastel checked curtain and cheap framed art.

A gray drizzle runs down the window outside and intensifies the gloom and depression that descends over both of us like a cloud. It's a palpable force, like another person sitting in the only other uncomfortable chair on the opposite side of the bed.

I find my place in my book, but after ten minutes I've re-read the same paragraph three times without making any sense of the words. I give up and get my phone out, opening Facebook, wanting a passport to the world outside of this death place. She has a DNR order and I feel a little bit guilty about looking forward to the moment it will be used, but I want all of this to be over. Yes, I want her suffering to end—I'm not completely unsympathetic—but I want this divided nature of mine to end just as badly. I look forward to the day I don't have to return and swallow back this bitter taste in my mouth. I want the sweet purple mulberries and stained fingertips.

Lunch arrives and I help her sit up, spooning the soft mush into her mouth and wiping her chin when it dribbles. She reminds me of an infant and I hate this. She seems dim, somehow. The skin on her hands is paper thin, age spots and veins crawl over them, and they're almost hooked into claws from her contractures. I wonder what would happen if I just walked out and left her here in the care of the nurses. It seems fitting somehow to allow her to be cared for by strangers in her final hours. But I stay, because I'm not really here for her. I'm here for Ben. And for myself, to prove I gave her all the opportunity I could to find resolution and peace.

I'm frozen in place, spoon in hand, looking out the window when she grunts at me and opens her mouth like a baby bird for another bite of pureed soup. I grimace, but it's unnoticed behind my mask.

Her eyes flicker a little, so maybe she can see it after all. Whatever. It doesn't matter to me one way or the other. I'm too focused on the hurt I feel.

*Days of Our Lives* begins as I crank her back down so she can spend the afternoon napping while I sit next to her with my own thoughts.

She grabs my wrist—harder than I imagined she had the strength for. I look at her in surprise, searching for meaning in her face. She grunts and gestures for the table. I pick up the peppermint-smelling mouth swab, but she shakes her head slowly and points to a pad of paper Ben and I have been using to keep notes on, her fingers crooked and bent with arthritis.

"You want to write?" I ask.

She nods, and I can almost hear the cords in her neck creaking with the effort. I'm surprised; she hasn't asked to write anything down in weeks. I hand the pad to her but she drops it. She's too weak to hold it steady. I sigh, pick it up off the blanket, and hold it for her while she scrawls two words and then drops her hands away in exhaustion. I turn it toward myself and read.

My breath stops. My heart refuses to beat. My legs will not hold me up for long. Just two words and they change everything.

"I'm sorry," it says.

I look into my mother's eyes and see that they're leaking. I lean my hip against the bed, weak and panicked. This is not what I expected. I assumed I would be burying my grief and hurt in the same coffin as this woman, unresolved. I wanted to carry my indignation with me away from her memorial like a badge and wear it on my sleeve forever. But the unthinkable has happened and now the next move is up to me.

I shuffle to the recliner and sit down hard, holding my head in my hands with my elbows on my knees. The world around me swirls in and out of focus. All those nighttime horrors infuse me as if injected through an IV like the one in her left arm. My hands shake and I feel like I might vomit. She's grunting next to me again, but I don't want to look at her. The formula runs through my head like ticker tape: F=A+A+C.

I summon the strength to look into my mother's dying face. I see it there. That thing I've been waiting for the last three decades. The first two A's in the formula. Acknowledgement and Apology. It was too late for the C—the Commitment to do better. But I've finally found Forgiveness in my heart.

"I forgive you, Mom."

She closes her eyes, and I note the peaceful smile on her face.

---

She died later that evening after I left. Ben was there to hold her hand.

Later, I told my therapist the C could be changed to Closure instead of Commitment. She agreed and congratulated me on finding peace. I don't know what happens in the afterlife, but I hope my mother's found that same peace for herself.

# 40

# THIS POEM IS NOT ABOUT THE DREAM

## MEGAN E. FREEMAN

the dream was inconsequential
entirely
the fleeting contents flew
at the first invitation
of consciousness
and whatever caused
the release of cortisol
adrenaline
the paralyzed scream

none of that matters to the point I'm making here

the consequential moment was
when I cried out and
immediately
your arms flexed around me
already embracing as we slept
but tightening more
instantaneous dissipation of dream
dissolution replaced with relief

in the same second I fell
you caught me
rocked me in the lullaby of your love
back to deep safe sleep

the immediacy of your response
the instance of my awareness
the bliss of coming to in your arms

that's what this poem is about

# 41

# LEARNING YOGA SLOWLY

## VALERIE SZAREK

I learn 3 poses every 5 days. I suspect I'll make 100 salutations to the sun from my backyard and be able to do a downward dog with Felix the cat before this world quarantine takes her bow, freeing us to the reverse fly and clanging dropped dumbbells at the gym again.

Sometimes I feel a little yogini waking inside of me. She drinks spicy chai in the morning before easing onto her mat and leaves 30 minutes for a Savasana meditation at the end. She's fearless, leaving the TV off and phone muted, no longer afraid that when she glides off her mat she'll find 11 messages on her silenced phone and watch two towers collapse into soot and asbestos over and over for days on end. Sirens and planeless skies keeping the sun occupied. Lockdowns and no-fly orders. Everybody staying home, holding breath and looking twice at every stranger.

Like now. A 40-day quarantine that will stretch past 64 poses, and she should be an expert by the time we can leave home again. She will be thin and lithe and have a healed right wrist in spite of 48 years of leatherworking. She will do tree pose as balanced as her silver maple and warrior pose in her hotel room before taking the stage to give a keynote address and signing books at the poetry festival. She will have black and lavender spandex hugging her legs and midriff. She'll take walks barefoot, bow Namaste to neighbors, will never need a chiropractor, and will probably give up meat.

(In response to "Learning Italian Slowly" by David Shumate)

# 42

# BELLY RING

## AMY BELLEFEUILLE

Yeah, ok, I admit it—I've been going through some early midlife crisis thing. At thirty! I've been dreading this milestone for some time and attempting to devise ways to deal with, if not defy, the evidence of my advanced years.

It doesn't help that, for years, my mother-in-law has been repeating some variation on the following theme: "Well, Amy, at least you're young. Even with a child on your hip or in your car, men still find you attractive. I was like that too. But I tell you, when I turned thirty, that was it. No one gawked or even glanced my way. Even the crudest construction-worker types stopped whistling when I passed by. Once I realized that no one was noticing me anymore, I began to *feel* unattractive: like a boring, overworked, over-the-hill housewife. Just you wait."

Great. And so along came thirty, smacking me in the face with the birth of my second child, my eighth wedding anniversary, and for the first time ever, my mother deciding to abandon her denial and admit loudly over dinner for six, "Oh my goodness, girl, you really *do* have a lot of gray!"

Determined to make something of my it's-all-downhill-from-here year, I blazed forward with a plan to accomplish something big. I trained for a marathon. Hard. Even when I'd been up all night with a screaming baby or a four-year-old with nightmares, I got up at five-thirty and ran in the dark, determined to make it happen. And happen it did. After six months of training, I completed the marathon—*running*—and met the time goal I'd set. And only eight months postpartum. What a thrill.

But enough of a thrill for me to call this a successful year to remember? Not quite.

I still needed to do one more thing. Call it a memento, a keepsake, a memory marker. I needed something semi-permanent, semi-noticeable, semi-controversial. Something.

That something was a belly ring. I simply *had* to have one. They were sooo cool. And if other people could get away with one, why couldn't I? I just wouldn't be referring to it as a "navel piercing." Ugh. Even off-handedly referring to my belly button as a "navel" made me feel like a big, round, *old* orange. I'd have none of that.

Otherwise, it was the perfect vice. Not as permanent as a tattoo (I'm too prone to change my mind), discreet if necessary (no one at church needed to know), yet unexpected enough to shock the modest one-piece swimsuits right off some of the moms in our infant swim class.

Yes! Now, how to make it happen? Clearly it would take some strategizing. After all, how often was I in the vicinity of a tattoo parlor (the only caliber of establishment offering body piercings) without my children, wearing something that would expose my midriff? Certainly not often enough to make it easy.

After several failed attempts involving erroneously daring to think—among other things—that ten o'clock in the morning was a reasonable time for at least one such place to open, I finally settled on my last resort, Plan D, and presented it to my husband for approval. We would do the deed on the way to a dinner party over the weekend when the place was sure to be open, when we had a babysitter, and when I would so cleverly arrange to wear swim suit bottoms underneath my sundress. Right, Babe?

He agreed. What else could he do? He was married to an aging weirdo with an agenda.

When the fateful night finally arrived, I marched into Tattoo Palace (or some such oxymoron) and spoke to a teenager at the front desk with piercings in what seemed every available half-inch of facial skin—eyebrows, nose, lip—OUCH! Suddenly, several bits of lint on my dress required my full visual attention while I told him I wanted my belly button pierced and asked about the details.

"Oh, you want your *navel* pierced." He corrected me, elegantly. "It hurts pretty bad, you know."

I didn't ask him how he knew—I thought it was a girl thing.

"It's thirty bucks and we only take cash," he said.

Ready for this (from another of the aforementioned failed attempts), my husband and personal cash carrier had come in with me. He sat down on a black vinyl bench surrounded on all sides by ultra-colorful illustrations of scantily clad fantasy women, deadly fanged reptiles, and numerous variations on the theme of death: skeletons, crossbones, skulls. As hip as my husband is, and as much as he's lived, I was pleasantly surprised to notice how out of place he looked sitting there.

I signed away my rights to legal action against "The Palace" should something go awry, chose the smallest sterling silver ring I could find on the tray, and followed a very tattooed woman into the back room.

Meanwhile, my husband attempted to be sympathetic to a balding, middle-aged, beer-bellied, Harley-riding gentleman in a dilemma—he couldn't find the precise skull design he wanted for the three square inches of available body-art space on his forearm.

The woman stopped short in the hallway when she realized I was wearing a dress and said, "Do you have shorts on under there or something because there are some men back here . . ."

I assured her it was all taken care of. She led me to a mirror, asked me to lift my dress, and drew a dot on my belly button with a purple marker.

"How does that look to you?" she asked. "Centered?"

"Yep, looks good to me."

"Okey dokey."

She had me lay down on a lounge-chair-ish contraption. While she swabbed on some alcohol and got out a few tools I purposely avoided looking at, she whispered, "Can you hear those guys?"

I had just started to pick up on some of the conversation of the three men getting tattoos in the chairs nearby. One was saying, "Oh man, that's gotta hurt!"

"Yeah," another one said. "You know, it was the Vietnamese who invented body piercing in the late sixties to torture prisoners of war!"

These men were having ink injected under their skin with needles—*repeatedly*—and they were talking about how painful piercing my belly button was going to be. Yeesh.

My "piercing artist"—proper title?!—was amused and said, "Okay, are you ready? This part *is* pretty painful."

I was perfectly fine until she started chanting, "Start breathing deeply. Breathe in, breathe out, breathe in . . . now hold it!"

Choonk! I could hear it as much as feel it, and I thought, *That can't be it, can it? There's probably more to come.*

She said, "You okay? How are you feeling?"

I said, "Fine. Was that it?"

"Yep," she said as she came at me with a huge pair of pliers I wished I hadn't seen. "I've just got to tighten it up and you'll be done."

The thought of those pliers possibly slipping was worse than the actual piercing. But it was done in a second with not so much as a tug. Phew. She asked me again if I was okay and said if I needed to lay there a minute or two, that was alright.

I said, "No, that's okay. I've had two children—one with no drugs. Believe me, this was no big deal."

She let out a whispered "Ohhh . . ." and I got the impression she really understood.

She had me check it out in the mirror. "What do you think?" she asked.

"Very cool," I decided.

She agreed. "Yeah, looks great on you. You're young, so it really works."

My new best friend then gave me the details on keeping it clean and led me back to the front of the store. By this time my husband was sitting with three men who suddenly all looked at me as if I were some kind of hero.

As we climbed into the truck and I lifted my dress to get my husband's opinion, he clued me in to his fifteen minutes of tattoo parlor fame. Turns out, right after I'd gone into the back, the Harley-riding, skull-seeking fellow had asked my husband what we were doing there. When he found out, his immediate response was, "Cool. How on earth did you talk her into that?!"

# SUPERPOWERS

## SUNNY BRIDGE

I am now at the age where
I have superpowers—

I am a *shape-shifter*.
I can melt into a puddle of tears at the slightest sympathetic glance,
    a song on the radio,
    a road once traveled,
    a note forgotten in a book.

I have a *forcefield*.
I can walk into a store and come back out without buying one single
thing.
You might call it grief or depression—but
    I don't actually need much anymore.
    Sometimes I go out only to be among other people
    and it turns out

I have a *cloak of invisibility*.
I can go nearly anywhere completely unnoticed.
    I belong to the tribe of women over sixty
    who fade into the background unless they're
    driving too slowly in the left lane.

I have *night vision*.
I can assure you things look their worst at 3 a.m.,
    emptiness stretching across un-mussed
    sheets on the far side of the bed,
    a pillow turned to stone.

I think I need new superpowers.
On the plus side—

I am a *time-traveler*.
I visit the past
    reliving days of sun and laughter,
    nights of love and tenderness,
    hours of pain, yet years of joy.

I have super-*human endurance*.
I am enduring
    what humans have had to endure
    since the beginning of humans.

I am now at the age where
fear is somehow smaller;
the worst has already happened
and I am still breathing—

# 44

# RUN LIKE HELL

## CALVIN GIROULX

*I'm the best runner ever!*

Fox burst through a wall of mist and charged up Grey Mountain. Frost stuck to her skin and snow tingled between her toes as her leather sandals made fresh tracks in the powder. Thirty miles was a long way to run, especially when the run ended with this steep climb. At least the next thirty would start downhill. But no matter how much she hurt, Fox refused to let up. She far preferred the pain to being at home. Every day she sprinted dozens of miles across the southern peninsula to prepare for next year's Gauntlet. This was her first time running over half the distance in one go, and it was exhilarating.

All her life, Fox had been treated like swamp trash and told females weren't strong enough to survive racing a hundred miles. She'd prove them all wrong. She hated losing more than she loved winning. Losing wasn't an option. If she didn't win, she'd die trying.

Somewhere behind her, Blackstar and Wakerobin struggled to keep up. For supposedly being two of the greatest runners in the tribe, they were surprisingly far behind. She hadn't just hung with the best, she'd dominated them halfway into this run.

*Only a taste of what's coming.*

As the mountaintop grew closer, the giant cathedral-like ponderosas thinned out. Golden afternoon sunlight radiated off the snow to create thousands of sparkling crystals that shimmered in waves so blindingly powerful, Fox had to shield her eyes. Distracted by the rhythm of her stride, the chatter of squirrels, the singing of birds in the trees, and the rustling of rabbits through the snow-topped underbrush, she almost missed how the ground suddenly ended.

She skidded to an abrupt halt inches from a cliff's edge and sent a spray of snow showering down toward the smoking, disc-shaped lake some one hundred feet below.

"Whoa!" she shouted as sulfur-smelling steam hit her in the face and a rush of vertigo spun her head while her stomach flipped over on itself. Her arms flailed as she wobbled for balance before backpedaling.

Beads of sweat dripped down her limbs as she pulled her disheveled mat of soaked ginger hair into a loose ponytail. Despite the protests of her muscles, she forced herself to stand tall and show no weakness while she waited. She put on her best smile for them.

And waited.

Convinced that something must have happened because she couldn't have had *that* big of a lead, she started to go back—only to have her tall, thickset fellow runners burst out onto the ridge, loud enough to spook every animal within shouting distance.

Wakerobin's long, loose hair bounced in strands over his straining red baby face, while the setting sun reflected off the glistening sweat on Blackstar's shaved and way-too-big head. Fox couldn't stop herself from checking out the elaborate ink designs that covered their muscular arms like sleeves on their dark-soil skin. The ink-workers tattooed every runner who completed the Gauntlet.

As her future competitors ran the final yards up to her perch, Fox stared at her light-skinned, freckle-covered arms and imagined what they'd look like all inked up. Even aside from the lack of tattoos, Fox could not have appeared more different, descended as she was from the rare line of Malpaso with pale skin and hair like fire.

When they reached her, Wakerobin and Blackstar stumbled around in drunken circles, wheezing, with hands linked atop their heads. Then they both collapsed onto their hands and knees, chests heaving like their hearts might explode. They were acting like elders instead of twenty-one-year-old men in their prime.

*Really?* Fox frowned at them. *I wasn't going that fast.* "Geez, took you two long enough. Did one of you stub your toe?"

They coughed responses that contained more phlegm than actual words.

Fox shook her head and turned to admire the majestic view. She'd never been to the top of Grey Mountain before, and it didn't disappoint. The world unfolded like a painting, everything so small and tranquil. A large red-tailed peregrine passed over the miles of dense, snow-dusted, forest-clad mountains with their many hot springs. She watched as the regal bird banked south and rode the wind toward where the mountain range's sharp icy peaks flattened into the long sinuous frozen Aurora Lakes that merged at various points. Beyond the tiny dots of kids playing on the ice as if the day would never end, she could just make out the Malpaso gem of the southern peninsula—Brighthaven, the city hidden in the hightrees.

High above ground, safely out of reach of dangerous predators, her people had built their home on the miles of massive wood rings that circled trunks and platforms resting atop branches, accessible only by lifts, ladders, and bridges. Tens of thousands of Malpaso had thrived here for generations, guarded by archers who patrolled Brighthaven's formidable watchtowers and outer palisades.

Fox's gaze was drawn towards the one dark blotch between here and Brighthaven that stained this endless beauty, like some giant had spilled black ink onto the Dark Forest's haunted trees, rumored to be home to raithtu and evil forest spirits. None from her tribe had ever returned from the Dark Forest.

Fox wanted to stay here and appreciate the vista, anything to delay her inevitable return to her odious job and miserable family in Brighthaven, but her light furs protected very little of her skin. That, and night approached. Being outside the Brighthaven palisades at night was suicide.

The labored breathing behind her faded, and when she glanced back over her shoulder, she caught Blackstar staring at her butt. She turned and glared. "Is there something I can help you with?"

Blackstar wore a dumb grin. "Is that an honest question?"

If it had been Wakerobin asking she might've answered differently, but Blackstar made her cringe. She hawked a fat loogie at his feet. "Hell no."

She glanced at Wakerobin, hoping her speed and fortitude had impressed him. But that dream was crushed when he said, "You must've found a shorter path we don't know about."

Fox's irritation flared at their denial. "That was too easy. You two sure you aren't losing a step?"

"Maybe next time we'll actually try," Blackstar said and strained to puff out his chest with dignity.

"Ha! Yeah, right. Is that why you're both so out of breath?" Their silence told her she'd touched a nerve. *Careful; they hold the key to your freedom*, she reminded herself as she forced a laugh. "Relax, it was just a joke. You gotta convince the Elder Chiefs to let me race. You know I'm ready."

The two exchanged dark looks.

"You're not ready," Blackstar said. "Just because you run a lot doesn't mean you can push yourself through dehydration and hunger when you're so worn out you can barely stand."

"I'd spend all my free time running too, if I had your parents," Wakerobin added.

Fox couldn't tell if that was meant as an insult or an actual attempt at sincerity. Either way, it stung. She didn't need some pretty boy with a perfect life reminding her of the tribe's worst kept secret. The bruises hidden beneath her furs did that well enough.

She shifted and stared at the horizon so they wouldn't see the pain in her eyes. "We need to go now while there's still light," Fox said. "You two ready or are you just going to sit there playing with yourselves?"

"You want to tell her or should I?" Blackstar said with a glance at his friend.

"Tell me what?" Fox asked, narrowing her eyes at him.

Wakerobin smiled and nodded at the edge of the cliff. "We always get at least one jump in."

Fox gave the hot spring below a skeptical glance. "You're full of crap." She'd made some high dives before, blowing off steam during a fishing expedition, but she wasn't sure she'd ever dived that far.

"We do it every time we come up here. It's awesome," Blackstar said with an equally mischievous smile. "There's hand- and footholds carved into the rocks to make a ladder back up here. It's a fast climb."

"Trust us, you're going to love it."

*Assuming I don't get killed.*

"Plus, you need the bath to wash off that fish smell," Blackstar said. He plugged his nose and batted at the air.

Fox rolled her eyes. No matter how many jokes she heard about stinking from being a fishmonger, they still bothered her. "You're so funny. I think you're just mad you got beat by a sixteen-year-old girl."

"And I think you're just scared," came Blackstar's snappy retort.

All she had to do was say no to this terrible idea. But she'd never hear the end of it back home, and the Elder Chiefs might not respect her or believe her fearless enough to race.

They both watched her, probably waiting to mock her if she backed down. She'd shown them no weakness so far and she refused to do so now, no matter how crazy and stupid this felt. "Let's do this."

"That's the spirit!" Wakerobin said and clapped. "Here's how it goes: we line up against that tree and when I say go, we run. Last one to hit the water has to buy drinks at the Wildflower tonight. 'K?"

She couldn't afford to buy them drinks. She could barely afford to buy food. Good thing she was faster than both of them combined. "Okay."

They removed their satchels and weapons and set them down for when they'd ascend the face of the cliff back up here. The three of them lined up like the start of a race, each with one hand touching a tree. Fox's nerves went ballistic, like someone was tickling the inside of her stomach. Terrified, she drew in a deep breath of the sweet air and closed her eyes. *You got this.*

"Go!" Blackstar yelled as he stole a half-step lead.

*Cheater!*

Fox sprinted after him and just caught him before the edge.

Then she was airborne.

The world rushed up, whistling loud and throbbing against her eardrums as she counted away the seconds of the long, floating one-hundred-foot freefall. Further than she'd ever dived before.

She took one last breath just before her feet broke the surface.

Warm liquid welcomed her, and she sank to the bottom until she stood on her feet. Water plugged her ears with a dull ring, and the sun cast a faint orange glimmer over the surface far above. As if standing in an almost weightless sensation in some murky, misty, fog-like substance, she held her breath until her lungs almost burst.

She tasted sweet air as she resurfaced and floated on her back like a corpse. Overwhelming, refreshing euphoria from being alive, like a wonderful drug, filled her until she realized she was alone.

Blackstar's voice shouted from atop the cliff, "I can't believe you're not dead."

"Congratulations," Wakerobin shouted next to him. "You're the only person dumb enough to jump off this cliff."

Fox's head shot up, stunned. "What are you two chickenshits waiting for?"

"We were just messing with you. We've never jumped," Wakerobin yelled.

*Should have seen that one coming.* "Ha ha ha, you got me. At least tell me where the rock ladder is."

They broke out into cruel laughter. "There's no ladder," Wakerobin said.

Never had his voice sounded so annoying. She was so furious she wanted to bash his pretty face in with a rock. Her jaw clenched, and her eye twitched so hard she thought she'd pop a vessel. "You two better run now, because when I scale up this cliff I'm going to kill you both."

"No way we're waiting that long. By the time you reach the top it'll be midafternoon, and then you'll still have the thirty miles back to Brighthaven. Plus there might not even be a path up. You're going to have to take the looonnnggg way back," Wakerobin said and laughed some more.

"But since you're such a better runner than us, you shouldn't have any problem," Blackstar said.

"Hey, don't worry though. If you make it back before night, we'll vouch for you. If not, well . . ." Wakerobin started cackling and Blackstar joined in. Their laughter seemed endless as it rained down on her.

"Assholes!" Fox screamed.

"Well, we gotta go, it's pretty late," Wakerobin said.

"Have fun getting back by yourself," Blackstar said.

They left.

Fox hollered every curse word she knew until her stomach hurt and her echoes faded from the cliffs.

She should have suspected something when they'd finally asked her to run with them, but she'd been so excited to prove herself. She knew they didn't care for her, especially now that they'd failed to beat her to the top of Grey Mountain and prove she wasn't as good a runner as she claimed. But to leave her in the wild without her spear, satchel, food, or water after a run up a mountain seemed too malicious.

*This has to be a joke. They would never leave me out here. This is murder.*

She got her answer when they failed to reappear.

Fox stared at the cliff face, searching for anything that resembled handholds. She shook her head. The rock looked impassable. Besides, she wasn't a climber. She was a runner. Only one option remained, no matter how crazy or impossible the path.

Taking a deep breath, Fox swam to the only beach among the encircling cliffs as the afternoon sun cast shadows over the hot spring. Out of the water, dripping wet with furs soaked in the crispy cold, she felt like the temperature had dropped ten degrees. But this wasn't the time to feel sorry for herself. She had to survive this so she could embarrass Blackstar and Wakerobin in front of the entire tribe in the Gauntlet.

Without her compass, she would have to make her best guess as to which direction she headed, and her body might crash before she made it back. But desperate times called for desperate measures when racing the sun.

She ran angry into the Dark Forest.

---

*This is an evil place.*

Her breath no longer visible, the hairs inside her nostrils thawed until she tasted a dominating aroma of foul muck and blighted leaves. As her eyes adjusted to the gloom, the thicket of bizarre, gnarled black trees exposed a creepy, poisoned realm of decay so unlike the lush life of Brighthaven. The twisted trees looked as if they might devour her. She'd never experienced woods so eerily quiet, as if something had scared away all the animals and insects. Yet, she had the unpleasant sensation that hundreds of hidden eyes watched her.

She ran for what felt like hours, with no way to tell time or direction under the thick canopy of interweaving leaves and thorn-like branches. The deeper she ventured, the more she believed the trees had her in their grip, like a fist slowly clenching. She'd give anything to be inside her family's busted hut within the Brighthaven swamplands, a warm blanket wrapped around her shoulders and a bowl of steaming broth in her hands.

She panted and stumbled. Knots formed on her calves, quads, and hamstrings as her stride faltered. Her feet rustled through piles of rotting leaves that covered the forest floor, the cold slush under-neath like ice against her feet. Sickening nausea hit her so fiercely she had to stop and lean on one of the rotting trees so she wouldn't collapse. She covered her eyes as the world spun. Desperate for any form of moisture, she scooped handfuls of black snow sludge to her mouth. She gagged against the dirt and small rocks that scraped down her throat and into her belly, which only made her stomach churn more.

The silence of this dark, dead world continued to unnerve her. She should have been out of the Dark Forest by now. For all she knew, a pack of unseen wolves or forest demons now stalked her.

*You did this to yourself, you stupid, stupid girl.*

Though angry at Blackstar and Wakerobin, her real fury came from how she'd embarrassed herself because of her stupid eager-ness over some stupid race. Even if she made it back alive, they'd surely come up with some other excuse not to let her run the Gaunt-let. She'd always been an outcast with no life and no friends. Aside from her little brother, Mud, she doubted anyone in Brighthaven would notice or care that a piece of swamp trash disappeared.

Thoughts of Mud only increased her anger at herself. When not at work, Fox had spent most of her free time running. She should have spent it with him. The guilt of not reliably being there for him had always haunted her, but she also wanted to be free. Nothing matched the freedom running gave her, always pushing herself to go farther and faster until she felt like she was flying. She couldn't imagine a life as depressing as one where she couldn't run. But what did that say about her, when she knew how much he looked up to her, how much he wanted to spend time with his older sister, and she still pushed him aside for running?

And where had that gotten her? A legacy of dying helpless and alone in this desolation. She wasn't ready to die, but she suspected that death never cared.

Footprints in the mud provided a spark of hope. Until she realized they belonged to her, and that she'd been so lost, she'd depleted the last reserves of her energy running in circles.

What little composure remained inside her broke. She vented her fury with a loud howl laced with fear at the thought of Mud trapped with their father. The man who liked to beat them when he drank too much—or simply whenever the thought occurred to him —while their mother watched.

She screamed and punched the trees until her knuckles bled. As she tried to kick a rock, she slipped and hit her head on the frozen ground. Her vision fogged and spun, and the sting made her eyes water. She reached for her throbbing forehead and felt where a welt blossomed underneath the mud now matted in her hair.

Fox lay there and wept, until she grew so tired she closed her eyes and hoped to never wake.

Something warm and wet licked her face. She moaned and forced her eyes open.

Beneath pointed triangular ears, the dark eyes of a red fox stared at her. She flinched back, expecting a bite, until she felt another slurp, followed by its warm, stinky animal breath. The fox nudged its wet nose against hers. Its whiskers tickled her cheeks, and she giggled—half mad with relief—as she caressed its thick silky auburn fur.

*What are you doing?*

Fox glanced around but didn't see anyone beside the fox. "Are you talking to me?"

The fox cocked its head in amusement. *Who else would I be talking to?*

Fox touched her head. How hard had she fallen?

She eased her back against a tree and hung her head in despair. The fox stared at her with curiosity. Fox sighed and glanced up. "Come to watch me die?"

*Stop feeling sorry for yourself. You only wasted around twenty miles running in circles. You can make it the last twenty to the edge of the forest. At least die by the lakes.*

"Piss off." She swatted at the fox, and it bit her hand. Genuine pain and blood followed, which put to rest any notion of this fox being a dream or hallucination.

"That hurt!" she yelled and rubbed the wound on her hand. "I should kick you."

*Like you could. You're too slow.*

Her old defiance flickered to life in the pit of her stomach. Fox rose and spat off to the side. "We'll see about that."

Dizzy and drained, she felt her empty belly sucking up against her spine as she staggered into pursuit. She chased the fox, matching its pace through the Dark Forest, and tried to grab it by its long bright bushy tail, but no matter how fast she ran, she couldn't catch her namesake.

When the fox at last stopped, Fox wondered if she'd stepped through an invisible portal into another world.

Bright bushes, purple moss, blue ferns, and glowing fireflies brought the Dark Forest to life, filling the air with hypnotizing warmth and humidity. The songs and chirps of insects mixed with the scurry and scamper of animals to create pleasant forest melodies. Fox listened and lost herself in the harmony.

She spotted a lone albino deer with magnificent antlers and gorgeous fur like snow. Something about its peaceful red eyes and graceful glide soothed Fox. She told herself everything would be all right.

In a flash, something grabbed the deer's neck with claws like sharp blades and bit its head off in one savage jerk.

*Raithtu!*

Fox swallowed a scream and went silent as the frightening strange mix of bear and lizard munched away, squealing with ravenous bites and spraying blood everywhere.

She stood in place and trembled, too scared to run. Now more than ever she yearned for her fishing spear, even though she doubted she could have pierced its heart between those thick hairy reptilian bladed scales—if that's where its heart even was.

The fox tapped her leg with its paw. *Follow me.*

As they snuck away, Fox imitated the fox's trot that betrayed no noise as it avoided sharp rocks, broken branches, pine needles, and decaying animal droppings.

Twilight appeared through the trees, and Fox realized they'd reached the edge of the Dark Forest. She emerged from the trees and stood atop a hill, looking down upon a sheet of frozen, wind-scarred turquoise that made up one of the Aurora Lakes.

Excited, she ran past the fox, but her feet got tangled up and sent her tumbling hard down the slope to a brutal stop.

*Are you okay? I did say you could die here, if you want.*

Fox sat up and checked out her right ankle, which had swollen to almost twice the size of the other. She took a calming breath and slowly rotated the joint, wincing at the pain. Not broken, but her range of motion had become very limited.

She stood, favoring her good leg, and sighed relief that instead of her ankle snapping, it only hurt like someone had smashed it with a hammer. The agony grew as she bounced on her toes, but at least she could still walk. "I'm fine. No dying for me today."

*Good. Only thirty miles to go.*

The number sent Fox's heart plummeting to her toes. Then she took a deep breath and strengthened her resolve. Thirty miles. Just half of what she had initially planned to run today. She'd run that much before easily. She could do this.

Starting with a slow jog, she began to follow the bank toward Brighthaven, but a fuzzing image of bluish green sent a jolt of terror down her spine. She halted and tried not to piss herself.

The raithtu had followed them.

Fox took small steps away from it and onto the ice. She shivered against the bursts of freezing evening wind.

As the ball of her foot touched down ever so gently, the ice made a loud tearing noise. The raithtu's ugly head shot up, and its four pupils expanded like four small suns that blazed together to create an intense angry glower.

Fox quivered. Her heart skipped a beat, and her bowels almost spilled onto the ice.

They stared at each other, as if breathing through their eyelids, neither ready to make the first move.

The raithtu's tongue clicked inside its mouth like a beetle buzzing and stepped onto the ice after her. It slipped and fell.

A loud crack resounded through the air, and the ice gave way underneath it. Its back two legs sank under water. A miracle.

The raithtu dug its front two claws into the ice and pulled itself out of the water, much angrier.

The fox dashed across the ice. *Now or never!*

Fox spun in a half circle, spat, and took off after the fox.

Without cover, the powerful wind hit her like a slap and hissed as its invisible wrath stung her exposed skin. The ice was slick and unstable underneath her feet, so she focused hard to maintain her rhythmic flow. She tried not to put too much weight on either leg, fully aware that if she went under, that was it.

The fox had gained a tremendous lead on her. The gap only continued to widen until the fox had shrunken into a little copper smudge and she no longer heard its voice in her head yelling at her to keep up.

The vicious growls and scrapes of claws from behind told her the raithtu was coming at her with everything it had. Fox stopped trying to listen for cracks or scan the ice with her eyes and just focused on not breaking stride. Nothing else mattered other than to run.

*Run.*

*Like.*

*Hell!*

Adrenaline pushed her through the mighty gusts of howling wind that pummeled her. She didn't dare waste an ounce of energy looking back, but she heard the raithtu getting closer, felt its warm breath on the back of her legs.

But she refused to lose. She hated to lose.

*You lose, you die. You lose and Mud is alone. You lose and Dad has no one to oppose him.*

Around the bend of the trees, she recognized the evening lights from the Brighthaven palisade on the far side of the lake. No matter how long she sprinted her heart out with a bad ankle, the lights kept moving farther away, cruelly taunting her like Wakerobin and Blackstar.

Fox glanced around frantically but couldn't locate the fox.

She cut right, using the raithtu's stumble at her misdirection to gain the few precious steps she'd need to get off the ice, climb up a tree, and wait out the beast.

She'd almost made it when she saw a group of kids playing on the ice. Time froze as the horrible choice confronted her. *They should know better than to be out so close to nightfall!* Fox swallowed her anger. She still had enough of a lead to climb up a tree, but the raithtu would slaughter those kids.

Her life or theirs.

Not much of a choice if saving herself meant a bunch of kids were eaten alive instead. Even if they belonged to parents who had shunned and humiliated her as swamp trash, who had told her she wasn't good or strong enough to run the Gauntlet. That didn't mean the kids deserved to die.

She zagged hard left, hoping the raithtu would take the bait and continue the chase.

It did.

*Come and get me!*

She hadn't been born with talent and skill for any job considered respectable. The only way she knew how to go at adversity was face to face, give everything she had and see how long she could hold on. Fuck the Gauntlet—*this* was the greatest race she'd ever run. Maybe she'd lose and become the raithtu's dinner, but if that bastard wanted her, she'd make it work for it. And she'd prove her entire tribe wrong in the process.

Horns sounded in the hightrees as hundreds of Malpaso poured onto the palisade. No doubt they recognized the only small redheaded runner in the tribe. And no doubt they recognized the raithtu.

Arrows fell from the sky and whistled past her head as archers in the hightrees tried to take down the enormous beast. But the creature dodged them all.

Fox had never run so fast. The hightrees to the right swirled past her as she searched for the willpower to make herself go just a little quicker. Out of the corner of her eye, she saw the group of kids rush to a lowered lift, which whisked them up the moment they were onboard.

They were safe.

More of the tribe packed onto the palisade. They screamed down at her to pick it up, push harder, kick faster. Fire arrows rained down, some tipped with incendiaries that exploded like fireworks around her, but the raithtu continued to evade them, undeterred from its frenzied bloodlust that wouldn't end until it feasted on her flesh.

Snarling like the monster, Fox let spittle fly from her lips as pebble-like snowflakes pelted her face. She fought to stay light on her toes as the ice cracked all around her. Her heart thundered like it might punch through her chest, her body on the verge of immolation.

She flew.

Thousands of Malpaso in the hightrees cheered her on and chanted her name. "Fox! Fox! Fox!"

Her ankle twisted again, having finally suffered enough abuse, and it felt like she'd run into a wall. She could no longer ignore the massed pain of muscles burning, knives digging into her ribs, and tendons tearing inside her.

Fox heard a bark and looked up to see the fox. It jumped up and down, urging her into the trees. She darted right.

The fox led her through the trees toward a steep pile of red rocks, where it scrambled up and launched itself into the trees.

Trusting the creature implicitly, Fox ran up behind it, jumped, and soared over a wide, deep ravine hidden behind the red rocks and trees. Her arms and legs spiraled. As she started to fall, she slapped her hand around an overhanging branch at the other end of the gap. Sweat on her palms made her grip slip, but her fingers tightened and held on. She kicked her legs up to avoid the raithtu's teeth by inches.

A sickening, bone-jarring crunch rang out as the raithtu's skull smashed into the rock cliff below and snapped its spinal cord. The beast fell limp until it impaled itself on the ravine's jagged rock bottom.

A second snap, this one from the breaking of the branch she still held on to with one arm, sent Fox plummeting down after it.

---

*Still alive!*

Fox clung to the side of the ravine by her fingers and toes. Each breath produced shooting pain in her ribs, probably cracked from when she'd smacked into the side of the ravine to break her fall and then barely managed to hold on.

Entire body on fire, she grit her teeth and, inch by inch, crawled to the top of the cliff.

Once she made it, she lay on her back and sucked wind. Tears in her eyes, she laughed despite the sharp pain in her ribs.

She rolled to her side to look down the ravine at the raithtu's mangled corpse. She sent a red gob of saliva down onto it and pointed her thumb to her chest. "Winner."

Actually, that wasn't technically true. The fox had beaten her.

Fox scanned her surroundings but saw no sign of her namesake, either up here or at the bottom of the ravine. She carefully touched the big lump on her forehead from when she'd fallen in the Dark Forest. Had she imagined the whole thing?

The ground shook from the footsteps of the Malpaso who swarmed the trees and descended lifts and ladders down to the forest floor. Fox forced herself to her feet. She would stand tall and strong. Disgust filled her to see Wakerobin and Blackstar arrive first. They smiled like the three of them were best friends.

"That was incredible!" Blackstar said.

"I've never seen anyone run that fast!" Wakerobin said.

Fox glared at them.

"Hey, don't be mad at us," Wakerobin said and threw his hands up defensively. "We were just having a bit of fun. You were the one who decided to jump."

"Having a bit of fun? I could've been killed, you assholes!" Fox took two swift steps and kicked him in his fruits as hard as she could. Wakerobin crumbled, and she stumbled past as Blackstar backed away. "Still think I'm not ready?"

More Malpaso arrived to congratulate her, overwhelming respect shining in their eyes, especially in those of the little girls. No one dared to challenge her worth after what they'd just witnessed, and they all talked about how excited they were for her to run the next Gauntlet. But maybe the best reward was little Mud running up and hugging her around the waist. "That was incredible!"

She buried her face in his curly red hair and squeezed him back. *I'm going to get you out of here,* she silently promised him. *We're almost there.*

When she looked up, she saw a reddish-brown smudge through the moisture in her eyes. As she blinked the tears away, her gaze focused on her savior. As if it sensed her gaze on its back, the fox stopped and turned back to meet her eyes.

*Well done. You might want to do the math.*

Then the fox disappeared into the forest.

*Do the math?* Fox shook her head at the cryptic comment, hurt to see her furry little friend go. She wanted to believe that one day they'd meet again, particularly so she could beat it the next time they raced.

"How far did you run?" Mud asked, breaking her from her reverie. "When those two dimwits came back without you, I was scared. They said you'd fallen down a cliff."

Anger at their lie almost made Fox forget Mud's question. *Do the math,* the fox had said. And then her eyes widened.

She smiled and faced the tribe.

"Bet everything you own on me, because I'm going to destroy the competition," Fox said. She turned to stare down Wakerobin, who still squirmed in the fetal position, and Blackstar, who stood in bewilderment. "I'm the best runner ever!"

# 45

# THE GATHERING
## MELISSA HUFF

Such a tiny thing
delicate to look at
yet weighted with age
a made thing
a slender cylinder
altered    to make music.
Those who crafted it
must have cut it
smoothed it
constructed the tools
to drill those holes
with chosen spacings
undeniably intentional.

I stand     where they once stood
surrounded by stone.
I see     what they once saw
deep scrapings in walls where cave bears
sharpened their claws.
I step     into the hollow
where these makers gathered around fire
forty     thousand     years ago
its warmth penetrating their flesh
as it would have penetrated my own.

The clear notes sounding
from this hollow instrument
would have attracted others
would have attracted me
to join the gathering
this circle of early humans
sitting     squatting     breathing
sending air     from lungs like mine
through the chambers of this flute
made     by hands like mine
this flute fashioned     of bone
from the wings of a swan.

# 46

# ON THE OTHER SIDE OF THE WORLD

### SANDRA MCGARRY

A sky of night light wished upon
vanishes in the morning—
Dissolved by the sound of jets.

Everything crumbles and piles
on itself and lost coins among
the ruins stay lost with pots and pans,
love letters, photos, a baby's crib.

And there's a foot wedged
between the rocks, all toes attached.
Its body gone as well as its path.
Contour lines on the foot's bottom
make a topography.

Dust has made the lines into a map.
It is useless as the dust.
Yet, even without its life blood,
it still anchors to a place as people do.

The gatherers will come and
sort through the rubble, find
once tan cats and stone cold bodies.

Others will come and lift loads
carrying the weight
of architectures bombed into oblivion.

A work hum rises from behind
the cloth masks. A genetic root?

*Find the bodies. Bring them home.*

# 47

# WHITE FEATHER

## MIKE KANNER

The small firm of Miller and Son had done well tailoring suits for London's upper-middle class. In the back workshop, Miller and a few journeymen tailors did most of the work. The front was decorated to give customers a sense of modest elegance. Mahogany shelves lining the walls were filled with bolts of fabric, from merino wool to the satins used for lining to cotton fabrics for shirts and traveling outfits for those visiting the tropics. The shop also featured a small stand where customers stood while being measured. Three full-length mirrors around the stand provided customers a complete viewing experience.

"You're not in uniform?" Burton, a middle-aged banker, stood being measured for a new suit and shirt.

"No, sir, now your arm, please." Thomas, the son in Miller and Son, was used to this question. In 1916, the War was part of almost every conversation. Young men in civilian clothes were often asked why they were not in the service. Thomas tried to avoid war talk with customers, most of whom were simply happy to get a well-made suit.

But some were not. Mr. Burton raised his arm and continued his questioning. "Why not? You seem fit."

"Quite fit, sir." Thomas pinched the tape, walked over to a small standing desk, and wrote down the arm measurement. "I've applied as a conscientious objector." Then, taking the tape in both hands, he stepped back to Burton. "Now, if I can measure your neck, please?"

Burton was staring at Thomas's reflection in the mirror. "A conchie? I thought you were a Jew. They're not pacifists."

Thomas tempered his initial reaction and tried to respond pleasantly. "Jews are not. I am. I believe war only causes suffering and does not settle anything. Now, if you will please step down so I can measure your neck."

Burton stepped down but raised his hands to block the tape. "No. I think I'll take my business elsewhere."

Thomas politely tried to persuade Mr. Burton not to leave. "Perhaps you'd prefer to be measured by my father? He's served."

Burton donned his brown tweed Ulster coat, taking his time buttoning the double row of buttons up the front. "No. I'm sorry, Miller and Son have done good work for me in the past, but I cannot support an establishment that is not supporting the War." He cinched the belt to emphasize his final point and left.

Hearing the door close, Thomas's father, Henry, walked into the front room from the workshop.

He frowned at his son. "Thomas. You shouldn't talk politics. It's bad for business."

Thomas avoided his father's stare by returning the bolts of cloth he had pulled for Mr. Burton's selection. "I was just taking his measurements when he asked why I wasn't in uniform. I thought he wanted a suit, not a philosophical discussion."

"I know, I know." Henry had long since resigned himself to his son's position.

Having finished with the bolts, Thomas faced his father. "Papa, you were the one who told me how horrible war was. Your experiences turned me against it."

Henry, born Heinrich in Hamburg, Germany, met his son's gaze. Years ago, Thomas had come across pictures of his father as a young soldier at the end of the Franco-Prussian War. His father had told him about the brutality of combat. How he had seen his best friend die clutching at his stomach after a French soldier cut him open with a bayonet. What it looked like when he fired his rifle point-blank at the French soldier's head.

"I understand, my boy, but this is not the time, especially for us. Germans and Jews are suspect. That's why I changed our name." Henry placed his hand on Thomas's shoulder. "Maybe you should work in the back. Less upsetting to customers."

Thomas stared at the floor and murmured, "Yes, Papa."

———

Thomas finally received notice to appear before the local tribunal. Though he didn't have high hopes for the hearing's outcome, at least his status would be finalized. When he entered the room, his heart sank as he saw Burton seated with three other prominent individuals—all of whom had been customers—and the local recruiting officer. Thomas took a seat, maintaining the pleasant manner he had developed after years of waiting on customers. Mr. Burton opened a folder. "Mr. Miller, you have requested to be excused from military service as a conscientious objector."

"Yes, sir."

"And this is not for religious grounds?"

Thomas saw this would be a continuation of the conversation in the tailor shop. "No, sir. As you might recall, I believe war does nothing but cause suffering and settles nothing. If—"

The local recruiting officer interrupted. "It says here you were born Thomas Mueller." He looked up from Thomas's file. "Sounds German."

Thomas sighed; he knew his family's German origin would not help his case. "It is. My father came here from Hamburg. He changed his name when he started his business. I was born in the East End and lived there my whole life. I would note that his Majesty also has a German name, but no one questions his loyalty."

"Don't be impertinent!" Burton exclaimed. "It is not helping your case."

Thomas took a moment to control his frustration. "I was merely pointing out that there are many loyal Englishmen with German names. I am loyal to the Crown. I just don't believe I can best serve the King in a war."

The recruiting officer stared at Thomas before continuing. "And your employment?"

"As members of the Tribunal, including the Chair, can attest, I am the son in Miller and Son, Tailors."

Mr. Burton addressed the board. "If there are no other questions?" Since none were raised, he told Thomas he could leave while the panel deliberated.

Thomas stood and left the room to wait in the hall with the rest of the conscientious objectors. Most sat hunched over with their elbows on their knees, heads hung down. Deferments were not often granted. Even if they were, alternate "work of National importance" or service in the Army's Non-Combatant Corps was required. Refusal of either option would result in a court-martial and prison, as per the Military Service Act of 1916.

Finally, Thomas was called back in. The chair he'd sat on during the hearing had been removed, forcing him to stand. Mr. Burton read out the decision. "The tribunal has granted an exemption with alternate service in the Royal Army Medical Corps as a stretcher-bearer. You are to report on Monday to the London

Hospital for training. Failure to do so will result in your arrest and jail."

"Yes, sir."

---

Although Thomas was not particularly religious, Mr. Burton's reference to his religion and the probability of serving in the trenches inspired Thomas to attend synagogue that weekend. The reading was from Deuteronomy about the conquest of Canaan. The Rabbi explained that while Jews were peaceful people, they were not pacifists.

"While peace is a virtue, so is justice. When faced with the atrocities we have seen coming out of Belgium and the murder of innocents such as Edith Cavell, who wanted no more than to serve her fellow man and relieve his suffering, it is time for good men to stand up. To do otherwise is to be on the side of evil. As Joshua said, 'Be strong and of a good courage, fear not, nor be afraid of them: for the Lord thy God, he it is that doth go with thee; he will not fail thee, nor forsake thee.'"

Members of the small Jewish community in his part of the East End knew Thomas had refused to fight. Many avoided him, choosing to say hello only to his parents. So, it was exceptional when Reb Mordechai approached. As the head of the local *yeshiva*, he had taught Thomas religion for years. When he was in front of Thomas, Reb Mordechai spat in his face and gave him a white feather.

Thomas took out his handkerchief and wiped the spittle off. He stared at the feather for a moment and then placed it in his jacket pocket.

"Don't mind that," his father said. "His only son was killed last year. He still says *Kaddish* for him."

On Monday, Thomas reported to London Hospital. He and the other recruits were met by a sergeant whose ribbons showed he had already served in France. The burn marks and absence of his left ear partly explained why he was assigned to the hospital. "All right, you lot, you're here because you're not willing to fight for your country. Well, then you'll get a chance to bleed for your country. Stretcher-bearers have a nasty habit of getting themselves killed." The coughing spell that followed his short talk explained another reason for his current assignment. He was a gas victim. Seeing this living example of the war's horrors reinforced Thomas's objection to the brutality of warfare.

Once he recovered, the sergeant came back to attention. "RIGHT FACE." Thomas and the other recruits pivoted right as directed. The sergeant continued his orders. "We will now proceed down this hall to get you your uniforms. You are now part of the King's Army. FORWARD!"

The first weeks were spent learning what it took to be a soldier —how to march, set up their bunks, and maintain their equipment. Thomas and his fellow trainees had mixed feelings when they were told they would not receive any rifle or bayonet training.

"What do they think, sending us to the battlefield without learning how to defend ourselves?" Thomas' bunkmate was an avid socialist who objected on political grounds. He saw it as a rich man's war.

"You can step down now and hand me the pants." Uniforms rarely fit well, so Thomas reworked them for the other trainees. Using thread and needle from their issued sewing kit, he started the alterations. "That's part of being an objector. Because we don't want to fight, they think they shouldn't waste the bullets teaching us how." After a few minutes, he finished the stitching and cut off the extra thread. "Now, here's your pants. They shouldn't grab you anymore."

His friend put on the pants and did some squats. "Oh, that's a marvel. You're a real whiz with that needle."

Thomas grinned at him while he put away his sewing kit. "Come by our store after the war, and I'll give you a discount on a suit."

Medical training followed their military training. In addition to basic first aid, they were taught how to carry litters, improvise litters, and move soldiers without litters. Those who knew how to drive were selected for additional training on ambulances. At the end of their training, they were turned over to the Royal Army Medical Corps and given their specific assignments. Thomas was assigned to the 12th Infantry Brigade, which was already stationed near Ypres, Belgium.

---

At brigade headquarters, Thomas was told his battalion was already at the front. He was given a map that showed the route through the reserve and communication trenches and sent out to find his way.

Once he was in the forward trench, he saw a sign that said "Aid Post" hanging on a reinforced dugout. Relieved at finding his post, Thomas paused and took in his surroundings for the first time. What he saw was not the pristine view from the London papers or the postcards available at the newsstands. The odor almost overcame him. The trench smelled like the open sewer it resembled. Mud spattered everything. Wooden slats and chicken wire were used to hold back the dirt and muck. That was a battle being lost in several areas, despite soldiers shoring up the breaks.

Next was the noise. There was nothing quiet about this "quiet sector." Distant artillery echoed off the clouds while the trenches were filled with conversations, snores, and the groans of the men in the Aid Post awaiting evacuation. The real horror was that the clay soil kept the blood from draining, so the mud had a red tint and the air smelled of copper.

Two soldiers were tossing lime and dirt on a pit filled with amputated limbs. Thomas turned away, feeling nauseated.

Outside the dugout, a soldier sat on an upturned ammunition crate, smoking a cigarette. His tunic was off, and the right sleeve and cuffs of his shirt were covered in blood.

Thomas swallowed to quash his nausea and cleared his throat. "Can you tell me where the medical officer is?"

The man looked at him and drew on his cigarette. "Why? You look healthy."

"I'm the new stretcher-bearer."

"Really? Who did you whiz off?" The soldier tossed his cigarette into the mud.

"My tribunal. I'm an objector."

The man stood up, grabbed a tunic hanging from a bayonet jammed into the side of the Aid Post. "I object to this shite also, but here we are." He turned around, pulled on his tunic, and shouted. "SERGEANT!"

A middle-aged man with sergeant stripes came out of the Aid Post. "What now, sir?"

"I've got your new bearer." When the man turned around with his tunic on, Thomas saw he was an officer. He began to salute, but the officer grabbed his arm. "We don't do that out here. Tends to shorten the lives of us officers." Turning to the sergeant, he said, "Get him settled and put him on the rota starting tonight. I'm going to get some kip before the next go-round." The officer set off down the trench and disappeared into a dugout.

"Well, you've met the doctor," the sergeant said. "He's not bad, as they go. Don't get underfoot when he's working, or you'll catch the blazes."

They walked a few yards until they reached canvas hanging

over a chamber dug out of the side of the trench. The sergeant pulled back the canvas and pointed to a bunk. "Here you go. Just pack up the stuff on that bunk, then report back to the Aid Post."

"It looks occupied. Won't he mind?"

"No, he's not goin' to mind anything ever again. We just haven't had time to pack his kit and send it home. Bring it up with you when you report for duty."

The sergeant left Thomas to settle in.

---

Thomas had just laid out his kit when a lance corporal and a private came in. The corporal spoke up. "So, you must be the new man. Sergeant Hawkins said we got a replacement."

Thomas put his hand out to shake the two men's hands. "Thomas Miller. I'm assigned as a stretcher-bearer."

"Well, you're up for a job," said the corporal. "The name's Jones, by the way. The youngster's name is Ryan."

The younger soldier chimed in. "Yeah, nothing like crawling through the mud hauling a body to make you wish for your own Blighty. Nothing major, mind you, just enough to get home and have the girls more friendly."

Thomas couldn't imagine wishing for a wound to get out of the war. With no idea how to respond, he changed the subject. "So, what's it like here?"

Corporal Jones loosened the collar on his tunic and lay down on one of the bunks. "Not bad. Better than last time."

"Last time?" Thomas asked.

"We were here last November. Got pushed back. Retook back in April. Been here ever since. The only difference is more dead and more mud. Say, where's your weapon?"

Thomas shrugged. "I refused it when it was issued."

"Refused it! What kind of idiot are you?"

Thomas didn't know what the reaction would be but went ahead and told the corporal. "I'm an objector. I don't believe in harming others. This is my alternative service."

Corporal Jones leapt to his feet. "A bloody conchie! Hell. Well, don't expect me to save your ass if you won't save your own." The corporal stormed out into the trench.

"Don't mind him," Ryan said as he unwrapped his leggings. "He lost a lot of mates the first time he was here. Got a few holes himself. He'll be okay in a bit."

"And you?" Thomas asked Ryan.

"I just want to get through all this. As the Frenchies say, C'est la vie." Ryan had his boots and socks off and was inspecting his feet. "But, we'll see how long your objections last when the Krauts start shooting at you."

There was no assault that night, but patrols were still out, cutting wire and mapping German trench locations. It was quiet until one of the patrols hit an old shell. The calls for "Medic" and "Bearer" introduced Thomas to the reality of his situation. He and Jones used the moans and cries of the wounded to guide them as they moved in the dark. Suddenly, they were bathed in white light.

"FLARE!" Jones shouted. Thomas dropped to the mud just before bullets traversed No Man's Land. In between the bursts, Jones crawled to where Thomas lay. "You okay?" he asked. Thomas was panting from the adrenaline rush that came with being shot at. All he could do was nod.

"Okay." Jones waited while he recovered. "Well, it won't get any better. Let's push on." They crawled over to the soldiers. A trench mortar had been fired at the patrol, creating a hole in which they found some safety. One of the men was dead; his tags would be collected and the body left there. Another had superficial wounds that Jones field dressed. The problem was they also had two wounded who could not walk and only one stretcher. Jones had to choose which would be carried back, knowing that the other man would probably be dead before they could get back to him.

"We can put one on the stretcher, and I'll carry the other," Thomas suggested.

"You're daft," Jones said. "Fritz has the hole pegged. You'll be dead as soon as you stand."

"I'll crawl out. You go first with the stretcher. I'll follow a few minutes later."

"You're a bloody fool." Jones told the walking wounded to grab an end of the stretcher.

Thomas loosened the injured soldier's web gear and found a discarded bandolier. As he'd been trained, he grabbed the soldier's uninjured arm, turned so he could hold the arm to his chest, and rolled so the soldier was now on his back. Pushing up, he tied the two shoulder straps of the soldier's web gear together with the bandolier to secure him to Thomas's back. Thomas spoke quietly to the injured man. "If you would be so kind as to not moan or scream, it would be greatly appreciated."

The man nodded grimly, his face wracked with pain.

Jones just shook his head and asked Thomas, "You sure you want to do this?"

"Go!" Thomas answered and then threw spare gear to the side of the crater to draw off German fire. Jones and the stretcher moved out of the crater during the burst of fire. Thomas waited a few minutes before preparing to leave. Taking a breath, he threw more equipment to the crater's other side and waited for the machine-gun burst before clambering over the pit's lip.

He could hear Jones calling from the British lines. Thomas crawled over with the man strapped to his back until he was challenged and recognized by an observation post. Jones and Ryan met him in the trench and carried the wounded man back to the Aid

Post. Once in the trench, the wounded man repeatedly thanked Thomas for not abandoning him.

After stand-to, Thomas returned to his bunk and realized what he had done. Crawling through the mud with a man strapped on his back, machine-gun fire impacting all around him. This was not the act of a sane man. But the soldier's appreciation for not being abandoned confirmed Thomas's commitment to serving others and relieving their suffering.

Over the next few months, patrols or an assault would go forward and then Thomas, Jones, and Ryan would follow to retrieve the wounded. Although many thought it odd that Thomas never carried a weapon (most bearers carried a revolver at least), no one made any remarks after the first few weeks.

Thomas acquired the nickname "The Clerk." In his tunic pocket, he carried a small notebook and pencil. He would stay with fatally wounded soldiers so they did not die alone. When he and the soldier realized it was the end, Thomas would ask, "Do you have a message for someone?" He would write down the particulars and then take the soldier's identity tags. If it was possible, he would then bring the body back to their lines. In most cases, it was not. Thomas would close the soldier's eyes and say a prayer for the dead before crawling back to their trench.

Jones asked him once, "Hey Miller, why do you risk your neck to wait and write all that down?"

Thomas took the notebook out of his tunic and held it. "Because there's nothing worse than dying alone and unremembered." He put the notebook back into his pocket. "I'm with them, and I will remember."

---

Thomas and Ryan were in No Man's Land, searching for any survivors from that day's skirmish. It was the middle of the night, but a full moon gave No Man's Land a gray tint that let them look for wounded but unconscious soldiers. They came across a clump of bodies and separated the Brits from the Germans, finding mostly dead on both sides. Identity tags were taken from the dead Brits so families could be notified.

Thomas respectfully collected letters and pictures to put in his notebook. The next day, he would write notes to the families to go along with the commander's letters and send the effects back to them.

Bodies and parts of bodies were neatly piled with the hope that a ceasefire could be arranged so both sides could retrieve their dead. Thomas found a dying German soldier gripping his stomach. The young man was terrified at seeing a British soldier approach. Because German was still spoken at home and among his parents' friends, Thomas spoke the language passably. He crouched next to the German soldier. *"Ich bin ein Sanitäter. Ich bin hier, um zu helfen."*

Thomas pulled the soldier's hands away and saw that the soldier was holding a grenade. The brass wire trigger had been removed. He looked at the grenade, knowing that when it exploded, he and the soldier would be blown apart. Terror filled his belly.

"GRENADE!" Thomas shouted. He and Ryan scrambled to get out of the hole, but Ryan slipped in the mud. He was only partway out when the grenade exploded. Both felt the explosion's concussion and were showered by dirt, blood, and body parts.

Thomas spit out the dirt he had inhaled. "Fuck." He looked over to see Ryan lying in the mud. "Ryan, you alright?"

"No." Ryan turned over on his back. Thomas scrambled over. "Can you pull this bit of bone out of my leg? I don't think it's mine."

Thomas looked down and saw a bone shard with bits of German uniform still on it sticking out just below Ryan's left knee. Below that, Ryan's leg was a bloody mass with bits of muscle and Ryan's own bones exposed. Thomas could see that Ryan's boot was flat, meaning that the foot was no longer attached. He resisted the urge to vomit, then pulled the bone out, put a tourniquet on Ryan's thigh, and gave him some morphine.

"Looks like I got my Blighty," Ryan said as the morphine began to work. "It's back to London for me. And you get to carry me." He passed out after that.

Tying Ryan to his back as he had already done with so many soldiers, Thomas dragged him to one of the forward trenches. From there, he got help bringing Ryan to the Aid Post and placing him on the operating table.

"He's still breathing. Now get the hell out of my way." The doctor bent over Ryan while Thomas waited by the door. Jones had gotten back from his mission and joined Thomas. The platoon sergeant brought them tea laced with some cognac they had found in an abandoned basement. The moon, which had illuminated the scene, gradually set. They heard the order to stand-to, which meant it was almost dawn.

Finally, the doctor came out of the Aid Post. "Well, Ryan's out of it."

"He said he had a Blighty," Thomas noted in relief.

The officer snorted. "Some Blighty! He's dead. The German's bone sheared every vessel and artery in the leg. Bled out."

Thomas worked to contain his nausea. Ryan was dead because some soldier who was already dying decided to 'do his duty to the Kaiser' and take some of the enemy with him.

Jones pressed Ryan's pistol into Thomas's hand. "If you've changed your mind about shooting the damn *Boche*."

Thomas curled his fingers around the grip and felt the weight. Taking up the weapon would make sense given all he had seen and experienced at the Front. But he also remembered the fear in the dead German boy's eyes before the grenade exploded. Thomas looked back into the Aid Post and then at Jones before handing him the pistol. "No. Just because the German was a swine doesn't mean I need be."

Jones checked the weapon was safe and then tucked it into his belt. "Well, then you're a better man than me. Next Kraut I see is getting what for."

---

As patrolling intensified in preparation for the next push, the number of wounded increased. A shortage of trained stretcher-bearers throughout the Army meant that Ryan was not replaced. As a result, Jones and Thomas were out every night. Most of the time, they retrieved the wounded and dying using their screams and groans to navigate. Both sides' increased activity resulted in Jones and Thomas dealing with a collection of British and German wounded.

Sent out in the late evening, they came across a crater occupied by soldiers from both armies. Jones went to work bandaging the British, ignoring the pleas of the German soldiers. Speaking German, Thomas assured the other soldiers that they were there to help.

Jones looked for Thomas to assist and saw him treating the Germans. "Miller, what are you doing? Those are *Boche*."

Thomas was busy treating a German private who was more severely wounded than any of the Brits. "I'm here to help the wounded. If you want, report me when we get back."

Jones shook his head. "Daft bugger. Okay, but we bring our boys back first."

"Fine." He said something to the German that got a smile.

Finishing with the private, Thomas looked over at the next German and saw that he had a pistol in his hand. He raised it and began to aim at Jones and the British wounded. Thomas jumped up and yelled "*Nein*" before throwing himself on the German.

Jones heard two shots fired. He turned just in time to see Thomas jump on the German to block the bullets. Instinctively, Jones picked up one of the dropped rifles and shot the German in the head. He scrambled over to the two bodies and rolled Thomas off the German and onto his back.

The expanding stain on Thomas's tunic, the blood coming from his mouth, and the hissing sound meant Thomas had been shot in the lungs.

"Miller . . ." Jones leaned over to see if the man was still alive.

"Notebook," Thomas whispered.

Jones choked back his emotions as he pulled out the now blood-tinged notebook from Thomas's tunic.

"Write," the dying man ordered.

"Ready." Jones held the small pencil Thomas kept with the notebook, trying to control his emotions and waiting for Thomas's last words.

"Write: Papa. I did not die without purpose. I helped where I could." He coughed. "You have that?"

Jones scribbled frantically, choking back his tears. "Yes, you did, mate. Anything else?" There was only silence. He looked over and saw that the bubbles around the wound had stopped.

Thomas was dead.

Jones took a breath, swallowed, and then put the notebook in his own tunic. "All right, you lot." Talking to the infantrymen and walking wounded, he said, "You're now stretcher-bearers." He organized them to carry the British wounded back so he would not have to think about his dead companion.

Jones knew that with an assault scheduled in the next day or so, there would be no truce to pick up the dead. He was not going to leave Thomas there to become part of the waste on the battlefield. Jones loosened Thomas's web gear, grabbed his arm, and rolled him onto his own back, tying the web gear's straps with the sling from a rifle. With Thomas secure, he pushed off the ground and stood up. "Now, Thomas," Jones's voice cracked, "if you will be quiet on the way back, it will be greatly appreciated."

---

The following day, Jones entered the medical officer's dugout carrying Thomas's duffle bag. "Sir, here's Miller's kit."

"Set it there with the others." The officer was writing letters to next of kin.

"One thing, sir. This was in his things." Jones held a packet of letters. "Do you want me to include these?"

The officer glanced up to see the letters and then returned to what he was writing. "They're his correspondence. They go in with the rest of his personal items."

Jones hesitated, feeling the slight bulge in one of the envelopes. "The thing is . . ."

The officer looked up. "Yes, Corporal?"

"They're not from his family. These are all from some bloke named Burton, and they're full of white feathers."

The officer took a drag from his cigarette, stood up, and took the packet from Jones. He walked over to the small stove warming the dugout and threw them in before sitting back down at the table.

"Must be some pillock's idea of a joke. Dismissed."

"Yes, sir."

Jones left the dugout and looked at the men spread out in the trench. Rifles in hand, waiting for the next push. The new litter bearer was waiting to go over the top. Jones looked at the parapet and prepared to mount the assault ladder. "No cowards out here."

# 48

# BEDBUGS AS SAND MEN
## LAURA MAHAL

"At Terezin" by Teddy, 1943. "When a new child comes, everything seems strange to him. What, on the ground I have to lie? Eat black potatoes? No! Not I! I've got to stay? It's dirty here! The floor—why look, it's dirt, I fear! Am I supposed to sleep on it? I'll get all dirty! Here the sound of shouting, cries, and oh, so many flies. Everyone knows flies carry disease. Oooh, something bit me! Wasn't that a bedbug? Here in Terezin, life is hell and when I'll go home again, I can't yet tell." Terezin concentration camp, Bohemia.

*In 1991, I attended the fiftieth reunion of childhood survivors, as Arnošt Lustig's guest.*

I have a hand in nothing; I am an observer, only
the fiftieth reunion of survivors of torture
Five decades of silence.

A cardboard sign of "welcome," in Czech, it's "vítejte"
Terezin—Theresienstadt; language is important
A cold holding station, one blanket per person.

So many were shipped on to Auschwitz by train
a river of railroad that fed a death ocean
by dark one arrived, and by day one was gone.

The children stayed children, performing sweet
songs, plays, and poems
the cellists, the flutes, "undesirables" from all over.

Everyday people, Jewish and Roma
scholars and poets, entertaining the Germans
an orchestra composed from the talent of Europe.

Dancing for their captors
frostbitten toes purple, bodies sour from
far-too-close quarters.

Death-delivering dysentery,
bedbugs as sand men,
bringing flea-bitten dreams.

I had a hand in something
I am not just an observer
Teddy, my child, long may you live.

# 49

# ALEPPO, 2014: THE BOY BY THE FIRE
## SUZANNE LEE

Television screens, newspapers
overflow with photographs of war,
of civil war, of wars uncivil;
of children no longer young
whose work is scavenging for food,
for water, for a reason to go on—
although a child excels the rest of us
in accepting what is, at persevering
in the face of fear, great darkness,
insufferable odds.

Not long ago, the boy would shy at danger,
seek mother, father, home; now, stripped
of refuge, he stands warily on the fringe
of a scattered gathering of young men
around a smoking rubble-fire.
Their silhouettes loom black
against buildings streaked grey with soot.
In rough, anonymous clothing,

hunched with exhaustion and the cold,
the men radiate alertness. The boy watches
for scraps of warmth, of food, listens
for fragments of news
about where the fighting is most intense,
where the water is not laced with mud
and dysentery, where there will be food
tomorrow—if God is gracious—
and ponders in his hungry, war-dazed heart
the possibility, or impossibility, of hope.

## 50

# BATH

MEGAN E. FREEMAN

coming through the door
contracted and brittle
crusty and hard
then into the hot hot hot
of the most civilized
of inventions
blessed and baptized
so hot hot
I turn pink
rivaling lobsters
and prawns
but no one waits for me
with bibs and lemons
and safely into the kettle I sink
as the molten relief
sears me inch by tender inch
seeping into all my crevices
and cavities
being absorbed

into the expanding cushion
of my self
until I am once again
supple and soft
and able to exhale
the steam of the day

# 51

# FIRST COMMUNION, SEVILLE
## DEBORAH KELLY

I saw the stone bridge arch
for a camera.

On its back, a girl.
As if her skirts were a saint's first miracle,
holy bells of tulle.

Net gloves pulled
imprints on her fingers,
her toes, pressed into blanched shoes.

Gray doves flocked her family for churro crumbs,
swans turned again, unmoved.

I wanted to dye the water blue.

But tulle, yes, white like suds,
for the first time she tastes body and blood.
A bridal child, wed
to a drop of wine and pressed bread.

And I wanted to dye the water red.

Another girl, younger, naked as butter,
waded with her mother.
They let the clear water rise above their shins.

I joined in.

The pool cooled our feet.
Quartzite edged our skirts' damp hems.

While the cameraman
positioned the wed-child for another still—

parakeets tore the leaf canopy
and, at the bridge's foot,
a goose tucked away his bill.

# 52

# THE PEONY HOUSE

## KATIE LEWIS

Rabbit rushed through her afternoon chores, polishing the wooden floors of the long entertaining room to a shine. Though she was only ten, she had been living with Auntie for several years now and had long ago become an expert at cleaning the big room by herself. She wiped the sweat from her brow and smiled to see that the sun was still high when she finished; the sooner she finished, the more time she could spend watching her Sisters get ready.

No one at the Peony House was actually related to her, but all of them treated her as a younger sibling. Only the Madam, her austere "Auntie," showed any hint of sternness toward her. Maybe it was due to her age. Or maybe they simply pitied her. Rabbit had seen beggars in the street who looked like her, after all, and she was old enough to understand that she lived here, in a Red Light District House, because none of her remaining blood relatives had wanted a child like her in their home.

Their motives didn't matter to Rabbit, however, who kept her fingers off the freshly polished banister as she dashed up the stairs. She was lucky just to have their kindness—she was also old enough to know not to question such things.

"There's our little bunny!" Sister JiaJia cried in delight as Rabbit slid the door back to slip into the crowded room. The room filled with a chorus of distracted greetings, not unlike the chirping of a flock of birds. Her Sisters were in various stages of dressing: some of them still wearing their plain robes as they did each other's makeup, others already draped in their silks for the night. Rabbit loved the vibrant colors and the intricate embroidery that decorated their Night Clothes.

JiaJia waved her over and Rabbit flushed with delight as she ducked and weaved her way through the room. Rabbit loved all of her Sisters, but JiaJia was her favorite. She was one of the stars of the House, and that meant she had some of the most beautiful silks and pieces of jewelry in her collection. Of course, that also meant that some of the other girls were a bit cold to her, but JiaJia was never anything but warm sunshine to all of them.

And especially to Rabbit.

"Come, come. Sit down," Sister JiaJia said. She was seated on a cushion herself, but patted the bare floor beside her. Rabbit sank to her knees on the floorboards without any complaint. "And what has my Little Sister Bunny been up to this afternoon?" she asked, dipping her middle finger delicately into a pot of rouge and applying it to her lips with the aid of a polished bronze mirror.

"Cleaning," Rabbit announced with a giggle. "But you knew that!"

"Of course I did," Sister JiaJia said, pausing to pucker her lips and tilt her head back and forth in the mirror. "I just wondered if our great, magnanimous Madam might have finally given you a day off."

This earned a few trills of laughter from the girls around them.

"Well!" JiaJia said, placing her hands on her hips and twisting to face her Sisters. "She ought to at least give our little bunny time to practice her music."

Rabbit sat up very tall. "I don't need to practice, Sister JiaJia," she said proudly.

JiaJia smiled down at her, not the painted-on smile she often flashed to her customers, but something warm and real. "Of course you don't," she said. Then she twisted around on her cushion to face Rabbit and dipped her finger into her rouge again. "Here, look this way." Rabbit did as she was told, forcing herself to hold still and not smile while JiaJia rubbed her reddened finger in small circles on each cheek and finally traced Rabbit's lips. This was the other reason Sister JiaJia was her favorite. If Rabbit could finish her chores quickly enough, sometimes the girls would dress her up like a favorite doll, but none of the others did so as often as Sister JiaJia.

It made Rabbit feel like she was truly one of them, though she knew she never would be. Not even when she grew older. Not with her looks.

The door flew open hard enough to clatter loudly in its frame, and all the twittering stopped abruptly.

"I can hear you from downstairs," Auntie scolded them. Rabbit kept her face toward JiaJia, but from the corner of her eye she could clearly see that Auntie was leaning heavily on her cane today. Pain never helped her mood.

"Look at you! None of you are even halfway ready and we open in an hour. Enough dawdling!"

Auntie limped heavily into the room, sharp eyes silently counting each girl and stopping at the corner where Rabbit was still sitting. Beside her, Sister JiaJia had returned to tending to her own makeup. Rabbit, however, didn't dare to move. She knew better than to try to look away to hide her face.

"And *you*," Auntie huffed, pointing a finger at the girl, "go change and wash your face. You look like a ghost!"

"Yes, Auntie," Rabbit said demurely. She got to her feet and bowed in silent apology for bothering her Sisters before slipping past Auntie to flee to the safety of her own room, bare feet pounding hard against the floorboards.

Rabbit's room was down on the first floor beside Auntie's. In truth, it was more of a closet when compared to her Sisters' luxurious quarters, but there was enough space for bedding and her few belongings. She washed her face in the basin and peered into a bronze mirror that was barely half the size of Sister JiaJia's and gave off a slightly warped reflection. Red eyes stared back at her, set in a pale face as round as a full moon. The wisps of hair that had escaped her bun were whiter than an old man's beard, as were her eyebrows. Even her eyelashes, which still had a few water droplets clinging to them like morning dew, were white. Streaks of red now stained her plump cheeks and smeared across her mouth like a wound.

She splashed her face again and rubbed it raw with her little bar of soap. Auntie was right. The rouge against her milky skin really did make her look like a ghost. She'd rather be a rabbit than a ghost any day.

Once the makeup was gone, Rabbit settled into her own routine of getting ready. The rough, cotton-spun clothes she wore to do chores were replaced with soft, peach-colored robes that bore an embroidery of simple flowers along the edges of the flowing sleeves. Her robes weren't made of silk, but they were still pretty— and in the end that was all that mattered. No one would be touching *her*, after all. Her tongue poked out of the side of her mouth as she squinted at her warped reflection, trying to secure her hair into a fresh bun with a wooden flower pin. She was never very good at this part and often asked one of her Sisters to help, but she'd already been chased out of their room once today. If Auntie caught her bothering them again, that cane would do more than thump on the floor.

It took half a dozen tries, but she finally managed to fashion a pleasant bun, tucking in any flyaway strands that tried to escape.

The pink of the hairpin's painted petals stood out brilliantly against her white hair. Enhancing her girlish beauty required a delicate balance, or so Auntie griped every time Rabbit grew and needed new robes. Too much red and the contrast was ghastly, but a mix of lighter peaches and pinks stood out nicely against her pale complexion and complemented her eyes. Rabbit wished she could wear more blues and greens like her Sisters, but she didn't dare to question Auntie's judgment on the matter.

By the time she had finished with her hair and made her way out to the main room, lantern light was fast replacing the dwindling sunlight. She wasted little time in rushing to her corner where her *guzheng* waited.

The instrument was longer than she was tall, already tuned earlier in the day as part of her chores. Rabbit sat before it and plucked every string one at a time, touching each movable bridge to ensure everything was positioned perfectly. Once she was satisfied, she closed her eyes and settled her hands in her lap, waiting.

A few girlish shrieks of laughter echoed from upstairs, followed quickly by Auntie's cry of warning, and then the doors were thrown open for the night. The voices of men and the heavy clomp of their boots came next, some she recognized and some she didn't. Soon enough, each customer was answered by the chirp of a female voice. Rabbit kept her eyes closed and her head bowed, listening to them pair off and fan out from the door to gradually fill the room around her.

As she waited for a sizable audience, Rabbit heard a particularly familiar call of "JiaJia, where are you hiding?" followed by her favorite Sister's twinkling laughter. Her fingers curled into fists in her lap, but she forced them to relax after a few deep breaths.

Once she'd regained her concentration, the voices were numerous enough to echo off the high ceilings, and it was time to begin.

Rabbit opened her eyes and stretched her hands over the

strings. The first few plucks were soft, but the sound swelled as she moved her fingers. The right hand led the melody while the left kept the strings vibrating on the other side of the row of bridges, sometimes pressing or sliding to change the pitch. The *guzheng* came alive under her fingers: not merely an instrument but a living being in its own right. While Rabbit was the master of the song, she always felt they worked in tandem more than anything else.

The strings directed her just as much as she directed them.

The music rose around her so thick in the air that sometimes she felt she could see it if she only squinted hard enough, like trying to focus on her reflection in her tiny warped mirror. She had played this song a thousand times, and yet each performance was new because there were always little differences. She might be the only one who could tell, but the truth was that each night's song was tailored to the guests of the Peony House.

She didn't need to look at the customers to know what to play for them—listening had been more than enough. One of the first men through the door had carried a slight tremble to his voice, so Rabbit's fingers plucked a bright set of notes to help him relax for the Sister attending him. Another's voice had carried a different kind of nervousness, the sour tone that meant wine was needed. Rabbit sent a quick flurry of notes in his direction, encouraging him to drink. However, she'd also heard the slurred speech of a man who had already had his fill of wine before entering the Peony House, so she quickly chased that melody with a slower one directed at the opposite corner of the House, lest the man get too drunk for any of her Sisters to offer him company.

And so it went. Rabbit fulfilled each customer's needs by weaving the music around them, sensing whatever was necessary in the way they talked and moved and breathed. Every so often, one of her Sisters asked her how—how she knew—and how her music could relax and excite men and even do the same for her Sisters.

But Rabbit had never been able to explain it and Auntie was always quick to put an end to such questions.

If JiaJia was the star of the Peony House, Rabbit was its secret weapon. The vast majority of the customers never had any idea, but every so often her music would attract a curious eye. She never liked that. She preferred being ignored and would always breathe a sigh of relief when one of her Sisters inevitably led such curious customers upstairs where they couldn't stare at her anymore.

An explosion of laughter burst from behind a privacy screen at the far end of the room, and Rabbit's fingers nearly fumbled the next few notes before she found her rhythm again. She closed her eyes and willed herself to concentrate. JiaJia's special customer was here tonight, and Rabbit knew well what he required above all else.

*Soothing.*

Rabbit didn't know much about him except that he had money. Only those with a certain amount of wealth and status were afforded such luxuries as a private partition or the ability to be served by more than one girl at once, though JiaJia was his favorite. This, in turn, improved JiaJia's popularity so Rabbit couldn't outright hate him. Still, he felt . . . *dark* to her somehow, and more than once JiaJia had refused to come out of her room for an entire day after he visited the House.

Rabbit pulled a string too harshly and a single ringing note shattered her melody. No one noticed—or almost no one. She caught Auntie staring at her from the entryway and quickly ducked her head. Though not musically talented herself, Auntie always seemed to know when a mistake had been made. Rabbit kept her head bowed as her small fingers returned to their work, weaving her song anew like a spider gathering up broken strands of silk to remake her web.

*Relax. Drink more. Drink less. Be calm. Repeat.*

She didn't count the customers or keep track of time. Without any signal at all, Rabbit knew when to change songs, just as she'd known when to begin. When enough food and drink had been served, her fingers nimbly adjusted a few of the instrument's bridges and began a different tune.

This one was not as bright as the previous. It utilized more minor notes and a darker, more sultry tone. This was the song that helped her Sisters do their work. The song encouraged a different kind of hunger in the Peony House's customers. Her Sisters told her that it affected them as well, though they only mentioned it vaguely and never gave specifics, merely saying that it made them feel "nice."

Rabbit supposed that a few of them must imagine that she didn't know what went on upstairs because of her age, but even a child of ten could recognize they were being raised in a brothel without having to see any of it firsthand.

But what did that matter, really? Auntie had given her a home when no one else would, just as she'd done for all of Rabbit's Sisters, and living inside anywhere was better than living on the streets. So she did her part, she played her songs—gladly—not just to earn her place but also to help her Sisters.

To make them feel "nice" while they earned their own place.

The first to go upstairs was the man who had come in drunk, though by now he'd eaten a full meal to help balance him out. Next was the nervous man, a full pot of wine braver. Then JiaJia's special guest left his private corner and ascended the staircase with a gaggle of giggling girls, JiaJia displayed prominently on his arm.

Rabbit closed her eyes when she saw that and concentrated harder on her music. She didn't want JiaJia to lock herself in her room tomorrow, so Rabbit wove a bit of her previous notes into this new song of hunger, pouring all of her will into the strings and listening to the *guzheng* sing out in answer.

*Be calm. Be calm. Be calm.*

The laughter of JiaJia and her entourage was cut off abruptly as her door slid shut and Rabbit let her eyes wander up to the balcony for a moment before refocusing on her work.

More customers came and the cycle started over again. Her music invited them, lulled them, and encouraged them all at once. As the night wore on, her melodies became more complex as she saw to the needs of those downstairs while still directing a few measures to the ones who had already gone upstairs. It wasn't easy, but luckily the *guzheng* was an instrument built for harmonizing with itself with its multitude of strings. She sometimes wondered if that wasn't why she'd been drawn to it over a flute or a simpler zither.

Hours passed and her fingers grew sore. Rabbit wasn't expected to play the entire night through. She was allowed her breaks when she needed them. But JiaJia's special guest was still here and something about his presence tonight made the back of her neck tingle. She didn't want to stop until he left.

Despite her determination, the longer she played, the harder it became to concentrate. Like most of the members of the House, she slept during the day. Weaving her music, however, could be draining. Indeed, she felt almost as though her beloved instrument were leeching something from her the longer she went on. Something warm and vital, leaving her fingers chilled and her head fuzzy.

Rabbit gritted her teeth and pushed through it, silently willing JiaJia's special guest to leave. Before she knew it, she'd woven the wish into her music, harsh cords nearly shouting *"LEAVE!"* through the House.

Her fingers immediately flattened against the strings, stopping all sound. This time, when she looked up, nearly everyone was looking at her. A cold sweat broke out on her forehead under the weight of so many eyes. Her vision swam and her stomach roiled until she thought she might be sick or pass out, or both. The sudden silence was painful.

Until it was shattered by a scream.

All eyes turned quickly upward and Rabbit's followed suit, her spine straightening and fingers tingling as she focused on the balcony, on JiaJia's door. Not even a moment later it flew open and girls in various states of undress poured from the room, hugging their silks to them to preserve what little modesty they had left.

Then the special guest appeared, bare from the waist up, holding JiaJia by the hair. His face was red with wine and rage and his uncovered gut shook with every word he spat at JiaJia, but Rabbit heard none of it.

She only heard JiaJia's screams of pain. She only saw JiaJia's makeup ruined by tears, her hands too busy gripping her own scalp to cover herself.

Every part of Rabbit that had been cold only moments ago was suddenly aflame. Her battered fingers reached for the strings before she could think. What came out wasn't a song but a sharp, atonal strum of notes that cut through the air like a knife. She could almost see the ripple of sound shoot across the room, aimed directly at the man's head.

JiaJia's guest stumbled back a step. His hand let go of her hair and reached up to feel his own head while JiaJia skittered away on all fours like a frightened animal. Rabbit watched him pull his hand away and stare, dumbfounded, at the smear of red now staining his palm, blinking more of it out of his eyes. He wavered on the spot for a moment before pitching forward. When he collapsed, his weight broke the railing into splinters and sent him crashing from the balcony into the freshly polished floorboards below.

Rabbit could only stare, her numb fingers automatically pressing on the strings once more to quiet the lingering vibrations.

An explosion of voices followed, louder than the crash had been. Customers and Sisters alike shouted, streaming either toward JiaJia or the unconscious guest. Above it all, Auntie was pounding her cane against the floor in an unsuccessful attempt to restore order.

Rabbit didn't realize she'd stopped breathing until her chest began to burn. Every breath seemed to scorch her lungs, and her face was wet. When she stood, she swayed for a moment. Then she was running, her numb legs carrying her though the curtained entranceway where her small room nestled beside Auntie's. Her speed didn't account for the size of the room, and she slammed into the wall, rattling the entire space and sending her bronze mirror flying. It gave a hollow ring as it landed face down on the floor, warbling in increasingly quick circles before settling at last.

In the quiet, Rabbit could finally hear her own breathing coming in wet, ragged gasps. She scrubbed at her face with her palms, the way she'd scrubbed the rouge off her cheeks, but the tears kept slipping between her fingers faster than she could wipe them away. She made no noise, aside from her breathing, however. With her room so close to Auntie's, she'd learned quickly how to be sorrowful in silence.

By now all of her limbs were numb and her head felt stuffed full of cotton. It only took another moment for her knees to give out, leaving her slowly sliding down the wall until she was a heap propped up by the corner.

Time passed, though she would never be able to say how much. Her tears dried up and her breathing gradually grew easier and more even. The muffled noises from the rest of the House quieted as well. The customers, the outsiders, *the men*, were the first voices to disappear. Then, when the Peony House had returned to its natural state, housing only the chirruping of females, she listened to her Sisters. Their voices continued for some time, likely trying to comfort JiaJia and the other unfortunate girls who had been with her in that room. Rabbit rested her head against the wall and listened to them until, at last, even those began to taper off.

Finally, she heard the shuffle of Auntie's limp and the thump of her cane. It paused for a moment outside her room. Rabbit watched the door slide open through a curtain of white—her hair had come undone at some point, the decorative pin lost either when she fled the main room or collided with the wall.

The skin around Auntie's eyes and mouth were pinched, but she didn't seem angry. Rather, she appeared tired.

"My poor little bunny rabbit. Come to my room," she said, leaving the door open. Rabbit listened to the shuffle and thump of her steps for a moment before using the wall to climb back to her feet. The numbness had hardened to a lead weight and she nearly stumbled, but by keeping one hand on the wall, she managed to cross her small room and make it out into the hall.

Auntie's room was barely ten steps from her own, but it seemed to take an eternity to get there. Usually at the end of a night she would sing a final song for Auntie, one that eased the pain in her bad leg and helped her sleep. That song was the reason Auntie had taken her in when no one else would, and Rabbit was always glad to sing it. Sometimes, after hearing it, Auntie didn't need her cane at all the next day. Those were always the days when she was in the best mood.

As Rabbit forced one foot in front of the other, however, she mulled over how to tell Auntie she couldn't sing for her tonight. She wasn't sure how to explain it, other than a simple *knowing* that attempting any more music tonight would not only be unsuccessful, but potentially harmful. Especially after . . .

Rabbit's feet stopped only a step away from Auntie's waiting doorway. She'd hurt that man, somehow. She'd hurt a customer. An important customer. Not only that, but there was also the damage he'd done to the balcony railing and the floor. A chill ran down her spine and her throat seemed to close. Girls had been thrown out for hurting customers. Would Auntie throw her out too?

But Auntie hadn't looked angry, Rabbit reminded herself. She knew better than anyone what Auntie's anger looked like. A thundercloud took over her whole body, and as muddled as Rabbit felt, she'd sensed no sign of such a storm in the older woman.

*She's not angry. She's not. She's not.*

With a final breath, Rabbit slid the door open and stepped inside.

Auntie was sitting on her bed, freeing her salt and pepper hair from the ornate pins that kept it piled on top of her head. She didn't pause her work when Rabbit entered, though she did pat the spot on the bed beside her.

"Auntie . . ." Rabbit began, and was surprised by how raw her voice was. She sounded almost sickly. Clearing her throat she tried again. "I'm sorry."

"Sit," Auntie said in response. When Rabbit only blinked at her, she narrowed her eyes slightly and repeated herself, her tone a touch sharper. "Sit."

Rabbit hurried to the bed and sat, staring down at her hands clasped in her lap. The tips of her fingers were red, especially those on her right hand. She touched one with her thumb and winced, wondering vaguely if she would even be able to use her hand come tomorrow.

The drag of wooden teeth through her hair made her jump, but when she tried to turn, a gentle hand on her head forced her to remain still.

Auntie was combing her hair.

"My poor, scared bunny rabbit," Auntie said with a sigh. "Who would have guessed that such a small little thing could cause so much damage?"

"I'm sorry," Rabbit gasped again, tensing her shoulders. The comb kept moving through her hair, the gentle pressure urging her to relax.

"Shhh. He's not dead, and I'm sure his wife would rather he pay for the damages than let it be known that he caused a scene in a wine house," Auntie said in her sensible business voice. She paused, however, and Rabbit's shoulders began to bunch toward her ears again. "Still, you're lucky he's only wealthy and none the wiser about what exactly you did."

The comb paused and Rabbit swallowed.

"I don't know . . . what I did," she whispered at last. Auntie sighed and the comb resumed its slow drag through her hair. The repetitive motion was beginning to make her sleepy.

"You never know," Auntie said, clicking her tongue. "From now on you need to be more careful, understand? I know you love JiaJia. I even thank you for saving her. But subtle influence is one thing; the power to attack someone is something else entirely."

"I didn't mean—" Rabbit began, but Auntie cut her off with a sharp tug of the comb through a knot in her hair. She winced.

"You never mean to, my dear bunny rabbit, but that's just the trouble. If word got out about what you can do . . . I'm afraid I wouldn't be able to protect you."

This time Rabbit wasn't rebuffed when she turned her head to stare up at Auntie. She barely remembered her life before the Peony House, and all she'd known since was gratitude for being allowed to stay.

"Protect me from what?" Rabbit asked. Frowning made pain blossom between her eyes, but she didn't understand. Worse, she was again struck by how tired Auntie looked. And how sad.

"The Peony House is our domain," Auntie said, beginning to run the comb through her own hair. "It's a world within the wider world: cut off from all that exists outside of it. For someone like you, though . . . you're simply too big to exist here forever. Someday, my little bunny rabbit, you'll outgrow us."

Rabbit frowned harder and rubbed her forehead when the pain grew sharper.

"Auntie . . ."

"Never mind," Auntie said suddenly. "Never mind. This has all been more than enough for one night. You're dead on your feet. Go to bed, Rabbit."

Rabbit paused, but only for a moment. Auntie truly would grow angry if she had to repeat herself, and the dismissal meant she need not make excuses for why she couldn't sing tonight. Her limbs were still stiff, but she managed to leave Auntie's room with a polite bow and somehow made it back to her own without tripping over her own feet.

She didn't bother to clean up or undress, but simply crawled into her bed while questions danced around her head. She had known she was different and that it was a secret, just as she'd known the true nature of the Peony House without needing to be told. But if she could "attack" someone, as Auntie had put it, what else could she do? What else hadn't she yet discovered? And why would that mean she needed protecting?

Too many questions made her head hurt too much to dwell on them. The exhaustion that had been weighing on her more and more throughout the night finally overtook her until she no longer had the strength to keep her eyes open.

Tomorrow she would sing the healing song for Auntie, and for JiaJia, too, if she'd let her. Then she could practice keeping her emotions in check while she played. As long as she did that, as long as she continued serving the customers, she could stay. She would never outgrow the Peony House. She could stay here, in their own little world within the world. She would never have to step outside her sanctuary.

Auntie would see. Rabbit had enough self-restraint to stay. Though she was only ten, she knew she could accomplish anything she imagined with her music.

# 5POEMS IN MY PURSE
## GIA NOLD

i'm busy holding a flower

she made a fine necklace      with the pearls of her disappointments

tea on a cold morning          ginger scented          hungry body
            i      am      blessing      this      ground

i made a mask        out of a small cork
like other things
it ached for a smile  kisses      lilies      olive eyes

the sun is still crying and the moon—singing

# LUCY'S MONSTER
## DAVID E. SHARP

"Did you check under the bed?" asked Lucy, her eyes scanning the room.

Lucy's father knelt, lifted the bed skirt, and made a theatrical production of peering into the depths. He rose with a smile on his face. "No, pumpkin. No monsters under the bed."

Lucy pressed her lips together. "In the closet? Check the closet."

Her father walked to the closet and cracked the door. He peeked inside and made a face of comical shock before throwing the door open to reveal nothing but hanging clothes and piled boxes. "Monster free. Anywhere else?"

Lucy offered a seven-year-old scowl in return for her father's antics. "How about the window?"

Lucy's father moved to the window and pulled back the curtains. He wrinkled his nose at the sight of some crumbling remains on the sill. "No monsters, but how long has that been there?"

"What is it?" asked Lucy.

Her father picked it up with two fingertips, held it to his nose, and took a tentative sniff. "Is this a *dog biscuit*? Lucy, you know the dog is not supposed to be in your room."

"Lucca doesn't come into my room, Daddy. She's afraid of the monster. She's a big scaredy."

He held the crumbly remains of the biscuit out to her. "You mean to tell me that *you* were snacking on this?"

Lucy didn't hide her disgust. "I don't even like your grilled cheese. Do you really think I would put *that* in my mouth?"

Her father narrowed his eyes, a clear sign he was activating his parental lie-detecting gaze. "Then *who*, young lady, should I believe is responsible for this disgusting, half-chewed dog biscuit in your window?"

Lucy leaned in and spoke in a conspiratorial whisper. "Monsters *love* dog biscuits."

Lucy's father clicked his tongue. "Lucy, there *are* no monsters. We've checked the entire room. Besides, you're old enough to know that monsters aren't real." He sat down on the bed and placed a finger on her forehead. "They're all in your mind."

Lucy brushed her father's hand away and thrust her finger in his face. "You're sure about that, are you? Well, won't that be good news for Cheryl Carson? She had to see the school counselor today on account of her ang-ziety. Bet you can't guess why she had ang-ziety. I'll give you three tries."

Her father stroked his chin. "You gave her one of my grilled cheese sandwiches?"

Lucy rolled her eyes. "Strike one."

"Hmmm," said her father, "Did you force her to play a pointless guessing game?"

"Strike two. And I know you're just messing with me. You're not as funny as you think you are."

"Shhh!" said her father, his finger to his lips. "I've got a good feeling about this one. It's coming to me. Is it . . . monsters?"

"Of course it's monsters! She told Jenna Ludmeyer that a big ol' shaggy monster with horns and giant teeth and nasty scraping claws jumped out of her closet last night and scared her so bad she had to put on new pajamas."

"Cheryl Carson, huh? I thought you didn't get along with her."

Lucy thrust her hand on her hip. "I *don't*. She makes fun of my shoes, and she breaks all the purple crayons because she *knows* they're my favorite. If anyone deserves a little ang-ziety, it's Cheryl Carson."

Lucy's father picked her up and deposited her beneath her blankets. "You know, if Cheryl Carson is having anxiety about something, maybe we shouldn't be so hard on her. Even if she does break all the purple crayons."

"She's not having ang-ziety about *something*. She's having ang-ziety about *monsters*! Are you even listening to me? *Somethings* don't have horns and teeth and scraping claws. *Monsters* do."

Her father swept a finger across her forehead and tucked a few loose hairs behind her ear. "Just go easy on her, all right? You never know what other people are going through that makes them act the way they do. Monsters come in all shapes and sizes."

"Shapes and sizes? What do you mean?" asked Lucy. "Are you saying Cheryl Carson is some kind of a monster?"

"No, pumpkin," said her father. "I'm saying that sometimes people might act in a way we think is monstrous, but if we're willing to look a little deeper, we may find some surprising reasons for that. Maybe she feels vulnerable. Maybe somebody hurt her feelings in the past and she's mean so people will be afraid to hurt her feelings again."

"Okay," said Lucy, thoughtfully. "Just so long as you're not really calling her a monster. That's giving her way too much credit. At best, I would say she's a pest."

Her father kissed her on her head. "Good night, pumpkin. I'll leave the night-light on for you." He stood up and walked toward the hall, stopping for a moment at the door. "Love you, Lucy."

"Love you too, Daddy."

He clicked off the light and closed the door.

And there it was.

Standing next to the wall, where it had been veiled by the open door, was an enormous shaggy green monster. Two black horns protruded from its head. Moisture from its giant teeth gleamed in the glow of the night-light. The tips of its claws scraped against the carpet as it took one lumbering step toward Lucy.

Lucy's heart jumped in her chest. She stifled a scream, and nearly fell out of bed. "What is the matter with you? I *hate* when you jump out at me like that!"

The great, fearsome beast opened its enormous dripping mouth. A deep rumble in its throat rose and took shape in its mouth, forming speech that sounded like grinding stones. "Apologies, milady." The deep resonance of its voice sent vibrations through her bones.

Lucy shook off her trepidation. She stood up on her mattress and looked the beast in the eyes. "We were looking everywhere for you. Didn't you hear us? Would it kill you to stop making me look so stupid to Mommy and Daddy? Do you see how they look at me when I talk about you? They think I've lost my mind."

The monster lowered its bloodshot eyes and sulked. Nevertheless, it was the most horrifying display of sulking imaginable.

Lucy crossed her arms. "And *thank you* for letting me get in trouble for your dog biscuit! Is it asking so much for you to clean up after yourself?"

The monster shook its shaggy green head. "It won't happen again, milady."

"See that it doesn't." Lucy followed up her admonishment with a demonstrative huff.

The monster averted its gaze. "Forgiveness, milady. I'm so terribly shy. You know how parents frighten me."

Lucy took a deep breath and released her anger. "Well, I guess I can't be too upset. You did take care of Cheryl Carson, after all."

The creature genuflected before her bed. "Your bidding has been carried out, milady."

A wicked smile crossed Lucy's lips. "Yes. She'll be wetting the bed for a week. That'll teach her to break my purple crayons." She slid off the bed onto the floor. Lucy moved to the window, drew the curtain aside, and gazed at the panorama of stars and city lights.

"Then you are pleased, milady?" said the monster from behind her.

"For now," she said, glancing back at him. "There are fresh biscuits for you in the dollhouse. See that you don't leave any crumbs this time."

The monster glanced at the intricate dollhouse to its left. It fumbled with brutish claws to unclasp the hatch. It then gingerly opened the miniature building to reveal the delicious contents within. It smacked its wet lips. "So generous, milady. The liver ones are my favorites."

Lucy offered a dismissive wave. "Yes, yes. Eat up. Quickly, though. We have more work to do."

"More children in need of ang-ziety?" asked the monster between crunches.

Lucy turned her attention to the window with an evil smile. "So *very* many, Monster. I want to talk to you about a boy named Evan Matthews."

"Oh?"

"He pulled my hair at recess."

# CONTRIBUTOR BIOGRAPHIES

*Jonathan Arena* was born with a pen and cried for paper. Now he's older and you should be worried. Fiction is his lover and he struggles to go a day without her. It's why he has a past with novels, novellas, short stories, flash fiction, poems, film screenplays, television screenplays, comics, video games, and so on. It's also why he has a past with action, adventure, drama, thriller, suspense, mystery, historical fiction, alternate history, science fiction, fantasy, satire, literary, horror, and so on. He will never conform to a style or genre even if it hurts his marketability. He just loves words and stories too much and wishes to explore it all. Find out more about this strange man at www.cavewritingonthewall.com.

*Karen Betstadt* has had a career as a clinical psychologist, respiratory therapist, and community activist. Her poetry usually reflects socio-political themes and has appeared in such venues as the *Denver Post*; *The Colorado Independent*; the National Federation of State Poetry Societies' anthology, *Encore*, with her first-place poem "Lessons;" and other state and national anthologies. She has been a judge for several poetry contests, including the Utah State Poetry

Society's annual contest for the past three years. In her current position as vice president for the Denver Bicycle Touring Club, she started a poetry column, "Cycling through Words," in the monthly newsletter. Her aim is to promote member submissions, including limericks and the latest Haiku/Bike-u challenges, because she believes poetry exists within us all and anything can inspire its release.

*Amy Bellefeuille* is a wife, mother of three boys, nonprofit executive director, local entrepreneur, and writer of personal narrative living in Fort Collins, Colorado. An Arizona native, she's a desert-girl turned beach-girl turned mountain-girl, who seeks out new experiences wherever she goes.

With an extensive list of interests and sufficient brains and blessings, she's earned a BA and an MBA and pursued careers in a wide range of fields, including public relations, education, and communications—though writing has always been her through line.

Journaling has become a daily ritual since she received her first lock-and-key diary in second grade. Since then she's filled a ridiculous number of notebooks with her musings. More recently, she's begun to fill cyberspace with her words as well, with blogs detailing the ups and downs of a month spent in East Africa with her family and the chronicles of her self-declared Year of Adventure leading up to a milestone birthday. "Belly Ring" is her first published piece.

*John Blair* grew up in Denver and graduated from Colorado State University. He pursued a career in trust banking management, now retired. He served in leadership roles for many educational, arts, and social service nonprofit agencies along the Front Range. John and his spouse Anne enjoy a passion for performing arts, often attending concerts, theatre, dance, and opera. He began writing poetry twenty years ago to fulfill a childhood dream.

*Sunny Bridge* knows her name sounds like an organic farm, and she's okay with that. Sunny has always loved writing, but after imagination-killing advice from her  parents —write what you know—and recognizing that at age seven she knew nothing, her dreams of publication were shelved until quite recently. Her poem "You," written after cancer claimed the life of her husband, was included in the 2019 Lighthouse Writers Workshop anthology *All the Lives We Ever Lived*. She is the author and photographer of the blog "Movable Assets: Adventures in Wanderlust." Originally created to document the couple's year of adventure in France and beyond, it has since broadened to include thoughts on surviving loss and clinging to hope in these challenging times. Sunny is based in Fort Collins, Colorado, but spends as much time as possible in La Rochelle, France. Find out more about Sunny at MovableAssets.com.

*Monterey Buchanan* received her BA in English from Earlham College in 2012 and has been figuring out what to do with it ever since. She earned her MFA in Creative Writing from Regis University in 2019 and enjoys writing fiction and plays about fantasy, disability, the environment, and other social issues, usually through a comic female lens. Her recent pandemic love story, "The Toilet Paper Baron of Metro Denver," won third place in Denverite.com's pandemic fiction contest and was also featured on *Colorado Matters* and the Stories on Stage live-stream "Simple Pleasures." When not writing, Monterey is tutoring or enjoying the Denver sunshine with the family dogs. You can read more of her work at montereybuchanan.wordpress.com

*John Christenson* lives in Boulder, Colorado. His publications include short fiction in the *New Mexico Review*, as well as stories in *Rise: An Anthology of Change* and several other anthologies.

*Holly Collingwood* is a freelance writer and editor. She was raised on wild blueberries and basketball in cold, snowy states: Alaska, Montana, and Oregon. Her work has appeared in *Mamalode*, *Sierra Trading Post*, *Flash Fiction Online*, *The Molotov Cocktail*, *Glimmer Train*, and local publications. When she's not reading or writing, she loves hiking, skiing, kayaking, gardening, and meeting with her critique group. She lives with her family in Colorado.

*Lew Forester* is the author of *Dialogues with Light* (Orchard Street Press, 2019). His poems have appeared in the *Atlanta Review*, *The Main Street Rag*, *The Blue Mountain Review*, *Plainsongs, POEM*, *Slipstream Magazine*, *New Madrid* and other journals, magazines, and anthologies. A social worker and multiple myeloma survivor, Lew lives with his wife in Arvada, Colorado, and enjoys frequent hikes in the mountains. A favorite three-word phrase is "onwards and upwards." www.lewforester.com

*Megan E. Freeman* attended an elementary school where poets visited her classroom every week to teach poetry, and she has been a writer ever since. She writes middle grade and young adult fiction, and her debut middle grade novel-in-verse, *ALONE*, is available from Simon & Schuster/Aladdin. Megan is also a Pushcart Prize–nominated poet, and her poetry collection, *Lessons on Sleeping Alone*, was published by Liquid Light Press. An award-winning teacher with decades of classroom experience, Megan is nationally recognized for her work leading workshops and speaking to audiences across the country. Megan used to live in northeast Los Angeles, central Ohio, northern Norway, and on Caribbean cruise ships. Now she lives in northern Colorado.

*Calvin Giroulx* studied creative writing at Colorado State University. After graduating, he continued to hone his craft under awesome teachers like David Farland and Mary Robinette Kowal.

He wakes up way too early each morning and loves reading, audiobooks, running, good scotch, death metal, and yelling at the TV whenever the Nuggets, Broncos, or Avalanche are playing. He lives in Fort Collins, Colorado, and is probably writing as you read this.

*Michael Hager*'s writing credits include a novel, poetry, short stories, theatrical plays, and film scripts. He was formerly managing editor for the largest English newspaper in Mexico. His first novel, *Just Beyond the Edge*, was published in 2011. In August 2008, his play *The Last Ride* premiered at an international regional theater. In 2020, he completed his second novel, *In the Times of Clouds & Sun*. He has won awards and grants for his poetry and published an anthology of his poetry titled *Reckoning of the Heart*. His film scripts have received numerous laurels from major film festivals. He is currently working on a short story collection titled *Wayward Messages*. In addition to his writing credits, he is an accomplished songwriter with over forty songs recorded by a variety of artists. He lives with his wife of forty-nine years, Christina, in Fort Collins, Colorado.

*Heather Hein* is a horror and thriller writer, writing both full-length novels and short stories. She is the Creative Programs Director for Northern Colorado Writers, A host for the Fort Collins chapter of Shut Up and Write, and a member of Rocky Mountain Fiction Writers and Pike's Peak Writers. Her short story "Aisle 16" was published in the *TulipTree Review*, and she was featured on Off The Hook Arts with her short story "The Day I Met Stephen King." She read for the Fort Collins Book Festival in 2019 and 2020 with her short stories "Oma's Cookies" and "Offerings to the Spider Gods." She is the third-place winner of InkBot Editing's Colorado Short Story Contest with her horror piece "The Mechanism of Love." "The Formula for Forgiveness" is her first creative nonfiction submission. Heather lives in Northern Colorado with a menagerie of people, pets, and plants.

*Melissa Huff* feeds her poetry from many sources—the power and mystery of the natural world, the way humans everywhere connect, and the importance of spirit. She appreciates the value of reading poetry aloud and won awards in both 2019 and 2020 in the Black-Berry Peach Prizes for Poetry: Spoken and Heard, sponsored by the National Federation of State Poetry Societies. Recent publishing credits include the *Blue Heron Review, Persimmon Tree, Snapdragon: A Journal of Art and Healing, The Pangolin Review,* and *Frogpond.* Melissa enjoys membership in Poets & Patrons of Chicago, the Illinois State Poetry Society, and Columbine Poets of Colorado. She currently splits her time between Illinois and Berthoud, Colorado.

*Amy Wray Irish* grew up near Chicago, received her MFA from the University of Notre Dame, then fled the Midwest for Colorado sunshine. She has been published in *Progenitor Art & Literary Journal, Thought for Food,* and *Twenty Bellows Lit.* Her third chapbook, *Breathing Fire,* won the 2020 Fledge Competition and is now available from Middle Creek Publishing. For more information, go to amywrayirish.com.

*Mary Strong Jackson*'s work has appeared in journals and anthologies in the United States and England. Her chapbooks include *From Other Tongues, The Never-Ending Poem by the Poets of Everything, Witnesses, No Buried Dogs, Between Door and Frame,* and *Clippings.* She was included in a 2005 Nebraska Educational Telecommunications program featuring United States Poet Laureate Ted Kooser. As a social worker, her desire to give voice to those with mental illness resulted in a collaboration with clients to create a book of prose and poetry titled *Singing Under Water.*

**Barbara "Bo" Jensen** is a writer who likes to go off-grid, whether it's backpacking through national parks, trekking up the Continental Divide Trail, or following the Camino del Norte across Spain. For over twenty years, social work has paid the bills, allowing them to meet and talk with people living homeless on the streets of America. You can find more of Bo's work on *National Parks Traveler*, *Out There* podcast, *Wanderlust*, *Journey*, and *The Road She's Traveled* (2022). www.wanderinglightning.com

**Mike Kanner** writes historical fiction, having written and been published in other genres. A student of World War I and a retired Army officer, he tries to bring realism to stories of the trenches. He is currently working on additional stories in the "White Feather" series and a novel based on the tunneling companies of the Royal Engineers. He pays the bills as an instructor in international relations and security studies. Mike lives in Longmont and can often be found riding on the back roads of Boulder County.

**Deborah Kelly** is from Minneapolis and Chicago, but the high deserts and mountains of The West kept calling. She now lives in Boulder, Colorado. There and (frequently) on the road, Deborah writes as a way of life and a practice. Her poems can be found in several journals in the US and abroad.

**Lynn Kincanon** is a nurse practitioner with over thirty-five years in ICUs and emergency rooms. As a poet, she has been in several poetry exhibits and has been published in anthologies and online publications. Lynn is involved in keeping poetry alive in Loveland, co-creating collaborative performances of poetry, music, and storytelling for many years. She has written two self-published ekphrastic chapbooks coinciding with installations at Art Works and Loveland's Feed and Grain. She is currently writing a book of poems about her work as a nurse practitioner as well as her love of nature. Both underline the fragile intersection between life and death.

***Jim Kroepfl*** writes short stories of mystery and adventure, as well as YA science fiction novels with his wife, Stephanie, from a rustic cabin in the Colorado Rockies. Their debut novel, *Merged*, was published by Month9Books in 2019. His short stories and articles have been published in literary journals in the United States and England. Jim and Stephanie often speak at universities, festivals, and conferences. When not writing, Jim is a musician. He and Stephanie are mythology buffs and world travelers who seek out crop circles, obscure historical sites, and mysterious ruins.

Born in New York City, ***Lynda La Rocca*** is a freelance writer who has also worked as a municipal and general-assignment reporter for the *Asbury Park Press*, as well as a teaching assistant at the Timberline campus of Colorado Mountain College in Leadville, Colorado. La Rocca's poetry chapbooks include *The Stillness Between* (Pudding House Publications, 2009) and *Spiral* (Liquid Light Press, 2012). Her individual poems have appeared in numerous state and national poetry society anthologies, along with such publications as *The Wall Street Journal*, *The New York Quarterly*, *Frogpond* (Haiku Society of America), *Colorado Life Magazine,* and *The Colorado Sun*. She was the 2020 winner in the poetry category of the Soul-Making Keats Literary Competition, a National League of American Pen Women arts-outreach program. La Rocca is a member of the River City Nomads, a performance-poetry troupe based in Salida, Colorado, where she lives with her husband, writer-photographer Steve Voynick.

***Suzanne Lee*** is a historian and writer. She grew up in small town Arizona and New Mexico, where she developed a love of the landscapes, spirit, and people of the Southwest. Her poetry has appeared in journals including *Snowy Egret, Sow's Ear, The Snow Line, Trumpet,* and *Colorado Life*, and in the anthologies *Weaving the Terrain* and *Rise: An Anthology of Change*. As a professional writer of nonfiction, she has published investigative reports and military history as well as articles on various topics for organizational, professional, and denominational publications.

***Katie Lewis*** lives in the shadow of the Rocky Mountains with their partner, their furry son, and a vast collection of geekdom sundries. When not at their computer, they can be found taking long walks to catch digital monsters or rolling multi-sided dice to save the world. They created Rabbit in the fall of 2019 and have been obsessed with learning more about her ever since. Katie hopes that this will prove to be only the first chapter of Rabbit's life on the written page.

***Anne Macdonald***'s most recent short story, "That Donnelly Crowd," appeared in 2019's *Best American Mystery Stories* (Houghton Mifflin Harcourt). Her short stories have appeared in the *Belletriste Review;* the *Blue Earth Review; Matter: A Journal of Literature, Art and Movement; WOW! Anthology* (Galway); the *Dublin Quarterly Review;* and RMFW's 2018 *False Faces* anthology (among other journals and anthologies). Her first novel, *A Short Time in Luxembourg* (Gardenia Press), was published in 2004. Anne's nonfiction includes *Foreign Investment in the American and Canadian West, 1870-1914*. Anne is forever a librarian, sometimes a grant writer, and always an advocate for the local arts. Check out her work at www.annetheresemacdonald.com

***Laura Mahal*** is a writer, copyeditor, gardener, coffee swiller, and admirer of fine whisky. She's won prizes for the first three: two-time winner of the Hecla Award for Speculative Fiction, WOW's creative nonfiction contest, Lit Fest finalist, and a member of the editing team for *Rise: An Anthology of Change* (2020 Colorado

Book Award winner). Her work pops up in a plethora of places: *Fish, DoveTales, Veterans' Voices, Across the Margin, OyeDrum, Sunrise Summits, Fresh Starts, Encore*. A fellow in Lighthouse's Book Project for full-length fiction, Laura can't resist composing poems, personal essays, and lengthy snail-mail letters. She advocates for veterans, the LGBTQ+ community, and enjoys the occasional Scotch tasting. www.lauramahalwriter.com

*Sandra McGarry* was a former elementary school teacher in New Jersey for twenty-eight years. She retired to Fort Collins, Colorado, to be close to her family. She has published in *Pilgrimage, Rise: An Anthology of Change*, the *Paterson Literary Review, DoveTales*, and *Encore* by the National Federation of State Poetry Societies.

*Marilyn K. Moody* grew up on the pancake-flat prairie of Central Illinois—and still prefers open spaces and distant horizons. Two of her poems are included in the 2020 Colorado Book Award winner *Rise: An Anthology of Change*, published by Northern Colorado Writers. She has also published poems in *Progenitor Art & Literary Journal, The Great Isolation: Colorado Creativity in the Time of the Pandemic*, and *Fresh Starts: Tales from the Pikes Peak Writers*. Her poem, "Bomb Friday at the Library," is a 2020 Pushcart Prize nominee. She lives near Denver.

*Lynette Flanders Moyer* taught writing, literature, and humanities for many years at Virginia Tech in Blacksburg, Virginia, where she also raised three daughters. Her husband, Albert Moyer, at the time of his death, chaired the History Department. Lynette holds a BA in English from the University of Colorado and an MA and ABD from the University of Wisconsin. Her specialty is twentieth-century literature, though percolating through that specialty is a keen interest in sixteenth-century literature. She currently lives in her original hometown of Longmont, Colorado, where she delights in the return to high-mountain hikes and high-altitude recipes.

*Gia Nold* is the author of three chapbooks of poetry, including *Moon is Always Moon* (Green Fuse Poetic Arts). Her most recent project is a musical recording entitled "Lagrimas." She was selected for the 2004 international poetry exhibition, Barrington, Illinois, and received 2nd place in the 2012 ACC Writers Studio: Speak Peace Colorado Respond Contest. Gia holds a Master of Fine Arts from Naropa University and teaches visual arts in the Denver Public School District. Her latest works have appeared in *BlazeVox*, *#63 Channels (Magazine)*, *Cyclamens and Swords Publishing*, *Blazing Stadium*, *Mad Blood Poetry Series*, and *(Un)Settled: A Community Art Exhibition*. Gia is a native of Lima, Perú, who lives in Evergreen, Colorado.

*Kristine Otero*'s most recent publication can be found in "Sappho to Stonewall," Zine #5 through Sapphic Writers. She won best nonfiction essay in the 2019 Southeast Missouri University Press anthology, *Proud to Be: Writings by American Warriors*. Additional publishing credits include pieces in *Passengers Journal*, *0-Dark-Thirty*, Kleft Jaw Press, and in the Colorado Humanities anthology *Still Coming Home*. Forthcoming publications include a fiction story and a poem in volume ten of *Proud to Be*.

Kristine served in the US army, surviving two tours of combat. Wanting to share more than "her war," she has begun to write and publish in other genres. She earned her degree in psychology from Liberty University. Kristine lives in Denver, Colorado, with her dog, Dali. Find her at www.kristineotero.com

*Kari Redmond* is an online ESL teacher, trainer, and writer located in Fort Collins, Colorado. She writes novels, short stories, poetry, flash fiction, and essays. She is currently querying her first novel,

*This Story Takes Place in a Bar*, while revising her second novel, *What We Let Go*. She has been published in *Rise: An Anthology of Change*, *Brilliant Flash Fiction*, the *TulipTree Review*, and *Sunrise Summits: A Poetry Anthology*, among others. When she is not writing, she is traveling the world (pre-COVID), tending to her seventy houseplants, going to live music, and generally loving life. You can follow her at www.kariredmondwrites.com.

*Erin Robertson* teaches outdoor nature writing classes for children in Louisville, Colorado (www.wildwriters.org), and has been honored with residencies through the Voices of the Wilderness and Boulder County Open Space Artist-in-Residence programs. Find her poetry in the *North American Review, Poet Lore, Deep Wild Journal, Cold Mountain Review*, and elsewhere. www.erinrobertson.org, www.robertsonrambles.com

*Jennifer Robinson* is a Colorado native, born and raised in the northeastern plains, and is a Colorado State University graduate. By day she works in insurance, but by night she is busy writing her first novel. When not writing fiction, you can find her cooking, roller skating, and reading. She currently resides in Fort Collins, Colorado, with her cat and her soul sister.

*Emily Rodgers-Ramos* is a business owner and retired teacher living in Loveland, Colorado. She has had poetry published in the *Greyrock Review*, the *Dry Creek Review, Nanny Fanny,* and the *Lilliput Review*. Her YA novel, *Riding the Double Helix*, spent at least twenty-nine minutes as the number-one seller on Amazon for YA historical/time travel fiction AFTER she posted on Facebook that it would make a great Christmas gift. Her twenty-two-year-old son is impressed she even knows about Facebook. She dabbles in meditation and mixology, not necessarily in that order. Her favorite three-word phrase is "Dare to suck."

*Carolena Romee* has a house full of cats, a sunny writing room with window seats, and a fountain pen on a mahogany roll-top desk. They live one county over from where Willa Cather used to hang out with the love of her youth. Carolena is fun but fictional, one of several pen names for a notoriously prolific and saucy writer with a penchant for baseball and protagonists who do not follow typical plot arcs. "Hands-on Experience" is their effort to combat fat-shaming in a culture that often fails to look at the "bigger picture"—the summation of a complicated life.

*David E. Sharp* is a noisy librarian. While he insists his middle initial stands for intrEpid, this remains unproven. He never pronounces the *t* in often. He has written and produced three plays, as well as published various other works. His novel *Lost on a Page* is available on Amazon and chronicles the plight of fictional characters from various genres who intend to murder their authors. Were this a biographical work, he might not be with us today. Its sequel, *Lost on a Page: Character Developments* is due to release in 2022.

*Valerie A. Szarek* is an award-winning performance poet and Native American flute player. Her poems are healing, present, political, and shamanic and cross between the seen and unseen worlds effortlessly. Her words, music, and workshops are featured at festivals and events around Colorado, including the International Young Leadership Conference, the Mercury Cafe, the Telluride Literary Arts Festival, and Ziggies Poetry Festivals. She was named Poet of the Year at Blissfest 2018. Other awards include Colorado Author's League Best Poem in 2020 and 2021 and The National Poetry Federation Winner's Circle Award in 2016. Valerie offers "Writing into Sanity" workshops monthly.

Her new book, *Soar Ready: Medicine Poems for a Changing*

*World*, has won many awards and is available on her website, <u>www.</u>
<u>poetval.com</u>.

***Cristina Trapani-Scott*** is the author of the poetry chapbook *The Persistence of a Bathing Suit*. Her work has appeared in print and online publications, including the *Paterson Literary Review*, *Hip Mama* magazine, and the *Voices* journal. She was born and raised in Detroit and now lives in Lyons, Colorado, with her partner and their rescue pup. She is a thrift store junkie and an upcycle enthusiast, and she may or may not talk to the treasures that find their way to her.

***Celia Turner*** is a poet who waited a lifetime to begin writing poetry and was sparked by CSU Osher classes. She is going on two years of participation in The Daily Grind and has continued to study with talented teachers over the past five years. Poetry pervades her daily life and words consume her. All other forms of artistry have paled in comparison to the allure of poetry.

# EDITORIAL TEAM BIOGRAPHIES

## Lead Editors

*Bonnie McKnight* is the owner of Lady Knight Editing and has been a freelance editor since 2015—but she's been correcting people's grammar since she was two (ask about the legendary fog vs. mist debate of '92). One of her proudest editorial moments was accepting the Colorado Book Award for Best Anthology for NCW's 2019 *Rise: An Anthology of Change.* Born and raised in Fort Collins, Colorado, Bonnie sees the mountains as home. She enjoys playing games, doing cryptic crossword puzzles, baking (she and Sarah clearly need to get together for a baking party), and spending time with her family, including her adorable son who will be celebrating his first birthday the same day this anthology is released! www.ladyknightediting.com

*Lorrie Wolfe* is a poet, technical writer, and editor living in Windsor, Colorado. After a career in human services, she is still passionate about volunteering, creating community, and the power of words to unite and move people. Her work has appeared in

*Earth's Daughters*, *Progenitor Art & Literary Journal*, the *Tulip-Tree Review*, *Pilgrimage*, *Pooled Ink*, *Mad Blood*, *Encore*, and others. Her chapbook, *Holding: from Shtetl to Santa*, was published by Green Fuse Press in 2013. She edited and contributed to the 2017 anthologies *Mountains, Myths & Memories* and *Going Deeper*. Lorrie was named Poet of the Year at Denver's Ziggies Poetry Festival for 2014–15. She served as the lead poetry editor for *Rise: An Anthology of Change*, which won the 2020 Colorado Book Award. Her two-word mantra is "Show up."

---

## Poetry Editors

***Joseph Hutchison*** has published poetry, short fiction, and essays in over a hundred journals in seven countries. He is the author of twenty poetry collections, including the recently-released *Under Sleep's New Moon*. Previous collections include *The World As Is: New & Selected Poems, 1972-2015*; *Marked Men*; and the Colorado Poetry Award–winning narrative sequence *Bed of Coals*. Joe served as Colorado Poet Laureate from 2014 to 2019 and currently directs the Professional Creative Writing graduate program at the University of Denver's University College. A Denver native, Joe has lived for the past thirty years in the mountains southeast of Evergreen, Colorado.

***Veronica Patterson***'s full-length poetry collections include *How to Make a Terrarium* (Cleveland State University, 1987), *Swan, What Shores?* (NYU Press Poetry Prize, 2000), *Thresh & Hold* (Gell Poetry Prize, Big Pencil Press, 2009), *& it had rained* (CW Books, 2013), and *Sudden White Fan* (Cherry Grove, 2018). Her two chapbooks are *This Is the Strange Part* (Pudding House, 2002) and *Maneuvers: Battle of the Little Bighorn Poems* (Finishing Line,

2013). She lives in Loveland, Colorado, and teaches for OLLI. She received two Individual Artists grants from the Colorado Council on the Arts. Her poems have been nominated for a Pushcart Prize and have been selected for *Writer's Almanac* and *Verse Daily*. She is currently Loveland's first Poet Laureate (2019–2022).

## Prose Editors

***Sarah Kohls Roberts*** is an editor and children's book writer who lives in Fort Collins, Colorado. She served on the editing team for Northern Colorado Writers' *Rise: An Anthology of Change*. She published several technical papers and articles before retiring from chemistry to spend time with her three kids and experiment with words instead. She is a strong believer in the magic of reading with children and the power that brings to them. She enjoys baking, reading, being outside, baking, spending time with family and friends, and baking for them.

***Tara Szkutnik*** used to thrive on chaos but has since learned that *that* isn't thriving. Instead, she keeps the chaos to a minimum with two miniature versions of herself running—er, crawling—around. When not having toddler meltdowns over typos, she's questioning whether she can do it all while making a valiant attempt at doing it all, including but not limited to being a wife, mom, student, and advocate for persons with disabilities. In a former life, she was editor of *Magic City Magazine* and *Big Sky Bride Magazine.* Today a writer, editor, and astrologer. Maybe tomorrow an interior designer.

# ACKNOWLEDGMENTS

This anthology would not be possible without the tireless work and enthusiastic support of so many talented writers, editors, and readers.

Words cannot express how much we appreciate Maggie Walker stepping in to do our anthology cover design. She applied her brilliant artistic skill to our anthology concept and created a cover that represents our theme beautifully.

Thank you to our first-round readers, Matthew Starr, JC Lynne, Miranda Birt, Ronda Simmons, and Eleanor Shelton, who worked their way through hundreds of entries to ensure adherence to theme and guidelines.

As lead editors, Bonnie McKnight and Lorrie Wolfe developed an editorial team that spent months evaluating, debating, championing, and making cuts to select the stories and poetry that made it to publication. Thank you Bonnie and Lorrie, as well as Veronica Patterson, Joe Hutchison, Tara Szkutnik, and Sarah Roberts for your dedication to making this anthology the best it can be.

And finally, thanks to the team of proofreaders, including the entire NCW leadership team.

It is an honor and a joy to work with all of you!

# ABOUT NORTHERN COLORADO WRITERS

NCW supports writers via education, resources, networking, collaboration, submission, and promotion. A for-profit organization based in Northern Colorado, we embrace new technology and modes of outreach and communication to support all writers, wherever they may be. We are committed to creating an inclusive and welcoming environment by fostering community among our members, providing opportunities for writers to develop their unique voices, and celebrating accomplishments big and small.

www.northerncoloradowriters.com

# ALSO BY NORTHERN COLORADO WRITERS

Rise: An Anthology of Change

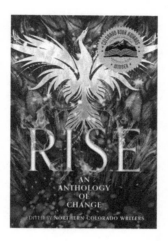

Sunrise Summits: A Poetry Anthology

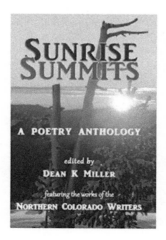

CPSIA information can be obtained
at www.ICGtesting.com
Printed in the USA
FSHW012253111021
85318FS

9 780578 976617